The United States of Storytelling

Folktales and True Stories from the Eastern States

Dan Keding

LIBRARIES UNLIMITED

AN IMPRINT OF ABC-CLIO, LLC
Santa Barbara, California • Denver, Colorado • Oxford, England

Library of Congress Cataloging-in-Publication Data

Keding, Dan.
  The United States of storytelling : folktales and true stories from
the Eastern states / Dan Keding.
      p. cm.
  Includes bibliographical references and index.
  ISBN 978-1-59158-727-9 (hardcover : alk. paper) 1. Tales—East
(U.S.) 2. Storytelling—East (U.S.) 3. East (U.S.)—History. 4. East
(U.S.)—Folklore. I. Title.
 GR106.K44 2010
 398.20974—dc22   2010021571

ISBN: 978-1-59158-727-9

14 13 12 11 10 1 2 3 4 5

This book is also available on the World Wide Web as an eBook.
Visit www.abc-clio.com for details.

Libraries Unlimited
An Imprint of ABC-CLIO, LLC

ABC-CLIO, LLC
130 Cremona Drive, P.O. Box 1911
Santa Barbara, California 93116-1911

This book is printed on acid-free paper ∞
Manufactured in the United States of America

To the children of the United States, who have such a rich and diverse cultural background. I hope these stories help you appreciate your past and those people who went before you, showing you the way. I hope you understand that in our diversity, in our stories, lies our strength.

Also, as always, to my wife Tandy Lacy, who encourages me, inspires me, and fills me with awe. Thanks, Tig.

Contents

Acknowledgments

First I would like to thank my wife, Tandy Lacy, who encourages me, believes in me, and was the first editor of many of these stories. I also want to thank Barbara Ittner of Libraries Unlimited, who came to me and planted the seed for this project. I thank her for her faith in me and for entrusting her idea to my pen. I also thank her for her patience and support as I made a personal journey while collecting Native American stories for this book. I want to thank the staff at The Center for Children's Books at the University of Illinois Graduate School of Library and Information Science, the people who supported me while I haunted their huge collection looking for stories. A debt of gratitude is owed to Art Thieme, not just for the stories he contributed but also for his constant encouragement and friendship throughout the years, and for leading the way for so many of us in our journeys in the folk arts. Thanks to my friends Donald Davis, Kevin Strauss, Tim Tingle, Jenifer Strauss, Alan Irvine, Bob Sanders, Dovie Thomason, Greg Rodgers, and Ceil Anne Clement, who contributed personal, original, traditional, and tribal stories. In addition, I thank the various Native American tribes that gave me permission to use their stories and Professor Debbie Reese from the University of Illinois for her thoughtful insight and advice concerning Native American issues. I want to thank Paige Osborn, who was my assistant and did endless hours of typing, and Christa Deacy Quinn for suggesting chapter glossaries and always asking, "How's the book?" A special thank-you to Rex Stephensen and Tina Hanlon for the story "Jack & His Lump of Silver."

Thank-you to all the folks who have encouraged me over the years to pursue my writing and storytelling, friends like Kendall Haven, Kevin Strauss, Betsy Hearne, Amy Douglas, Elizabeth Ellis, Susan Klein, and the all-too-many others.

Most of all, thank-you to the all the children who have listened over the years to my stories. Because of what I saw in your eyes as you listened, and because of your kind words in remembering me as adults, I know that the stories still live in your imaginations and memories and I continue to tell stories. You have given me the gift of purpose, and there are few gifts greater than that.

Introduction

It is diversity that makes America a great nation. Each state in this country is unique, having its own geography, climate, people, and their stories. That uniqueness makes the study of the stories of these states exciting and rewarding. In these pages you will find some characters you recognize—like Johnny Appleseed and Davy Crocket—and you will meet some lesser known heroes like Josiah Breeze, Betsy Dowdy, and Elizabeth Blackwell.

Stories are windows that allow us a glimpse of another time. We can see how people differed from us and how they were similar to us, how they acted under severe hardship and how they lived their daily lives. When we look through these windows, we see why people laugh and cry, why they try to break through unfair barriers and reach out for the new and exciting. We start to understand why someone fights against injustice and why he or she enjoys spinning a yarn for friends. We can see people's dreams, their fears, their hopes, and their courage. This is the power of the story.

The stories in this collection come from the states east of the Mississippi River. Some of the tales are traditional stories carried by native people who resided in the area long before the Europeans arrived, some are transplanted stories brought to America by settlers who came from other countries, and others grew up from the land; some feature historical characters and events and others the geography, flora, and fauna of a particular state. Virtually every type of story can be found in this collection—true stories, legends, tall tales, pourquoi tales, ghost stories, funny stories, and fictionalized stories based on true events. All, it is hoped, can help readers better understand specific states, their peoples, and their histories.

The chapters of this book by no means provide a definitive collection of the stories of the individual states represented. Instead, they hold a sampling of the stories that are found in the lore and history of the various regions of our country. Naturally it would be impossible to represent every immigrant culture, Native American tribe, historical event, or famous citizen of each state in a collection like this one. Instead, this story collection is meant as a resource—for students, who can find a state and explore some of the stories and legends and people that have made it what it is today, and for educators, who can find state-themed stories to add to curriculum units.

To select these tales I researched hundreds of books and other printed sources, locating several versions of each story before retelling the tale in my own words. I primarily used my own collection and the collections at the University of Illinois Library and the Center for Children's Books at the Graduate School of Library and Information Science at the University of Illinois. In adapting and retelling all of these traditional stories, I have tried to be as faithful to the story as possible—to its voice, content, and range of emotions—while still working to make these stories come alive for a twenty-first-century audience.

The stories that come from Native American sources are reprinted here with the permission of each of the various tribes represented, or by permission of recognized Native American storytellers. I contacted tribes from every state. Some tribes gave me permission, a few declined permission, and many others did not respond. Unfortunately, many chapters do not include a story or stories from Native Americans who live or once lived in that state. After much consideration and thought, and with the help and advice of my wife Tandy Lacy, Director of Education at the Spurlock Museum at the University of Illinois, and many friends and colleagues, including Barbara Ittner, my editor at Libraries Unlimited; storytellers Dovie Thomason and Lynn Moroney; and Professor Debbie Reese from the University of Illinois, I held back over 100 stories and included only those approved by tribal authorities or Native American storytellers. This was the decision of the tribes, a decision I honor.

Other tribes and Native American storytellers readily gave their consent, and I greatly appreciate their cooperation and contribution. I believe that the stories of Native Americans belong to them and cannot be treated as a general resource to be pulled from other printed materials and used without any consideration for the people who hold them sacred. Authors and storytellers need to approach American Indian stories as part of living cultures, still vibrant and alive in this country, and not as historical or public domain pieces to be read or told with no regard for their origins and the people who have kept them alive these countless centuries. I hope that my readers will also honor these stories and treat them with the respect they deserve. I encourage other authors and storytellers to do the same.

I also asked several of my storytelling friends to donate a story. Art Thieme, Dovie Thomason, Kevin Strauss, Tim Tingle, Greg Rodgers, Alan Irvine, and Bob Sanders contributed traditional or historical pieces. Donald Davis, Ceil Anne Clement, and Jenifer Strauss gave me true stories from their families or from their own experiences growing up in their home states. These glimpses into the not-too-distant past are meant to entertain and enlighten students and let them see that stories are all around them, even in their own lives.

Chapters are organized alphabetically by state name, and each begins with an introduction to the state and its stories. There are four to six stories for each state. At the end of each state's chapter is a short glossary to help the student understand words, people, and ideas that might not be familiar to a twenty-first-century reader, followed by a list of sources, which notes the titles only. The bibliography at the end of this volume lists complete information about all sources. This extensive bibliography can point students and teachers to books that contain more stories. I hope readers will use this resource to discover the many legends that are still told and perhaps some that are almost forgotten and thereby save them from being lost.

People often ask me, "Are stories still important in this modern world of the twenty-first-century where computers, cell phones, and iPods have become commonplace?" I say that stories and storytelling are more important than ever. Stories help us recognize that we are part of something greater. They help us to be human in the best sense of the word. They engage our imaginations and make us feel alive. Stories teach us about where we come from and what it means to be at this place, at this moment. They even open our imaginations to what the future may bring. Consider the incredible impact of the *Harry Potter* books, the lasting power of Tolkien's <u>Lord of the Rings</u> trilogy, and the universal popularity of Terry

Pratchett's <u>Disc World</u> series. All of these books have one thing in common: they tell great stories. This book, too, is filled with wonderful stories.

I hope that by reading this book students and teachers are encouraged to look into the lore of all states that make up America. Moreover, I sincerely hope readers will connect with the stories of their own states and their own communities, then search to discover more folktales and true stories of their past. I also hope that these tales encourage readers to seek out their elders and discover the living stories that can be more inspiring than any book. Perhaps students will start collecting stories in their own communities or writing their own stories, sharing their memories and thoughts about the places where they live and the people who live there with them. Their stories will become the new legends, myths, hero tales, and ghost stories of America's twenty-first-century communities.

Alabama

Alabama entered the union in 1819 as the twenty-second state. When European settlers arrived, there were already indigenous peoples living in the region—the Alabama, Creek, and Tuskegee. Slaves imported from Africa came not long after the settlers arrived. The original peoples of the state are represented here with the story "Journey to the Land of the Tie-Snakes" from the Creek/Muscogee people.

You'll also find a story about the yellowhammer, the Alabama state bird, as well a true story about the only city in the world that has a monument to an agricultural pest. The African American tradition is represented by "The Preacher and the Bear" and the well-known story "Wiley and the Hairy Man."

Yellowhammers

The state bird of Alabama is the yellowhammer, and often in the old days folks called Alabama the Yellowhammer State.

The story goes that a young man who had never left his part of Alabama was in Georgia with his boss. They had driven a herd of cattle there to a market. The young man was given the day off by his employer and decided to explore the town.

He walked through the city, admiring the beautiful items on display in the shops, and finally turned into a residential neighborhood and walked among the old houses, wondering at their size and the wealth that hid behind the walls and high gates. He came to one house, and as he walked by he heard a strange scream and then someone talking to him in an unusual voice.

"Who are you? Who are you?" asked the voice.

The young man looked up, and there in the window he saw a parrot. The young man had never seen a parrot before, and he thought it was a bird he was more familiar with, a yellowhammer, a bird native to Alabama.

The bird started to scream again and called the young man all sorts of nasty and insulting names. The young man yelled back at the bird. "Hey there, old bird. You better watch yourself."

The bird squawked and screamed and kept yelling insults at the young man. The young man just kept shouting back. Finally he picked up a rock and was just about to throw it at his feathered foe when a young boy ran out of the house and stopped him.

"What are you doing?" asked the boy. "That is a valuable bird."

"Valuable," snorted the young man, "well, we have hundreds of them in Alabama. It's just an old yellowhammer."

Word spread about the young man's encounter with the insulting parrot and his mistaken identification. Soon folks all over Georgia were calling Alabama the Yellowhammer State.

Wiley and the Hairy Man
(African American)

Wiley is the young trickster found in tales throughout the South. Hairy Man is a shape-shifting creature, similar to the Abominable Snowman.

Now Wiley had been warned about the Hairy Man since he was a small boy. People said that the Hairy Man had taken Wiley's Pappy because he'd been such a bad man. His mama told him over and over again to always be on the lookout for the Hairy Man.

"Wiley," said his mother "you have to always be careful and never go anywhere without your dogs, because the Hairy Man hates dogs."

"Yes, mama. I'll make sure I keep an eye out for the Hairy Man and always take my dogs with me."

One day Wiley took his axe and his dogs down to the swamp to cut some wood. When they got to a nice stand of trees the dogs scared up a wild pig and took off after it. Wiley took up his axe and started to chop away, but he kept looking over his shoulder. "I wonder if the Hairy Man is around this morning." He looked down the path and sure enough, there was the Hairy Man, running toward Wiley grinning from ear to ear. He was covered with hair and had feet like a cow and stank so bad that Wiley could smell him when he was still a little dot on the horizon. He was horrible to look at, and his grin made him even worse. Wiley threw down his axe and climbed to the top of the tallest tree he could find. He figured that with feet like that the Hairy Man couldn't climb trees.

"What are you doing up in that tree?" asked the Hairy Man.

"My mama told me that I should never get too close to you. She said you carried a big sack and kept things in there for your supper."

"My sack is empty, Wiley, but it won't be for long." The Hairy Man put his empty sack on the ground, picked up Wiley's axe, and started to chop down that old bay tree. He swung that axe, and every time it hit chips just flew away. Wiley held on to that tree for dear life, and every time the Hairy Man hit the tree Wiley would yell out, "Fly chips back to the tree, back where you belong."

The Hairy Man was chopping and Wiley was yelling, "Fly chips back to the tree, back where you belong." The Hairy Man just chopped faster and faster, and soon Wiley's voice was so hoarse that the Hairy Man was gaining on him. Just then Wiley heard his dogs barking and he called out "Hey dogs, come to me." The dogs came running toward the sound of Wiley's voice.

"I hate dogs, Wiley." The Hairy Man dropped the axe and started running as fast as he could through the swamp.

When Wiley came home he told his mama what happened. He told her about the sack and the dogs driving the monster off.

"Next time Wiley, I don't want you climbing up a bay tree."

"That's right, mama. Bay trees aren't big enough."

"That's not what I mean. I want you to stand right there and face him and say 'Hello, Hairy Man. I heard you are the best conjurer in the whole world. I bet you can't turn yourself into a giraffe.' If you tease and ask enough times he will. Then you ask him to turn himself into an alligator. Then ask him to turn himself into a possum, and when he does grab that possum and throw him into his own sack, tie it up, and then throw him into the river."

Wiley tied up his dogs so they wouldn't scare the Hairy Man off, then he walked into the swamp. He hadn't walked far when he saw the Hairy Man running through the trees, grinning and laughing as he came toward Wiley. Wiley just stood there as the Hairy Man got closer and closer.

"Hello, Wiley," said the Hairy Man.

"Hello, Hairy Man."

"I heard that you are the best conjurer in the whole world. Is that true?"

"I guess it is, Wiley."

"I bet you can't turn into a giraffe."

"That's too easy," said the Hairy Man.

"If it's so easy, then do it and let me see," said Wiley.

The Hairy Man turned once then twice then three times, and there stood a giraffe.

"I bet you can't turn into an alligator from being a giraffe," said Wiley.

The giraffe turned once then twice then three times, and a big old alligator took its place.

"Big things are easy," said Wiley, "but I bet you can't become a little old possum."

The alligator turned once then twice then three times, and a little old possum took its place. Quick as a thought Wiley grabbed that possum and threw it into the sack and tied it up. Wiley ran as fast as he could to the river and threw that sack into the deepest part.

Wiley started for home, when he looked over his shoulder and saw the Hairy Man running and grinning. Wiley ran right up the biggest tree he saw and sat on the highest limb.

"Wiley," said the Hairy Man, "I just turned myself into the wind and blew right out of that sack. I'm going to sit right here at the bottom of this tree until you get so hungry that you climb down."

"Well, you are pretty smart," said Wiley, "but I bet you can't make things disappear."

"Wiley, you don't know how powerful I am. Look at that bird nest up above you." Wiley looked up and the bird's nest disappeared.

"I'm not so sure there was one there to begin with, Hairy Man."

"Look at your shirt, Wiley." Wiley's shirt was gone.

"That was a plain old shirt. I bet you can't make this rope around my waist disappear. It's been conjured."

"I can make all the ropes in the county disappear," said the Hairy Man.

"I bet you can't," cried Wiley.

The Hairy Man got real mad and yelled as loud as he could, "All the ropes in this county have disappeared." Wiley's rope that held up his pants disappeared. So did the ropes that held his dogs tied to the fence. When their ropes disappeared, those dogs took off looking for Wiley.

"Hey dogs, come to me," yelled Wiley.

The Hairy Man heard those dogs barking as they got closer and closer. "Are those your dogs?"

"Yes, they are."

"I hate dogs."

"I know you do," laughed Wiley.

The Hairy Man took off running with the dogs on his heels. They chased him deep into the swamp and then came back and walked Wiley home.

Wiley told his mama how the Hairy Man escaped from the sack and how he fooled him into making the ropes disappear so his dogs could come and rescue him.

"Wiley, you fooled the Hairy Man twice. If we can fool him one more time he can never bother us again. I've got to give this a lot of thought."

While his mama sat there thinking, Wiley tied up one dog to the front door and one to the back door and brought one inside. Then he lit a fire in the fireplace. He felt a little safer now.

"Wiley," called his mama, "I have a plan. Go to the barn and get a young pig. And bring it here." Wiley got a little baby pig from the barn and brought it to his mama. She took it and put it into the bed under the quilts. She told Wiley to tie up the two dogs in the barn and then go up into the attic with one of his dogs and hide. Wiley did as he was told and hid near the wall of the attic and looked out through a little hole. Then he saw something running as fast as the wind and it landed right on the roof. Wiley knew it was the Hairy Man by the smell. When the Hairy Man touched the chimney he yelled out because it was so hot. He jumped down and pounded on the front door of the cabin.

"I've come for your baby," cried the Hairy Man.

"You can't have him," said Wiley's mama.

"I'll set your house on fire with my breath," said the Hairy Man.

"I can put out that fire with a bucket of milk I have right here by my side," replied Wiley's mama.

"I'll blow this house down with one blast," cried the Hairy Man.

"I can hold this house up with just one hand," laughed Wiley's mama.

"I'll burn down the barn, dry up the spring, make your hens stop laying eggs, and send boll weevils into your fields," sneered the Hairy Man.

"That's too mean even for you," cried the woman.

"I'm a mean man, the meanest you'll ever meet," cried the Hairy Man.

"If I give you my baby, do you promise to leave here and never bother anyone else again?"

"I promise, and I always keep my promises."

Wiley's mama opened the door, and the Hairy Man stooped down and walked into the cabin.

"He's over in the bed," she said.

The Hairy Man walked over to her bed and threw back the quilt, and there was a little baby pig. "This isn't Wiley. This is a baby pig," roared the Hairy Man.

"I never said I was giving you Wiley. I said I was giving you my baby, and that was my baby pig and now he's yours."

The Hairy Man stomped and snorted and swore and screamed, but he knew that he had been tricked for the third time. He grabbed that pig and took off running through the swamp, knocking down trees and causing havoc all along his path.

When the Hairy Man was gone Wiley came down from the loft and hugged his mama.

"The Hairy Man is gone, Wiley, and he can never hurt us again. You don't ever have to be afraid of him anymore."

Wiley and his mama had a good supper and told this story over and over again until Wiley fell asleep in her lap.

Monument to a Pest
(Based on True Events)

The people stood around the town square with anticipation. The city was unveiling a monument today that would be the pride of the whole county. It was draped in cloth, waiting for the unveiling, and as the covering dropped the people of Enterprise, Alabama cheered. The monument, over thirteen feet tall, is a woman, draped in robes with her arms stretched above her head, surrounded by a fountain. The monument itself wasn't nearly as unique as the bronze tablet on the base of the monument, which read, "In Profound Appreciation of the Boll Weevil and What It Has Done as the Herald of Prosperity, This Monument Is Erected by the Citizens of Enterprise, Coffee County, Alabama—December 11, 1919."

The boll weevil came to Coffee County, Alabama, in 1915. Three years later farmers were losing their entire cotton crop to the insect. The beetle just ate through their fields, leaving nothing behind that could be salvaged. Cotton had been king in that part of Alabama since before anybody could remember. Farmers were facing financial ruin when one of the townspeople, H. M. Sessions, convinced a few farmers to try their hand at planting peanuts. They did, and the crop was so successful that they worked their way out of debt and proved to the other farmers that the lowly peanut was worth their time and effort.

The new diversification of crops brought more economic prosperity into the community. When the boll weevil epidemic was over, farmers went back to planting cotton but also continued to plant peanuts and other crops that ensured their economic stability.

The actual figure of the boll weevil wasn't added until thirty years after the original statue was dedicated. But the lady now holds a replica of the cotton-eating insect high over her head. Enterprise, Alabama, is the only city in the world that has a monument to an agricultural pest, but who can blame them? The lowly boll weevil taught them an important lesson: Don't put all your eggs in one basket.

Journey to the Land of the Tie-Snakes (Creek/Muscogee People)

Tie-snakes are powerful and greatly feared mythological water spirits.

Once a long time ago a chief sent his son with a message to another chief. He sent a bowl with the boy as a gift and as a symbol of his authority.

The chief's son stopped along the way and began to play with some boys near a small lake. As he played he forgot about the bowl, and it slipped into the water and sank to the bottom. He was afraid to continue his journey or return home with out it. He jumped into the water and dove down to where he thought the bowl had sunk. The other boys waited for a long time, but after awhile they knew that he must be dead, so they returned to the village and told his father.

Now when the boy had dove into the water, Tie-snakes had come and taken hold of him and brought him to a cave deep beneath the surface. There he saw their king sitting on a throne that was made of hundreds of Tie-snakes. He was told to climb to the top of the throne and talk to the king. He tried once, but the throne just moved and grew. He tried a second time and again a third time, but each time the throne just moved and grew underneath him. On the fourth try he walked to where their king sat and stood before him.

The king looked at him, pointed to a corner of the cave, and said, "That feather over there is yours if you can grasp it."

The boy went to the feather and tried once, twice, three times to grab the feather, but it kept floating away from him. On the fourth try he finally succeeded.

Then the king pointed to a tomahawk and told him that if he could grasp the tomahawk then it was his. The boy again tried three times to grab it, but each time it moved away from him and he failed. On the fourth try he finally caught it.

The king of the Tie-snakes told the young man that he could return home after three days in the king's cave. "Do not tell your father about the throne or the feather or the tomahawk. If you and your people ever need my help, just walk toward the east, bow three times to the sun as it rises, and I will come to help you."

After three days he was carried by the Tie-snakes to the surface and the lost bowl was placed in his hands. He returned to the village, where the people were mourning him. The sadness turned into a celebration when they saw him walking toward them. He told his father about the king of the Tie-snakes and his message of help whenever it was needed.

Soon afterward an enemy approached the village and threatened the boy and his people. His father asked him to go and ask the Tie-snake king for his help. The boy put the feather on his head and the tomahawk in his hand and went to the east and bowed three times toward the rising sun. The king of the Tie-snakes appeared. The boy told him of their danger. The Tie-snake told him to return to his village. "Tell your people not to fear. None of them will be harmed. By morning all will be well."

The son returned and told his father the chief what the snake king had told him. That night the enemy attacked their village, but not one person was harmed. In the morning they saw that every enemy warrior was held fast in the grip of the Tie-snakes. All the enemy warriors were captured. The enemy was afraid of the powerful magic that had stopped them from destroying the village. The chief made peace with his enemies, and they were released by the Tie-snakes. They lived as neighbors from then on.

Used with permission from the Cultural Preservation Office of the Muscogee/Creek Nation, Okmulgee, Oklahoma.

The Preacher and the Bear
(African American)

Once a preacher was on his way to an appointment and decided to take a shortcut through some neighboring woods. As he walked deeper and deeper into the woods he finally came to a creek. The only way across the creek was a huge log that spanned the waterway from one side to the other. As the preacher put his foot on one end of the log he looked up and saw a bear that had come out of the woods on the other side of creek and had put his paw on the log's end on his side. The two stood very still, looking at each other. The preacher very slowly took his foot off the log. The bear took another step forward across the log. The preacher looked up into the heavens and said, "Please Lord, I have only one request to make of you. Help me if you can but if you can't please don't help that bear." With those words the preacher dove into the water. The bear watched as the preacher swam downstream and finally crawled out of the stream and ran on to town.

The preacher went to church that Sunday and told about his experience with the bear. When he finished one of the ladies of his church said, "Preacher, you should have prayed harder. You should have relied on prayer."

The preacher looked at her and said, "Sister, prayer is all right at a prayer meeting but it isn't worth much at a bear meeting."

Alabama Glossary

Alabama: A state that gets its name from the Native American tribe of the same name. The capital is Montgomery.

Boll weevil: A beetle that has a great appetite for cotton. It feeds on the buds and flowers of the cotton plant. This insect came to the United States in the late nineteenth- century from Mexico.

Creek/Muscogee people: A Native American people who lived in what is now Alabama and Georgia. They were a federation of several tribes. They were one of the Five Civilized Nations and were forcibly removed across the Mississippi River to Oklahoma, then known as Indian Territory.

Hairy Man: A shape-shifting creature that haunts the woods and swamps of the South in many African American tales. It is a cousin to the Abominable Snowman.

Tie-snakes: Mythological water spirits that appear to be about the same size as other snakes but have incredible strength. These spirits are greatly feared.

Wiley: The young trickster that baffles the shape-shifting Hairy Man. Many versions of this tale can be found throughout the South.

Yellowhammer: The state bird of Alabama. It is also called the golden winged woodpecker or the northern flicker.

Story Sources

Alabama Tales

Alabama, One Big Front Porch

American Folktales from the Collections of the Library of Congress, Volume 1

American Folktales from the Collections of the Library of Congress, Volume 2

American Myths & Legends, Volumes 1 & 2

The Book of Negro Folklore

Buying the Wind

Cultural Preservation Office of the Muscogee/Creek Nation, Okmulgee, Oklahoma

Every Tongue Got to Confess: Negro Folktales from the Gulf States

Folk Stories of the South

The Greenwood Library of American Folktales, Volume 2

Mules and Men

Myths & Legends of Our Own Land, Volumes 1 & 2

The People Could Fly: American Black Folktales

Southern Indian Myths & Legends

Stockings of Buttermilk

Sweet Bunch of Daisies: Folk Songs from Alabama

13 Alabama Ghosts & Jeffrey

A Treasury of Southern Folklore

Why the Possum's Tail Is Bare & Other Classic Southern Stories

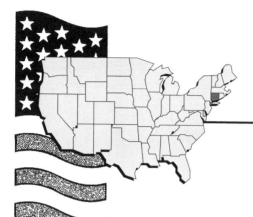

Connecticut

Long before the arrival of the Europeans, the Pequot people lived in the area now called Connecticut. One of the thirteen original colonies, Connecticut officially became a state in 1788. It is home to many wonderful folktales and legends. Two stories here, one about fearsome frogs and the other about a man concerned with getting to heaven, represent that great storytelling tradition of being able to poke just a little bit of fun at yourself. The soldiers of Connecticut were the first in the colonies to be referred to as Yankees, and their story and song are told here.

Like all of New England, Connecticut is known for its beautiful hardwood forests, where oak trees stand alongside maple, cherry, and other types of trees. Not many trees have played a part in the fight against tyranny, but the tale of the Charter Oak features a tree that served its people well. John Ledyard, who led a life of travel and adventure, appears in another story. This son of Connecticut could be called America's first world traveler.

Yankee Doodle Soldiers
(Based on True Events)

The frontier in 1756 was a dangerous place. Raids by the French and their Indian allies always threatened to disrupt the peace. In response, Colonel Thomas Fitch, the son of Thomas Fitch, the governor of Connecticut, had organized a colonial cavalry unit to accompany British regulars that were stationed near Albany, New York.

Colonel Fitch's "soldiers" were as unmilitary looking a group of men as you could find anywhere. Most of them were farmers and woodsmen who wore the clothes in which they hunted and farmed. Their muskets were suited for hunting rather than fighting in a war, but these men were motivated. They would fight to protect their families; and what they lacked in uniforms they made up for in knowledge of the woods, their incredible marksmanship, and their free and easy manner. As they gathered at Colonel Fitch's house before leaving to join the regulars, Elizabeth Fitch, the younger sister of the colonel, walked out to see them off. When she saw the ragtag group she declared that they needed something to identify them as soldiers. She and some other girls from the household went to the chicken and duck pens and gathered long feathers, then gave one to each volunteer to put into the band of his hat.

When the Connecticut volunteers finally rode into the camp of the regular British army, they were met with catcalls and laughter. Here was one of the great European armies, dazzling in their red and white uniforms, watching as the Connecticut colonial cavalry rode into camp with chicken and duck feathers stuck into their hats. One of the officers, Doctor Shuckberg, an army physician, laughed and pointed and called out that the colonials thought themselves proper macaronis. "Macaroni" was English slang for the continental European style of fashion that overdressed dandies preferred. The young soldiers from Connecticut, rather than being offended, joined in the fun. Dr. Shuckberg actually penned a little song to the tune of "Lucy Locket Lost Her Pocket":

> Yankee Doodle came to town
> Riding on a donkey
> Stuck a feather in his cap
> And called it macaroni.

That's the legend of "Yankee Doodle." The little ditty went on to be the song that colonial soldiers sang as they went to war against England in the Revolutionary War. It was the song that American soldiers have sung in many wars since. In 1979 it became the official state song of Connecticut. I'm sure those ragged colonial cavalrymen who served under Colonel Fitch would approve.

Yankee Doodle

Yankee Doodle went to town,
Riding on a pony,
Stuck a feather in his cap,
And called it macaroni.

Chorus
Yankee Doodle keep it up,
Yankee Doodle dandy,
Mind the music and the step,
And with the girls be handy.

Father and I went down to camp,
Along with Captain Gooding,
And there we saw the men and boys
As thick as hasty pudding.

And there we saw a thousand men
As rich as Squire David,
And what they wasted every day,
I wish it could be saved.

And there I see a swamping gun
Large as a log of maple,
Upon a deuced little cart,
A load for father's cattle.

And every time they shoot it off,
It takes a horn of powder,
And makes a noise like father's gun,
Only a nation louder.

The Windham Terror

On a misty night in July 1758 the people of Windham, Connecticut, were awakened by a sound they had never heard in their village before. The darkness that seemed to envelope the houses was pierced by unearthly screams and deep voices that seemed to rise from the depths of the earth. Men sprang out of bed and reached for their muskets. Women and children were ushered into the church, where they prayed and sang for deliverance from the terror that howled right outside the church. The men took up defensive positions around the village. One man was heard to declare that he would give half his fortune to anyone who could keep him safe until morning.

All night the people of Windham remained vigilant. As the light of the first rays of the sun started to streak across the sky, the voices and screams stopped. Armed patrols left the village and went looking for the source of the horrible sounds that had haunted the village all night long.

The next night the sounds again woke up the residents of Windham and kept them awake with the moans of the dead and the howls of fiends until dawn came, and with it, peace. It wasn't 'til that afternoon that the reason behind the nightly terror was finally revealed. During the recent drought a nearby pond had dried up, making hundreds of frogs that lived there homeless. The homeless frogs had all moved to a small pond right at the edge of the village, where they sang and croaked all night long. The moans of the dead and the screams of the monsters in the night were just some relocated frogs serenading their new neighbors in the village with their throaty songs.

The Oak Tree Conspirator
(Based on True Events)

The old oak tree had once stood surrounded by others like it, deep in the forests of a land that is now called Connecticut. Some say the oak was 400 years old when Columbus first caught sight of the New World. The Native Americans in the area had honored the tree for generations and had traditionally held their councils underneath its massive branches. Now it stood on the Wyllys property, still magnificent, still an object of awe and respect, and now part of a famous conspiracy that was trying to keep Connecticut free from a tyrant.

When the Wyllys family moved into Connecticut and bought the land where the huge oak tree stood, the local Native Americans came to Old Samuel and begged them to spare the tree. They told the family of its history and the councils that had taken place underneath its towering branches and of the peaceful coexistence it signified. Though Samuel Wyllys cut down the forest around it, he spared the old oak tree. So the old oak waited until it could once again become part of a legend.

When Connecticut decided to appeal to King Charles II to obtain a charter of liberties, John Winthrop, often called Winthrop the Younger to distinguish him from his famous grandfather, John Winthrop the governor of Massachusetts, went to England to hand deliver the petition. The colonists in Connecticut were hoping that the king might just remember that the elder Winthrop had been a favorite of the king's father. Besides his famous name, Winthrop also brought with him a beautiful ring the king had given his grandfather and a document signed by the Indian chief Sequassen. This document supposedly had given away Sequassen's lands and birthright to the English settlers at Hartford. Aided by the Duchess of Castlemain, the king offered the settlers of Connecticut the most liberal guarantee of rights and freedom of any colony in the New World. The charter was signed, sealed, and given to Winthrop on April 26, 1662.

The charter was so liberal and gave the people of the Connecticut colony such unprecedented rights that the next monarch, James II, tried to reverse it. He sent Sir Edmund Andros, the former New York governor and now the governor of all the New England colonies, to Hartford to take back the charter and revoke Connecticut's rights. The arrogant Andros was known as a tough administrator.

Andros sent word to the people of Connecticut that they should give the charter to him. But the people had lived peacefully and well for twenty-five years under their charter and were not going to give it up that easily. Andros threatened the colony of Connecticut with dissolution. Their eastern land would be made part of New York, while their western lands would be part of Massachusetts, he said. But the officials of the colony still refused.

Sir Edmund was at the end of his limited diplomatic skills and decided to go to Connecticut and demand that the colonists give him back the charter. He prepared to address the Assembly at Butler's Tavern. At one end of the table sat Connecticut governor Treat and the Assembly while at the other end sat Sir Edmund and his soldiers. Finally Sir Edmund Andros rose and began to speak. He reminded the colonists that he was an agent of the king and that he and all the colonists of Connecticut were his subjects. If they refused any longer to produce the charter then he would consider it treason.

Governor Treat rose and signaled for Captain Joseph Wadsworth to go to the Wyllys home and fetch the charter. The family had been hiding it in a blanket chest. After he had gone to fetch the document an angry debate arose among the members of the Assembly. One by one they stood and told why they favored giving it back or why they favored keeping it. Finally Captain Wadsworth returned with the charter case and turned it over to Treat.

Just as he did, Andrew Leete rose to his feet and began to speak. He banged his fist against the table and called for the Assembly to keep the charter. He walked around the room waving his arms, speaking with more and more passion until he made a sweeping motion with his arms that sent both of the candlesticks on the table crashing to the floor, plunging the room into darkness. Nathaniel Stanley jumped up and in the confusion and darkness grabbed the charter and passed it to Captain Wadsworth, who was waiting underneath one of the windows. Wadsworth ran back to the Wyllys home.

Ruth Wyllys was waiting, and the two of them tried to think of the best hiding place. They both knew that Andros and his soldiers would come there first and that hiding it in the house was a bad idea. Mistress Wyllys looked out her window and saw the old oak at the end of her yard. It was huge and twisted, and time had caused a crack of sorts that had made a crevice near its base that was just large enough to hide the precious Charter of the Colony of Connecticut. Wrapping it in his coat, Captain Wadsworth hid the charter in the massive oak.

Andros never found the charter, but that didn't stop him being a tyrant to the people in the colonies, especially Connecticut. The people suffered until James II was succeeded by William of Orange. Only then did the great oak give up its secret and return the charter to the people.

The tree had been on the verge of death when the charter was placed in it, but suddenly it began to spread again, and it lived for 170 years, until it was toppled in a storm on August 21, 1856. All the bells in Hartford tolled in mourning for what was called the Charter Oak, the last living conspirator against King James and Sir Edmund.

John Ledyard, America's First Explorer (a True Story)

John Ledyard was born in Groton, Connecticut, in 1751. The first great American explorer, he became a friend and associate of some of the most famous people of his day.

For a brief time John Ledyard attended Dartmouth College. Then he began his life of travel with a trip up the Connecticut River in a canoe that he made himself. He then signed on as a seaman on a voyage to the Caribbean and then on to the Barbary Coast. He was impressed into the Royal Marines and joined Captain Cook's third and final voyage.

From 1776 until 1780 John was with the Cook expedition. During this voyage they became the first Europeans to visit Hawaii. They also visited New Zealand, Tahiti, and many other islands in the Pacific Ocean. Ledyard also became the first American to visit Alaska, the Aleutian Islands, and the Pacific Northwest of what would later become the United States. He was with the expedition when Cook was killed in Hawaii.

Still a Royal Marine, John Ledyard was sent to the colonies to help put down the revolution. After coming ashore he deserted, and he eventually returned to Hartford, where he wrote his journal of the third voyage of Captain Cook. It was the first book to be protected by the copyright laws of the United States.

Later Ledyard tried his hand at the fur trade, but he wasn't really a businessman. He was an adventurer. His friend Thomas Jefferson suggested to Ledyard that he explore the western part of the North American continent by traveling across Russia and crossing over at the Bering Strait. He left London in December 1786 and traveled through Moscow and all the way to Yakutsk in only eleven weeks. He spent the winter there, only to be arrested on orders of Catherine the Great and deported.

John Ledyard then proposed an idea to the African Association in London to travel the African continent from the Red Sea to the Atlantic Ocean. Before the expedition could start, John Ledyard became ill in Cairo, Egypt, and died.

John Ledyard was a true adventurer and traveler. He visited parts of what would someday be his country long before any other European American. He traveled with the great Captain Cook and was with him when he made many of his discoveries. His dream of walking around the world was cut short, but his journey through life was a magnificent one.

If You Want to Get to Heaven ...

A long time ago there was a farmer named Josiah. He was a wealthy man who had remained single his whole life. In fact, he had no family to speak of at all. One day after church he sat on the front porch of his fine house looking over his garden and farm, his barn full of milking cows, his pigs, and his goats. He looked over his acres of wheat and corn and he was content. His life was perfect. He was a happy man. That's when he had a very unpleasant thought. "I am so happy and content that I would hate to leave this place. What will I do when it's my turn to go into the next life? I won't want to go. I've never been unhappy or troubled or poor or hungry. What will heaven offer me? I need some trouble in my life so I won't be sad to leave it someday."

Josiah joined some of his friends down at the local public house and listened as they all talked about their troubles. Now the problem was that all of their troubles had nothing to do with him. Some men complained of being poor; he wasn't. Some men complained of their terrible children; he had none. Some men complained of taxes; he had enough money to pay them without thinking. Some men complained about their cows or horses or crops. Josiah had no problems with any of these in his life. Then he heard a man complain about his wife, and Josiah had an idea. He might not have a wife, but he could get one, and he could find the most difficult woman in all of Connecticut to be his bride, and then he would have troubles enough to make him happy to leave this world.

The very next day he set out on his journey to find a difficult woman for his bride. He went from town to town. He listened in on conversations at taverns and public houses in case he might hear of some difficult single woman. But after days of searching he still hadn't found a bride.

As he was making his way home, he passed the house of a neighbor named Andrew and heard the most awful screaming and yelling and fussing. It was old Andrew's only daughter, Hannah. The sounds that came from that house hurt his ears. How could he not remember Hannah? She argued and fought with everyone in the village and with all her father's neighbors. You could hear her voice a mile away.

Josiah walked up to the door and knocked. The door opened. There stood the red-headed daughter of old Andrew.

"What do you want?" she demanded.

"Hannah, will you marry me?" Josiah heard a scream from the other room and then a feeble "thank you" coming from the mouth of old Andrew.

Hannah looked him up and down. To be truthful, Josiah was a handsome man and a wealthy man too. "Yes, I believe I will," she answered.

The two of them were married, and Josiah could not have been happier because Hannah was perfect. She argued and nagged all day long. She caused so much trouble that he was always shaking his head at his good fortune. She would start yelling at him even before he walked through the door at night. She argued with the baker, the preacher, the dressmaker, the postmaster, and the constable. He even heard her arguing with the cows and horses one day. Josiah was sure that he would be content in heaven and never miss his farm or life here on earth because he finally had his share of trouble. The only person who was really happy now was Hannah's father, who walked around the town with a beautiful smile.

One day Josiah was in the public house with his friends when one of them asked how married life was for Josiah.

"It's perfect," he said. "She scolds and hollers and argues and screams at me all day long." He smiled contentedly.

"That's an odd thing for a husband to say, Josiah. Why does her bad temper make you happy?" asked one man.

"Yes Josiah, why would anyone pick the woman in this area with the foulest temper and be pleased about it?" asked another.

"I'll tell you my friends why I chose her. You see, I had everything a man could want and I knew that when it was my time to go to the next world I'd miss my farm and friends. I never had any trouble or hardship and I knew that I would never enjoy heaven if I didn't have something to give me a bit of trouble here on earth. That's why I married Hannah. I'll be happy to leave now and can enjoy the afterlife with no regrets about leaving this one."

His friends listened in astonishment and just shook their heads sadly at his story. In fact the story was so good they all told their wives, and you know how stories travel. Soon it all came back to Hannah's ears.

She was sitting with some of her neighbors sewing and talking when one of the ladies, a longtime friend of Hannah's, spoke up and said, "My husband came home the other day with the strangest tale I ever heard. He told me that your Josiah told all the men at the tavern that he married you so you would make his life miserable and bring trouble into it so he would be happy to go to heaven and leave this world behind. He said that his life was too good before and he would have missed it in heaven, but now since you came along he's looking forward to leaving this world behind."

Hannah slowly stood up. Her face got as red as a beet. She made her hands into fists and started to scream and rant and yell and fuss. "Just wait until he gets home tonight," she said. "he thinks life has been hard so far? Wait until I get finished with him." She paced the room and looked as if she was going to explode at any minute. Then all of a sudden she stopped. She stood very still and a look came over her face that no one in that room had ever seen before. Then she smiled. The smile became bigger and bigger and brighter and brighter. It was as if all the smiles she had never used were all coming to her face at the same time, and it was beautiful to see. The ladies almost gasped at the beauty of Hannah's smile.

"Ladies, I will not be the reason my husband goes to heaven a happy man. I'll show him what a mistake he made when he chose me as his ticket to eternity." Then her smile turned to laughter and the ladies, all understanding what she was going to do, all laughed with her.

That night when Josiah came home she greeted him with a smile and a kiss. He stood there in the doorway in shock. She laughed and asked him about his day and was all smiles and joy. She had made his favorite meal and was actually happy to see him.

From that day on Josiah had the finest wife in the whole town, maybe in the entire world. It gave him no peace of mind at all because now he worried that he would not enjoy heaven since life here on earth was as good as it might ever get. Then one day as he walked across his field he thought to himself, "I can enjoy the next world as long as Hannah will be there with me, and I know she will." From then on he was truly a happy man, and Hannah actually enjoyed being a happy woman. Life was good for them.

Connecticut Glossary

Captain Cook: An English explorer who made three round-the-world voyages of discovery. He was killed in the Pacific Ocean during his final voyage.

Charter: A document given to a colony to legally recognize its right to exist under the British Crown.

Connecticut: A state whose name comes from the Native American word "Quinnehtukqat," meaning "beside the tidal river." The capital is Hartford.

Copyright: Legal protection for an author prohibiting other people from stealing his or her original written works.

Pequot people: A Native American people were once part of a larger tribe that included the Mohegans. After a split between the two factions the Pequot moved into what is now Connecticut. Pequot reservations can still be found in Connecticut.

Story Sources

American Folktales from the Collections of the Library of Congress, Volume 1

American Folktales from the Collections of the Library of Congress, Volume 2

American Myths & Legends, Volumes 1 & 2

American Traveler

Folk Tales of Connecticut

The Greenwood Library of American Folktales, Volume 1

Jonathan Draws the Long Bow

Legendary Connecticut: Traditional Tales from the Nutmeg State

Myths & Legends of Our Own Land, Volumes 1 & 2

New England Bean-Pot

New England Legends & Folklore

Spirit of the New England Tribes: Indian History & Folklore

A Treasury of New England Folklore

Delaware

Delaware was one of the thirteen original colonies, and it was the first to sign the Declaration of Independence in 1776. It officially became a state in 1787. In size, Delaware exceeds only Rhode Island, the smallest state in the union. The Delaware people, called the Lenape in their own language, were among the first people to make this land their home.

Later, from Europe came the Swedes and the Dutch, who colonized Delaware. Their history in the state is reflected in the story "The Lights of the Enemy." "The Phantom Dragoon" is a story from the days of the Revolutionary War, when Delaware was a battleground that saw both sides—those loyal to the Crown and those fighting for independence—win and lose on its soil. Delaware borders other states that held slaves and was itself a home to slaves before its agriculture changed. This period in Delaware's history is illustrated by the story "The Fiddler's Coin." Our last story is about Howard Pyle, one of Delaware's artistic sons, who is noteworthy for the profound influence he had on children's literature.

The Lights of the Enemy
(Based on True Events)

In the old days before America was a country and when the English were not the only Europeans settled in the New World, there was a colony of Dutch at New Amsterdam and a colony of Swedes at Fort Casmir and Fort Christina. Now the leader of New Amsterdam was the wily old fox Governor Stuyvesant. He was determined to take the land away from the Swedes and make it part of the Dutch colony. He would walk around his office and stomp his wooden leg and rant, "If we can take those forts then all the land of the Swedes in the New World will be ours." He decided to send two spies disguised as traders to keep an eye on the colonists at Fort Christina and find out how strong and well prepared they were for an attack on their lands.

The spies arrived in the fort on the same day that a boatload of settlers and soldiers arrived from Sweden. There was a great celebration in the fort and a great feast and dance was held in honor of the new arrivals. The spies saw the new soldiers arrive in their iron helmets with their muskets and swords. They also saw neat wooden cabins and rich pelts hanging from racks, bins full of corn, and a strong stockade. The new settlers and soldiers were happy to see how prosperous the colony was, but they were also having some second thoughts. This land was not like Sweden. This land had deep woods and marshes where some folks say lions and dragons and snakes with jaws as wide as a bear lurked and hid waiting for unsuspecting prey. They didn't trust the deep shadows and the noises that came out of them. Soon though, the soldiers and colonists fell into a routine and their fears were pushed further back into their imaginations.

One night in June one of the new soldiers was on guard on the wall of the stockade. The night was dark, with little light from the moon or stars. The young soldier walked his sentry duty back and forth along the wall, looking out into the darkness, wondering who or what was making all the dreadful sounds that filled the night.

After a while he was sure that he had caught a glimpse of a dragon, its long serpentlike tail coiled and curled around a huge tree. Then he was sure that he saw lions, their great manes shaking as they roared slipping from one shadow to the next. Maybe there were also giant magical birds that could carry him away roosting in the dark trees, watching him with their yellow eyes. He started to see frightening shapes everywhere he looked, and soon it seemed that the whole night was filled with creatures waiting to carry him off or attack him at any moment.

Then he saw a light, just one at first, blinking on then blinking off again. He stared at the light, trying to figure out what it could be. Then the light moved closer. Then another appeared and then another, and they kept moving and darting about in the night. The soldier started to see more and more of them as they filled up the night sky.

What could this be? he thought. Is it an attack by the native people? Is it the cursed Dutch led by old Peg Leg Stuyvesant? Is it the monsters of the night coming for him and the rest of the colonists? More lights appeared, coming from all directions, flickering on and off as they made their way toward him and the fort. When he heard the croaks and bellows of the frogs, he knew they were under attack and he sounded the alarm.

"Awake!! Awake!!" he cried. "The enemy is upon us. Defend yourselves!"

The people and the soldiers rushed from their homes, muskets in hand, and ran to the walls.

"What have you seen?" asked his commander.

"Look over there. The enemy is carrying lights to burn down the fort. They are attacking from all directions," he cried.

He pointed toward the woods and the people followed his arm. At first some of them were angry with the young guard, but soon they were all laughing. The beautiful shining lights were none other than fireflies flitting in the night.

Word spread about the foolish young soldier. Peter Stuyvesant also heard the story from his spies.

"If their soldiers are frightened of lights in the night, they should be easy to defeat," he said with confidence.

When the old Dutchman finally attacked the forts, he took them without firing a shot and without hurting a soul. He claimed he had outwitted them, but perhaps the Swedes were just too smart to fight back and start a war.

The Phantom Dragoon

Near the city Newark, Delaware, there is a high place called Iron Hill, where the British camped during the American Revolution. General Howe used it as his base as the British army was making its way to Brandywine. The American army made its outposts nearby, trying to keep the British in sight. They placed their picket posts near Welsh Tract Church. Every night the sentries would keep on the lookout for British patrols and any movement of the army.

During that first week a young American sentry was thrown into a panic as a wild horseman dressed in white came charging out of the mist straight at the young Continental soldier. When the sentry was found he begged not to be at that post again. The next night a new sentry was posted there, and again the rider in white came charging out of the mist, a mocking laughter accompanying his unearthly appearance. Night after night the rider came to the sentry post and approached the sentry, laughing and ready to run them over with his powerful horse. The men in the Continental Army who were from the area started to tell others the legend of the ghostly rider. They told stories of a man who had been chased along the road by demons and now chases others right to the gates of Hell. Others told stories of the devil himself, who rode at night trying to lure the unsuspecting into following him; if they did, they were never seen again.

The stories continued until one old Yankee sergeant from New England decided that he would stand guard himself that night. He wasn't afraid of ghosts, and he would prove to all the others that it was a trick of their imaginations, or that the rider in white was as real a man as any of them. The others were certain that the old sergeant would sing a different tune the next morning.

The sergeant stood behind a fence near the old church road and waited in the shadows. He had his musket primed and loaded. There was a mist that night, and he was certain that the rider in white would appear as he had on all those other misty nights. It wasn't long before he heard the beat of hooves coming down the road at a furious pace. In spite of himself the old soldier could feel a chill crawl up his back. He took his musket and raised t to his shoulder and waited for the rider to come into view. Suddenly the rider and horse seemed to fly out of the misty darkness right in front of the sergeant. The sentry took aim and fired. The ghost seemed to hold still for just a moment and then the white rider tumbled from its horse and fell to the ground. The old soldier vaulted over the fence and ran to the fallen figure. Turning the white rider over, the sergeant found not a demon hunting for lost souls but a British scout. The British army had taken advantage of the local stories about riders in white and had disguised one of their men as the ghostly rider so he could get close to the American lines and spy on the army. The scout was captured and brought back to the American camp, where his wound was tended. He gave his captors more information about General Howe's army than he ever collected about the Continentals as the white rider.

The Fiddler's Coin

A long time ago outside of Wilmington, there was an old road with a bridge that spanned a creek. The locals called it Fiddler's Bridge. The legend says that if you toss a coin into the water off the bridge a fiddler will rise from the waters and play you a tune.

Before Delaware became a state, when it was still a colony, an African boy would sit on the railing of the bridge and play his homemade fiddle, sing a song, or sometimes dance as he played. People would pass by and he would give them a song and sometimes they would hand him a coin.

The boy's name was Jacob, and he was born to slaves on a nearby farm. Jacob loved his music and played for anyone who would listen, and if there was no one there to listen he played for the joy of playing. Eventually his old homemade instrument was replaced with a real fiddle through the kindness of someone who liked his music. So Jacob sat by that bridge from morning to night almost every day, happy with his music.

Though most people found Jacob to be amusing, entertaining, and a joy to watch as he played, there were others who just considered the young boy a lazy nuisance. One of these few who didn't like the boy was the caretaker of the farm. One day he pulled Jacob aside and yelled at him for sitting on the bridge doing nothing all day. Then he lashed the boy until he was unconscious. The caretaker thought that a good beating would drive the music right out of the boy's head and put an end to his fiddling. For a while it worked, because Jacob was speechless and unable to move for several weeks after the beating. When he finally recovered, he had lost the power of speech and reason. But he could still fiddle, and now his fiddling became wilder and even more intense than it had ever been before. The caretaker, out of guilt or shame or just meanness, drove him off the farm. Jacob built a small shelter near the creek by the bridge and there he fiddled, day in and day out. He fiddled for the animals that lived near the creek and were his neighbors, and he fiddled for the passersby who heard his music as they crossed the bridge near his little shack. Sometimes they would throw him a coin and he would stop and solemnly tip his straw hat, and then begin to play again.

Jacob sat there fiddling for many years, growing old, and essentially became a fixture by the bridge. Sometimes people would stop and listen; other times they enjoyed the music as it followed them on down the road. The coins he collected paid for his food, and the animals kept him company.

Jacob never spoke, he never smiled, and he didn't dance like he did before the beating. He just played his fiddle. Late at night people could hear the soft notes drifting on the summer breeze. Early in the morning just as the sun rose, they could hear his tunes floating through the early morning mist in the fall. Jacob was always there, always fiddling.

One day the townspeople found his body floating in the creek. He had drowned. Some folks thought he fell in by accident, while others said he might have had a seizure, a leftover from that brutal beating. Now the fiddle was silent and the music was gone.

But not long after Jacob was buried, people started to hear things when they crossed the bridge down by Scott Run. They heard fiddle music. Some folks say that when they came by at night or in the early morning fog, they could see a figure standing near the bridge, fiddling a tune.

One night some young men who had been having a good time at a local tavern stopped at the bridge while they walked home. They remembered the stories about the old man who had lived in a shack and fiddled for anyone who would listen. Some of them actually remembered Jacob from their own boyhoods. One of them jokingly said it might be a good idea to toss a coin to the old fiddler and ask for a tune. He took a coin and threw it over the side of the bridge and said, "Come on Jacob, how about a tune?" Imagine their surprise when a shimmering apparition arose from the waters of the creek and floating in midair started to play them a tune on its fiddle. The music speeded up and became so intense that the young men were rooted to the ground. Finally they looked at each other and one of them looked at his pocket watch and said in a trembling voice, "Well boys, it's just about midnight. Maybe we should think about heading home." With that, they all ran as fast s they could across the bridge and into town.

Now the old bridge is gone, but the creek is still there, and if you ever are in that part of Delaware, it might be interesting to head down to Scott Run and toss a coin in the creek. Maybe you'll be lucky and get to hear some fine music from a real old master. Then again, you might not think it lucky.

Bringing Legends of the Old World to the New (a True Story)

A young boy sat under a tree with a book, reading an adventure story, his lips almost moving in anticipation of the next flight of the arrow. Vivid illustrations cemented in the young boy's mind what Robin Hood and his men looked like, and the images stayed with him for the rest of his life. In fact, the illustrations seemed to tell the stories themselves—Robin Hood being carried across the stream by Friar Tuck, Little John standing over a defeated Eric of Lincoln, Robin meeting Will Scarlet, and finally Robin shooting his last arrow as he lay dying in Little John's arms. The book he was reading was *The Merry Adventures of Robin Hood*, illustrated and written by Howard Pyle.

Howard Pyle was born in Wilmington, Delaware, in 1853. He taught at Drexel University and later started his own school of art and illustration. Famous artists such as N. C. Wyeth studied under him. Even though he was known as an art educator, it was his adventure books that brought him to the attention of the general public.

Pyle enjoyed the old legends and stories from medieval Europe. He took those old stories and the ancient ballads and rewrote them for a younger audience, adding his realistic but also romantic illustrations. In rewriting the old tales, he strove to present a good story, rather than an accurate revision of the ancient legends. Howard Pyle wrote stories about King Arthur and his knights, Robin Hood and his band of outlaws, and pirates in the Caribbean; and he illustrated stories and novels for other authors. He also wrote his own tales, including *Otto of the Silver Hand*.

Pyle died in Italy in 1911, but his books are still popular today as they grace the shelves of children of all ages, bringing the heroes and ladies, knights and villains, pirates and champions, kings and paupers, outlaws and archers to life for countless young readers.

Delaware Glossary

Delaware: A state named after the Delaware River, commemorating Sir Thomas West, Baron De La Warr. Its capital is Dover.

Dragoon: A cavalry unit in the British army.

Governor Peter Stuyvesant: Legendary leader of New Amsterdam.

New Amsterdam: The Dutch settlement that eventually became New York City.

Story Sources

American Folktales from the Collections of the Library of Congress, Volume 1

American Folktales from the Collections of the Library of Congress, Volume 2

American Myths & Legends, Volumes 1 & 2

Ghost Stories of the Delaware Coast

The Greenwood Library of American Folktales, Volume 1

Legends of the Delaware Indians and Picture Writing

Myths & Legends of Our Own Land, Volumes 1 & 2

Upstate Downstate

The White Deer & Other Stories Told by the Lenape

Florida

Florida was admitted to the union as the twenty-seventh state in 1845. The Seminole people lived here when the first explorers from Spain landed, and they fought many a fierce battle with Spain and then the United States over their homeland. Most of the tribe was forcibly removed to Indian Territory, now Oklahoma.

Two stories, "The Fastest Man" and "Uncle Monday, the Alligator Shaman," come from African Americans in Florida, who came not only as slaves but also as immigrants from the island nations of the Caribbean Sea. "Antonio the Woodcutter" shows the influence of Cuba (which lies just off the Florida coast) and its people on Florida. The hunting tradition has always been strong in Florida, and the tall tale, "A Peachy Tale," found here, is just the kind of story hunters love to hear. Every state has a real person who has entered into legend, and Florida is no exception, as we find in the story "The Barefoot Mailman."

The Fastest Man (African American)

Once there was a pretty young woman who was attracting a lot of attention among the young men in her town. Three in particular kept coming around to visit. All three seemed like hard-working young men and were always polite when they came to visit. Now her father was having a hard time deciding who was best for his daughter. And the girl couldn't decide which one she liked the best either. Finally her father came up with a plan.

"You are all decent, hard-working young men, and I can't decide which one would make the best husband for my daughter. I've come up with a contest. Tomorrow we'll decide which one of you is the fastest, and that man will marry my daughter."

The next morning the first man to arrive noticed that there was no water in the bucket and offered to get some. He was told that the spring was ten miles away. He took off running so fast that he was there almost in the blink of an eye. He filled the bucket and took off back for the girl's house. When he was halfway back, he noticed that the bucket was lighter and saw that the bottom of the old bucket had fallen out, and all the water was gone. He turned and ran back to the spring so fast that he caught the bottom of the bucket in midair and put it back with all the water without spilling one drop.

Now the father of the girl thought that was mighty fast, but the second man just shook his head. "Could you please get me an axe, a hoe, a plow, a harrow, and a bag of seeds?" They brought what he asked, and he walked out into a wooded ten-acre lot. He chopped down all the trees, dug up the roots, plowed the ground, planted the seeds, and harvested the crop in time for them to have green peas with their dinner.

Now that was fast, thought the father. Nobody could ever be faster than that man. "I do think you've won my daughter."

"Wait a minute," said the third man. "I still have a turn to try my hand."

The young man took a rifle and went into the forest. He saw a deer and took aim and fired. He ran back home and around behind the house and set his gun down and then ran back into the woods, caught the deer ,and held it still until the bullet hit it.

That was the man who won the girl.

The Barefoot Mailman (Based on True Events)

The man walked along at a pace few could even consider keeping up with; even horses had to trot to keep up with him. His long, strong legs just chewed up the miles. On his back he carried a large sack filled with letters and packages that needed to be delivered to the communities of Fort Ogden and Fort Myers. Since this was Florida, the mailman didn't need to worry about braving ice and snow, but unlike his northern brethren he had to brave alligators, panthers, and blistering heat. His name was James Mitchell Johnson, "Acrefoot" Johnson to most folks, Florida's barefoot mailman.

Acrefoot stood over six feet seven inches, with the longest legs you ever saw, and at 250 pounds he was as strong as an ox. He got his nickname because he wore a size thirteen shoe, pretty uncommon in the 1800s.' Since that size was hard to find in those days, he saved his shoes by walking barefoot most of the time. Acrefoot started as a mailman when he was thirty years old. He applied for the job, and the postmaster couldn't decide whether to hire Acrefoot or another equally strong, but not as long-legged, applicant, Big Ed. So the postmaster decided to have a bit of a race.

The two men started out from Fort Mead to Fort Myers. For a good part of that morning they were side by side as they walked along the dusty road. But in the afternoon the long legs and strong constitution of Acrefoot began to show, and soon the other man was left far behind. When Acrefoot got to Fort Myers the people were so happy to finally be getting mail delivery that they had a celebration in his honor.

Twice a week Acrefoot Johnson walked 154 miles from Fort Meade to Fort Myers and back, delivering the mail. The speed he walked at was legendary, as were the adventures he had along the way.

They say that one time a prominent judge offered Acrefoot a ride back to Fort Meade in his new buggy, but Acrefoot declined. He thought it might slow him up. The judge decided to teach the barefoot mailman a lesson and raced for Fort Meade, only to find Johnson sitting on the steps of the post office, smiling from ear to ear at the bewildered judge.

One day Acrefoot came into Fort Meade after his route and then walked twelve more miles to his sister's home in Bowling Green. After a visit he slept a few hours and then headed home. When he got into Fort Ogden, he learned that a dance was going to be held that evening. Now Acrefoot loved to dance, and with those long legs he was a wondrous sight on the dance floor, but all he had was an old worn pair of boots, and you need good boots to dance properly. He walked fifty more miles south to Fort Myers to purchase a new pair. He swam the Caloosahatchee River with his new boots in a bucket to keep them dry and danced all night. Next morning he headed back to Fort Meade with the mail.

One evening he returned home after walking 154 miles on his route, to find his son seriously ill. The nearest doctor was in Fort Myers. The giant mailman tied a wooden chair between his shoulders, and placing his son in it, he walked to find the doctor in Fort Myers. He swam the Caloosahatchee River twice with his son on his back, reaching the doctor in time to save the boy.

Sometimes Acrefoot had encounters with panthers and alligators, but he always got the best of them. The saying "the mail must go through" took on new meaning with this mailman, and the folks in Florida were proud of his adventures.

After seven years of faithful service the railroad connected the towns of Fort Meade and Fort Myers, and Acrefoot eased into retirement. He became a woodcutter, cutting more wood in a day than most men could cut in a week, providing timber to the railroad that had taken away his job. Later he became a blacksmith, but it was those years as a mail carrier that give us the legend of Acrefoot Johnson, Florida's barefoot mailman.

Uncle Monday, the Alligator Shaman (African American)

Deep in the swamps of Florida there lives a huge alligator. To call him the king of the alligators would be wrong—he is more than a king. Before he took on the skin of an alligator, Uncle Monday was a man. He was a great shaman, a medicine man in Africa, but was captured by the slave traders and brought to the shores of America. He was a slave on a plantation in Georgia before he escaped and joined the Seminole Indians in Florida.

Among the Indians and other escaped slaves he was considered a leader and a man of great power, a man of magic. He fought beside the Seminoles in their fight for freedom against the white man. One day there was a battle, and many of the warriors in Uncle Monday's band were killed. He and the others escaped and found their way through the forest to Lake Belle. There were only two choices, fight and die or run and hide. Uncle Monday didn't like either choice. He gathered his warriors around him and told them what he was going to do.

"My friends, in Africa I was a shaman for the crocodile clan. I learned my magic from others like me and from the beasts that roam the banks of the rivers of Africa. I will not fight only to die; neither will I run away. I will join my brothers who live in the lakes and swamps, and I'll wait until peace comes back to the land, and then I will return."

He began to sing while some of the men beat drums or hit their weapons against the sides of trees in time to his song. He raised his arms over his head, and then his skin began to get thick and very rough, his head became longer and full of menacing teeth, his arms and legs became shorter, and a huge tail sprouted from his tailbone. His voice was like thunder as he bellowed like a bull and hundreds of voices roared back, and his followers saw an army of alligators lined up ready to receive Uncle Monday as their leader and medicine man. He gave his earthbound brothers one more glance and then fell to his four short legs, slid into the water, and was immediately surrounded by the alligators that had come to greet him.

Through the years the stories of Uncle Monday have traveled all around Florida. People have heard about his magic and how he can change between man and alligator. Many a person claims to have seen or been chased by or even talked to Uncle Monday when he or she ventured too close to the deep parts of the swamp.

Now Judy Bronson heard these stories, and she didn't think they deserved the breath it took to tell them. She was a wise woman in her community and a healer. "I can do hoodoo magic as good as Uncle Monday," she proclaimed. Well, most folks thought she was bragging and that she was no match for the old, mystical, and mysterious shaman. Word finally worked its way through the settlements and into the swamp until it found the ear of Uncle Monday. He shook his head sadly and said, "The foolishness of tongues is higher than mountains." That was all he said.

One day old Judy thought she'd go fishing, so she told her young grandson to get her a pole. Her family was surprised because she had given up fishing years before, saying it was a waste of her time to just sit around waiting for the fish to decide to take the bait and being food for all the bugs that descended on her as she sat. They also thought it was foolish to go to Blue Sink Lake, which was so deep that if you stepped a few feet from shore the bottom seemed to go on forever. But she was determined to go and go alone, so that's what she did.

When she got to the lake it was almost dark, and she could barely see to bait her hook. She didn't like the dark and was about to try to work her way back home when she slipped into the lake. Her legs just seemed to give out from under her, and there she was, barely able to keep her head above the water, clinging to some roots. She seemed to have lost the strength in her legs and could not climb out of that dark, forbidding lake. Finally she found her voice and yelled for help, hoping that somebody from her village or one of her family might be close enough to hear her. But a booming voice silenced her. "Hush your tongue. Your bragging, lying tongue has brought you here, and here you will stay until I decide if you may leave or not."

Judy saw a huge shape walking across the lake. A clear, bright beam of moonlight shone on a man walking toward her across the backs of dozens of alligators. It was Uncle Monday. As he walked on by, each alligator fell in line behind, like a grotesque army moving in her direction. Uncle Monday was dressed with beads and shells and jewels around his neck and the skull of an alligator as a crown. He bore himself proudly, like a king. Judy thought she would die of terror if she didn't drown first.

Uncle Monday looked down at her and said, "I brought you here, and I put you in the water. You will stay there until you bow down and acknowledge that I am your better. It was your bragging and ignorance that brought you down."

Old Judy's pride rose. If she bowed down to Uncle Monday, she figured her position and livelihood in the community would fade away. She just couldn't give in to Uncle Monday, no matter how afraid she was of dying.

Uncle Monday looked down at her and said, "When you decide to stop trying to compete with me with your stubborn pride and stupidity, you can get out of the water. Until you do, I will have a guard here to keep watch. When you bow down to me as your better, then someone will find you." Uncle Monday glared down at her and then calmly walked back the way he had come, across the backs of alligators. One of the huge alligators swam close to her and stayed right next to her, motionless, so close she touched him whenever she took a breath.

After what seemed like hours, old Judy's will broke, and she bowed her head and said that she was weak and nothing compared to Uncle Monday. She begged for mercy. As soon as her words died away she saw a torch coming through the trees and heard her grandson calling her name. The huge alligator just slipped down into the water and disappeared. She called out, and they found her and took her home.

Old Judy never tried hoodoo magic again and kept to her ways of being a healer with herbs and roots. To her dying day, she told anyone who would listen about that night, and she swore it was the truth.

A Peachy Tale

One day an old farmer decided to go into the woods near his place and hunt a deer. As he walked toward the woods, he realized that he had powder all right, but no shot for his old musket. So, rather than go back to his house, he looked around and found some peach stones and loaded them into his musket and continued with his hunting. Now he hadn't gone very far when he saw a big buck with its head down, just grazing in the middle of a clearing. He raised his musket and fired, but just at the last minute the big buck raised its head and took one step forward. The peach pits grazed its side, and the startled animal ran away into the thickets. The old man went home empty handed.

About a year later that same man was walking in the woods trying to bring back a deer for his winter meat. As he walked along he saw a ripe, fresh peach just lying on the ground, but not a peach tree to be seen anywhere. Then he saw another peach and then another. He kept following the peaches that lay along the trail, picking them up and putting them into his hunting sack. Finally he came to a clearing, where he saw the biggest buck he had ever seen. Growing out of its two antlers were two peach trees, covered with big ripe peaches.

Now some folks will tell you that he shot that buck and that he and his wife had venison and peach pie for many a night, but others will say he just threw a rope around that buck and took it home. Every season he took it to town and sold the peaches that grew on its antlers. Everyone wanted to pick his or her own peach. Maybe money doesn't grow on trees, but peaches sure did grow on that buck.

Note: White-tailed deer are found throughout the wilderness areas of Florida.

Antonio the Woodcutter (Cuban)

Many Cubans immigrated to the United States, especially after the Cuban revolution in 1959; and many settled in Florida. This is a story they brought with them.

Once there was a boy named Antonio, who went to the forest to chop firewood so he could bring money home to his mother and buy food for them both. Antonio's mother was very old and feeble, and they lived on what the boy could make chopping wood and selling it in the village.

But one day the boy saw a man who was walking along with a sack. He was carrying a cat in the sack and was going to throw it into the water. The boy said, "Stop! Don't do that to the poor little cat. Why are you going to kill it?"

And the man replied, "This cat got into my pigeons at home and killed them all. If you want it, you can have it."

The boy said, "I'll take it then. At my house I don't have any pigeons." And he took it home.

When his mother saw that the boy was coming home with a cat she said, "My son, why are you bringing a cat home? How are we going to feed another mouth?"

And he replied, "Don't worry, Mama I'll just chop more firewood." And so he went out and chopped more firewood.

Soon afterward he saw a man who was carrying a dog, also in a sack, and was going to throw him into the sea. The boy said, "Stop! Don't be so mean. Give the dog to me and I'll take him home."

The man said, "Be careful! That dog bites people."

But the boy replied, "I'll take him home anyway. He won't bite me." And he took the dog home.

His mother was angry and said "Antonio, why are you bringing a dog here?"

"Don't worry, Mama. I'll just bring in more firewood."

Every day he went out with his dog and his cat to chop firewood, and every day he went home and gave the money to his mother. Antonio worked very hard, and his mother was pleased.

One day he went to the forest to chop firewood and saw that a man was about to kill a snake. The boy yelled. "Stop! Don't kill that snake."

And the man said, "It's a rattlesnake, but if you want it, take it." And the boy took it and put it under his shirt and took it home.

He went to his mother saying, "Mama, imagine there was a man in the woods and he was going to kill a little snake, the poor little thing. Look, I have it here!"

"Antonio! What are you doing with that thing! My goodness, take it away! I don't want it in my house!"

So the boy took it back to the forest. Every day he carried it some food and every day the snake waited for him.

But then Antonio got sick. A long time went by, and boy was very sad because he couldn't see his little snake. After he recovered he returned to chopping firewood with his dog and his cat. So he went to where the snake's nest was, but the snake was gone. He said to himself, "My snake has died because I wasn't here to feed it." The boy went home and was very quiet. His mother asked him, "What is the matter, my son?"

"Nothing, Mama, nothing."

One day he went to chop firewood and a terrible storm come up. Looking for shelter, he came upon a huge snake that opened up her mouth as if to eat him! But instead the snake said, "Don't be afraid of me. Once upon a time you saved my life and now I am going to save yours. Do you see this ring that I have here on my tail? It's a magic ring, and it is a gift for you. With this ring you can ask for whatever you want, and it will come true."

The boy took the ring off the snake's tail and ran home to his mother. He burst into their house and said, "Mama, we are going to be happy now! All our problems are over."

"What are you talking about?" she asked.

"The little snake that I saved one time, when they were going to kill her, has given me this magic ring and with this ring I can ask for whatever I want."

The dog said, "Make a wish, master, for whatever you want."

The boy closed his eyes and said, "I want to marry a queen!" Right away an enormous castle appeared where their old house used to be, and servants came with new clothes and fine food. The queen was beautiful, and she shared her treasure with the young man and his aged mother. Even the dog and cat were happy because the servants treated them as part of the family and brought them food and treats for them whenever they wanted it. They lived very happily for a while.

However, the queen did not like Antonio! One day when he was sleeping, she stole the magic ring away from him and wished that she and her castle and her servants would be brought to the other side of the river. The queen and the castle and everything in it, except the boy, his mother ,and his dog and cat, disappeared and was moved to the other side of the river.

The boy and his mother and the dog and cat fell into poverty again and were having a very hard time.

One day the cat said, "What are we going to do? There is nothing to eat. Our master has been so good to us. Now I think we need to help him in return."

The dog said, "Let's figure out how to get over to the other side of the river and get the ring back."

So the dog took a gourd and made a boat, and the two of them crossed the river to the other side. As soon as they got to the castle, the cat saw a mouse. He grabbed the mouse and said, "If you don't do what I say, I'm going to eat you!"

The mouse looked at the cat, and then at the dog, and said, "Whatever you want!"

The cat said, "I want you to find where the queen keeps the magic ring. Steal it and bring it back to us. You will go to where the queen is and take away the ring. If you do, you can come and live with us and our master."

The little mouse dashed off and found the queen sleeping. The ring was on the table beside the bed. The mouse ran up the leg of the table and took the ring in his mouth, and scurried back to where the cat and dog were waiting. The dog took the ring in his paw, and the mouse jumped up on his back, and they all began to swim across the river. The dog wanted to look at the ring as they swam and he opened his paw and dropped it into the sea. They saw a huge fish swallow it. Before they could get to the fish, a fisherman caught the fish on his line.

The cat said, "Don't worry. I'll get it out of the fish." While the fisherman was baiting his hook, the cat crept up behind him and removed the ring from the fish's belly. The cat ran back to where the dog and mouse were waiting.

The dog and the cat said to their master, "Look, master, we brought your ring back and a new friend, the mouse, who helped us. Please be careful with your wishes."

Antonio took their advice, and they all lived happily.

Florida Glossary

Cuba: A culturally diverse island nation in the Caribbean Sea. Due to its closeness to Florida and the number of refugee who fled to Florida after the revolution, it has had a strong cultural influence, especially in the Miami area.

Florida: A state that gets its name from the Spanish, who called it "Pascua Florida" or Feast of Flowers. The capital is Tallahassee.

Healer: Someone who uses traditional healing practices such as herbs and potions.

Hoodoo: The magical practices of the African American culture in the South, especially those with an African or Caribbean background.

Shaman: A wise man or medicine man. He keeps the stories and history of a people from generation to generation and is often a healer.

Story Sources

American Folktales from the Collections of the Library of Congress, Volume 1

American Folktales from the Collections of the Library of Congress, Volume 2

American Myths & Legends, Volumes 1 & 2

Every Tongue Got to Confess: Negro Folktales from the Gulf States

Florida Folktales

Folk Stories of the South

Folksongs of Florida

From the Winds of Manguito: Cuban Folktales in English & Spanish

The Greenwood Library of American Folktales, Volume 2

Legends of the Seminoles

Mules and Men

Myths & Legends of Our Own Land, Volumes 1 & 2

Southern Indian Myths & Legends

Tellable Cracker Tales

A Treasury of Southern Folklore

Uncle Monday & Other Florida Tales

Georgia

Georgia, one of the thirteen original colonies that fought for their freedom from the British Empire, officially became a state in 1788. That fight is represented here in a story about the legendary Nancy Hart. The African American heritage can be found in three stories, two from the mainland and one from the coastal islands of Georgia, where readers find African elephants as well as the well-known African trickster, Rabbit. There is also a Native American story here from the Creek/Muscogee people, called "The Game Between the Birds and the Other Animals." "The Preacher's Rabbit," a story from the rural area of Georgia, shows what happens when an honest boy meets his preacher, and in turn, the preacher meets his better.

Brer Rabbit and the Tar Baby
(African American)

One morning, before Sister Moon had even gone to her rest, Brer Fox was up and busy. He had mixed up a big batch of tar and made it in the shape of a baby. He walked down to the road where Brer Rabbit passed every morning and placing a hat on its head, he propped that Tar Baby where Brer Rabbit could not miss it. Then Brer Fox hid across the road in a ditch behind some bushes and waited.

He hadn't waited long before he saw Brer Rabbit coming down the road whistling a tune, without a care in the world. Seeing the Tar Baby standing there at the side of the road, Brer Rabbit tipped his hat and said, "Good morning, neighbor. Nice day today, don't you think?"

Tar Baby didn't say a word. He couldn't, of course, being made out of tar.

Brer Rabbit asked Tar Baby, "Are you deaf? If you are, I can talk a bit louder." Brer Rabbit yelled, "How are you? Beautiful day today, don't you think?"

Tar Baby just sat there and didn't say a word.

Brer Rabbit became a bit upset with Tar Baby's behavior. "Didn't your parents teach you any manners? What is this next generation coming to?"

Tar Baby just sat there and didn't say a word.

Brer Rabbit was so angry that he hauled off and hit Tar Baby. Rabbit's hand stuck fast to Tar Baby's face.

"You let me go right now or I'm going to really hit you." Brer Rabbit tried to get free but the tar held him fast. "I warned you," he yelled, and he hit Tar Baby again. Now his other hand was stuck.

"Let me go right now or you'll be sorry," he screamed. He kicked at Tar Baby, but his foot soon was held fast by the silent Tar Baby. He kicked with the other foot and then butted with his head, and now he was hopelessly stuck to the silent Tar Baby.

All this time Brer Fox could hardly keep himself from laughing out loud. When Brer Rabbit was firmly in the grasp of the silent but deadly Tar Baby, Brer Fox slowly walked across the road and stood over the helpless rabbit.

"Well I have you now, Brer Rabbit, and you know who is going to be in my pot for supper tonight, don't you?" Brer Fox could hardly hold back his laughter at poor Brer Rabbit's misfortune.

Brer Rabbit couldn't see Brer Fox because his head was still stuck on the Tar Baby, but he knew that he meant business and that he was in trouble.

"You won't be bothering people or making fun of anyone or playing tricks on folks ever again, Brer Rabbit. The only thing you'll be doing is becoming my supper. Time to start the fire and get the water boiling."

"Is it too late to mend my ways, Brer Fox?" asked Brer Rabbit.

"It has been too late for a long time," replied Fox.

"It looks like this is the day I get cooked, but at least you won't be throwing me in the briar patch. I'd rather be covered in barbeque sauce and simmered over a nice fire than ever be thrown in that nasty old briar patch. Do you have enough sauce there, Brer Fox?"

When Brer Fox heard these words, he thought to himself that to be cooked up as supper was too good for Brer Rabbit. He wanted Brer Rabbit to have the worst death possible.

"You know, I don't think I want to spend my afternoon standing over a hot fire making sure that you are properly prepared. I'm going to hang you instead."

"Hanging is an awful way to die, but thank you for that small mercy. At least I won't be thrown into the horrors of the briar patch."

Brer Fox heard him and said, "Small mercy, huh? Well I didn't bring a rope, so I guess I'll just drown you in the river."

"Drowning?" replied Brer Rabbit. "Well I can't stand the water, but it is a kindness next to being thrown into the briar patch."

"Kindness? Well it's too far to haul you all the way down to the river, so I'll just take out my knife and skin you nice and proper."

"Thank-you, Brer Fox. You can skin me and tear off my ears and cut off my legs and pinch my nose, but please don't throw me into the briar patch. Oh thank-you for not throwing me into the briar patch. That is the one thing I don't think I could bear."

By this time Brer Fox was sure that throwing Brer Rabbit into the briar patch was the worst possible end for him. He pulled that rabbit off of the Tar Baby and threw him over the road and into the thickest part of the briar patch. Then he waited and waited and waited some more. Just as he was sure that Brer Rabbit had met his painful and sorry end in that briar patch, he heard laughter. It got louder and louder and louder, until Brer Fox knew he had made a big mistake.

"Thank-you, Brer Fox. I am right at home in this old briar patch. I was born and raised among these thorns and thistles. Hope to see you soon."

Brer Fox watched as Brer Rabbit hopped out the other side of that briar patch and over the hill, still laughing as he ran off to play some more mischief.

Spanish Moss (African American)

A long time ago there was a man so evil that Death didn't have the heart to take him. He felt he at least needed to warn the man and give him a chance to redeem his life. So Death appeared to the man and told him that a week from that very day he was coming back for him. The evil man became frightened, and he begged and pleaded with Death. He dropped to his knees and promised to mend his wicked ways. He begged Death to give him a little longer to amend his life. He cried and carried on so much that Death finally said he would give him time to get his life in order, and that he wouldn't take the man until he had come again with another warning.

Well the years went by and the man only grew more and more evil. He cheated his neighbors and stole from those who were passing through. One day Death appeared to him again and told him that at the end of that week he was coming to take the man away. Well that wicked man was so scared that he fell to his knees and wrapped his arms around Death's legs, begging him to give him more time to straighten out his life. He cried and moaned and was causing a terrible racket. In the end Death told him he could live a little longer so he might correct all the mistakes he'd made throughout his life. He told the man that he would send him a token before he came to take him, a token that he could either see or hear.

Well the years went on and the man only went from bad to worse, and then even further down that lonely road of sin and wickedness. He grew older and older, and with each passing year he grew more powerful. As the years passed, he grew blind and he grew deaf, until one day Death came for him.

He said to Death, "You told me that you would send me a token before you came for me."

"I did," said Death. "I sent you a token you could see."

"But I'm blind now," said the old man.

"Well I sent you a token you could hear," replied Death.

"But now I'm so old and worn out that I'm deaf, too."

Well the man argued and he cried and he begged Death to let him live just long enough to make amends to all those he had wronged. Death washed his hands of that man and just walked away, leaving that evil man to stand there by himself.

Now that old man just walked the woods. His children were all dead and his grandchildren and even their grandchildren, but he still walked all by himself. All the people he wronged throughout his wicked life were dead, and no one could forgive him. Still he wandered the woods. He was blind, so he couldn't find food; and he was deaf. so he never knew if someone was speaking to him or not, and as the years rolled on he just walked, his hair getting longer and longer.

He walked and walked through the woods until he just became a shadow with long hair. Now his hair blows in the wind, and he can't die because Death refuses to come back for him. So he wanders through the woods until nothing is left but his long hair blowing around the trees, caught in their branches, hanging down as it grows longer and longer. The folks who live near the woods call it Spanish moss, and now you know how it got there.

The Game Between the Birds and the Other Animals (Creek/Muscogee People)

One day the birds challenged the other animals to a game of ball. It was agreed that all creatures that had teeth would be on one side, and all the creatures that had feathers would be on the other.

The day was selected, the poles erected, and the balls were prepared by the medicine men. The animals and birds came to the field. All those with teeth were on one side and those with feathers on the other. Bat came along and stood with the animals with teeth.

"What are you doing here?" asked the animals. "You fly through the air. Go on the other side with the birds."

Bat flew over to the birds' side of the field.

"What are you doing here?" cried the birds. "You have teeth, so you have to be on the animals' side."

The little Bat flew back to the animals' side of the field and begged them to let him stay with them.

"You do have teeth," they said, "so you can stay, but don't get in the way. You're too small to be of any use to us in this game."

The ball game began, and soon it was clear that the birds had an advantage. They could throw the ball high above the heads of the animals. No matter how high the Bear and Wolf jumped, they could not catch the ball and take it away from the birds. The Crane was the birds' best player. With his long beak and neck he could catch the ball every time.

The animals started to think that the game was lost when suddenly little Bat flew into the air and caught the ball right in front of Crane's outstretched beak. Bat was so quick that he caught the ball every time, and soon Bat had won the game for the animals.

All the animals agreed that though he was small, he was one of them, and he gained the honor of being their best player.

Used with permission from the Cultural Preservation Office of the Muscogee/Creek Nation, Okmulgee, Oklahoma.

The Preacher's Rabbit

A long time ago the local preachers would visit their parishioners. More often than not they would come at suppertime, especially the unmarried preachers. They would have a free meal while they talked about salvation and such. Now one such preacher was coming to visit a widow who had three young children. This family barely scraped by with enough to feed themselves, let alone another adult coming to supper. In a panic the poor woman told her oldest boy to take his dog out into the woods and try to catch a rabbit for their guest. "Now this is important son, because this will be the preacher's rabbit."

The little boy was proud and took the idea of finding their supper very seriously. Soon he and his dog saw a rabbit, and the dog took off after it, with the boy not far behind.

The rabbit saw a hollow log next to the road and ran right into it, safe from the two hunters. The dog barked and barked and the boy got down and reached as far as he could into the log, but his arms weren't quite long enough.

Just at that moment a buggy came down the road and the driver stopped and spoke to the boy, "Morning son. What do you have there in that log?"

The boy never looked up. "Good morning, sir. My dog and I have cornered a rabbit."

"Well son, do you reckon that you and your dog will bring that rabbit home to your mama?"

"I surely hope so, sir. This here is the preacher's rabbit."

"The preacher's rabbit? What do you mean by that son?" said the man, smiling.

"Well sir, the preacher is coming for supper tonight. We never have much to eat now that my Papa's dead, so Mama told me to go out and catch a rabbit for the preacher's supper. There's nothing else at home to eat, so I have to get this rabbit."

The man in the buggy didn't say a word, but his smile faded a bit and his face became just a little melancholy. "I hope you have a grand supper, son," said the man.

"Thank you, sir," replied the boy, still reaching as far as he could for the rabbit.

The preacher turned his buggy around and went back to his own home, allowing that family to have a fine rabbit supper without having to share it with their preacher.

Nancy Hart, Hero of the Revolution (Based on True Events)

At six foot tall with shocking red hair, Nancy Hart was an imposing woman. Like many frontier women in those days of the Revolutionary War, she was strong, independent, and able to handle a rifle. She was also known for kindness and her willingness to help her neighbors. And she was a staunch believer in freedom.

One day six red-coated British soldiers came out of the woods and surprised Nancy Hart while she was with her children. The men of the tiny settlement were out in the fields, not anywhere near the cabin. Normally Nancy would have fought the soldiers off with her own musket, but with the children all around her, the soldiers got the better of her. She was facing down six muskets with bayonets.

"Well, Mistress Hart, have you helped any rebels to escape lately? We'll just stay here for a while so you can't raise the alarm, and while we're waiting, how about feeding us?" The soldiers laughed.

"I'll not be feeding the King's soldiers," she replied. "Besides, every scrap of food we had was stolen by your army last time they came through. All we have left is an old rooster."

"That will be fine by us, Mistress Hart. I'll go fetch the old bird and you can start to cook it for us." The soldier that was doing all the talking leaned his musket against the wall of the cabin while the others stacked their weapons carefully by the door.

The soldier came back a few minutes later with the old rooster dead in his arms. "I'm sure you can make us a tasty meal out of this bird. Let's see if your cooking is as good as your reputation for fighting." The soldiers all snickered.

As he handed her the dead rooster, Nancy had an idea. "Of course I'll cook the bird for you," she said.

The soldiers sat down and waited for their meal while Nancy, with her young daughter Sukey by her, started to prepare the dinner. As they waited, the soldiers passed around flasks of liquor, and soon they were relaxed. Nancy walked back and forth, making a great deal of noise in her cooking preparations. As the soldiers laughed and joked, she whispered to her daughter, "Darling, I'm going to send you out for water. Now you know the old conch shell we use for calling your father? Get it and run as far away from the house as you can and then blow the signal for him and the others to come." Sukey nodded and smiled expectantly.

Nancy kept preparing the food and talking with the soldiers. She actually got them to laugh once or twice. She kept walking back and forth between them and their guns. When she was sure no one was looking, she would slip one of the guns out of the cabin through an opening in the wall. The soldiers were too busy drinking and laughing to notice what she was doing. She had slipped two guns outside when she turned to Sukey and said, "Sukey, go down to the well and get me a pot full of water." Sukey ran out the door.

Nancy took another musket and started to push it out through the hole in the wall when one of the soldiers saw her. "She's taking our guns," he cried.

Before any of the soldiers could even rise from the chairs, the musket was at her shoulder and aimed right at them. "Any Redcoat that moves won't live to see tomorrow," she said calmly.

The soldier who first saw her taking the guns made a move toward her. She shot him and had another musket at her shoulder as he dropped to the ground. A second soldier tried to get to her, but he dropped as she grabbed another musket and leveled it at the four remaining Redcoats.

"Who's next?" she asked. The soldiers all stood still. "Now sit down. You are all my prisoners."

Sukey ran in, yelling, "Father and the men are coming!"

The soldiers made a rush for the door, and another one dropped to the ground. The men captured the remaining three soldiers. Once again Nancy Hart had shown not just her cool judgment and courage, but also her belief in freedom from tyranny. She is still one of Georgia's most remembered heroes.

The Elephant and the Rooster
(Gullah—African American)

Note: In the Gullah dialect spoken by the African American people who live on the coastal islands of Georgia, Buh *means* Brother.

Buh Elephant and Buh Rooster knew each other very well. The two friends traveled together, and every morning Buh Rooster woke Buh Elephant so they could look for food before the dew dried.

One day they were talking together and the conversation turned to food. Buh Elephant bet Buh Rooster that he could eat longer than his friend could. Rooster took that bet. The next morning they got up early to see who would win this bet. Buh Elephant ate leaves and grass. He just ate and ate until he was so full he couldn't eat another bite. Buh Rooster scratched and pecked and hunted for seeds and worms. Finally Buh Elephant sat down under a tree to rest, and what do you think he saw? There was Buh Rooster just pecking away and eating one seed here or a worm there. He looked over at Elephant and tried to smile, even though he had a grasshopper in his mouth. Buh Elephant knew then and there that the man with the biggest belly isn't always the one who can eat the longest.

Georgia Glossary

Brer Rabbit: The trickster in many folktale collections, including *The Uncle Remus Tales*. He is found in the folk literature of Native American, African American, and even a few European American stories.

Buh Elephant: Brother Elephant.

Creek/Muscogee people: A Native American people whose towns comprised several hundred people. When one of these towns got too large, part of the population would move to a new location and start a new town. One of the Five Civilized Tribes, they were forcibly removed from their homeland to Indian Territory (Oklahoma) on the Trail of Tears.

Georgia: A state named after King George II of England. The capital is Atlanta.

Gullah: A dialect of English that is spoken by the African American people who live on the coastal islands of Georgia.

Redcoat: A term that referred to British soldiers. The British troops wore red coats, patterned after the Spartans and Romans, who wore red cloaks or tunics so their enemy would not see that they were wounded.

Spanish moss: An epiphyle, a plant that grows on another plant, in this case hanging off its branches. It absorbs its water and nutrients from the air and rain through its aerial roots. It is not a moss but a flowering plant, though its blossoms are so tiny they are difficult to see.

Story Sources

American Folktales from the Collections of the Library of Congress, Volume 1

American Folktales from the Collections of the Library of Congress, Volume 2

American Myths & Legends, Volumes 1 & 2

Buying the Wind

Cultural Preservation Office of the Muscogee/Creek Nation, Okmulgee, Oklahoma

Every Tongue Got to Confess: Negro Folktales from the Gulf States

Folk Stories of the South

The Greenwood Library of American Folktales, Volume 2

Gullah Folktales from the Georgia Coast

Myths & Legends of Our Own Land, Volumes 1 & 2

Southern Indian Myths & Legends

Stockings of Buttermilk

Stories of Georgia

Storytellers: Folktales & Legends from the South

The Tales of Uncle Remus: The Adventures of Brer Rabbit

Tall Betsy & Dunce Baby: South Georgia Folktales

13 Georgia Ghosts & Jeffrey

A Treasury of Southern Folklore

Illinois

Illinois, the twenty-first state to enter the union (1818), was originally the home of the Illini and Miami people.

A true tale relates the devastating horrors of the great Chicago Fire of 1871. A different kind of horror can be found in the famous Chicago ghost story, "Resurrection Mary." If you thought you knew everything about Abe Lincoln, check out "Lincoln and the Clary Grove Boys," where you'll meet Abe as a young man facing down a bully.

Illinois attracted people from all over the world to settle within its borders, on its prairies and in its cities. The true story "The Gypsy Wagon" describes growing up in Chicago in the 1950s. Finally, another true story about one of Illinois's most famous citizens is told in "A Life Worth Living."

The Great Chicago Fire (a True Story)

In October 1871 Chicago was the biggest city west of Pittsburgh, a sprawling metropolis that grew up around old Fort Dearborn and then just kept growing. Although it was a city, it still kept its rural, frontier roots, with most homes having a barn in which they kept livestock, grain, and wood to cook and heat their homes with during the harsh Midwestern winters. But those cold winters were far from their minds during the drought that plagued them in the summer and fall of 1871.

At that time the city of Chicago was virtually constructed of wood, with even some of the streets planked in pine and spruce. The city firefighters, considered among the most advanced at the time, were exhausted after battling twenty-four fires the week before. Along with the hot, dry weather, there couldn't have been a worse setup for a fire.

It started in the barn of Patrick and Catherine O'Leary. Neighbors who had been visiting that evening saw flames and raised the alarm. But the fire spread quickly, fueled by high winds. It raced through residential areas and swept through the lumberyards, mills, and warehouses, consuming the city like a dragon. In thirty-six hours the fire had claimed 300 lives and 18,000 buildings, burning three and a half square miles in the heart of the city. It left almost 100,000 people homeless.

Lincoln and the Clary Grove Boys
(Based on True Events)

New Salem was just a sleepy little village on the Sangamon River about twenty miles outside of Springfield, Illinois, when a young man by the name of Abraham Lincoln moved there in 1831. The folks who lived there were for the most part families, but like any community they had a few who were a bit rough around the edges. In New Salem that was the Clary Grove Boys, led by Jack Armstrong. Now the Clary Grove Boys were tough, loud, and boastful, and would brag to anyone who would listen that they could out-fight and out-wrestle any man in the village. Of course to be fair to those men, you should know that New Salem was a frontier town where people had to work together, and most of the time the Clary Grove Boys could also be counted on to help out.

Young Abe Lincoln worked in the general store that was owned by Denton Offutt. One day, listening to some of the Clary Grove Boys brag about their fighting ability, Offutt told everyone present that Abe was the strongest man in the village and could easily out-wrestle any one of the local gang. When Jack Armstrong heard that boast, he challenged Abe to a match in front of the whole town. Abe accepted.

Now Jack Armstrong was built like a bull and was a veteran of many a brawl, but Abe Lincoln was six feet four inches tall and weighed in at almost 190 pounds, a giant compared to Jack and most of the men in New Salem. The whole town showed up to watch, and many a bet was placed on both men. Denton Offutt himself wagered $10 that Lincoln would win hands down.

Jack and Abe circled each other, testing the other's weaknesses and strengths and finding few. Lincoln had the great advantage of size and strength, and he slowly began to wear his opponent down. Finally, he grabbed Jack Armstrong by the scruff of his neck, lifted him over his head and shook him, and then threw him down like a rag doll. The rest of the Clary Grove Boys started to close in around Abe, who put his back against a log wall and announced that he would take them all on, one by one. But before anyone had a chance to take Abe up on his challenge, Jack Armstrong got up and walked over to Lincoln and in front of the whole village offered his hand to him. He announced to his men that Abe was one of the bravest men he had ever met and he would be one of them from now on. From that day on Jack and Abe were the best of friends, and Abe would often stop by Jack's house to have a meal with him and his wife Hannah. Abe's example gave the Clary Grove Boys a new way of thinking and settled them down.

Years later, when Lincoln was a lawyer in Springfield, he defended Jack and Hannah's son Bill Armstrong in a murder case in Beardstown, Illinois. Through Lincoln's skill, the jury returned a verdict of not guilty. When Hannah and Jack tried to pay Abe for his service to their family, he replied that he could never charge them; they were friends and he would always be there for them.

Resurrection Mary (a Chicago Ghost Story)

It was a stormy night, and the two young men drove home after attending a basketball game at a neighboring high school. They had just passed the Willowbrook Dance Hall when they saw a young woman standing in the pouring rain at the side of the road, dressed in a white party dress, looking a bit lost and very scared. They pulled their car over to her and asked her if there was anything they could do to help.

"I'm on my way home from a dance and I got separated from my friends and I'm really going to be late getting home. I only live down Archer Avenue. Would you mind giving me a ride?"

"No problem," said the driver. The boy in the passenger seat got out and pulled the seat forward so she could climb into the back seat of their two-door car.

She was shivering so badly that the young man gave her his letter sweater to wear. "Thanks," she said, "I just can't get warm."

The young men tried to engage her in conversation, but they only got a yes or no from her. Suddenly, as they approached the front gates of Resurrection Cemetery, she called for them to stop. They looked into the back seat and she was gone. When they looked at the cemetery entrance they could see her walking through the bars of the gates and disappearing into the night. They ran to the gate, but it was locked.

The next day the two young men drove to the cemetery and were walking around when they noticed one of the groundskeepers cutting the grass. They told him about their strange adventure and the girl who got out of their car without opening the door and walked through iron bars.

The man slowly shook his head and asked them to follow him to the office. As they walked, he told them the story of the young girl who was killed as she left a dance at the Willowbrook Dance Hall and how she has been given a ride home to the cemetery for over fifty years. When they got to the office the man reached behind a counter and produced a letter sweater.

"This sweater must belong to one of you," he said. "She's always cold and usually someone is kind enough to lend her his sweater or jacket. One of us usually finds it on her grave the next day."

Resurrection Mary is one of the best-known urban ghost stories in America and probably the Chicago area's best-known ghost. She haunts Archer Avenue between the Willowbrook Ballroom and Resurrection Cemetery in Justice, Illinois.

A Life Worth Living (a True Story)

The audience grew silent as Halvdan Koht approached the podium. He looked out over the crowd of men and women and began to speak:

> In honoring Jane Addams, we also pay tribute to the work which women can do for peace and fraternity among nations. Twice in my life, once more than twenty years ago and now again this year, I have had the pleasure of visiting the institution where she has been carrying on her lifework. In the poorest districts of Chicago, among Polish, Italian, Mexican, and other immigrants, she has established and maintained the vast social organization centered in Hull-House. Here young and old alike, in fact all who ask, receive a helping hand whether they wish to educate themselves or to find work. She is not one to talk much, but her quiet, greathearted personality inspires confidence and creates an atmosphere of good will, which instinctively brings out the best in everyone.
>
> From this social work, often carried on among people of different nationalities, it was for her only a natural step to the cause of peace. She has now been its faithful spokesman for nearly a quarter of a century.—Halvdan Koht, Nobelprize.org

It was December 10, 1931, and Jane Addams was receiving the Nobel Peace Prize. She was the first American woman ever to receive this award.

Jane Addams was born in Cedarville, Illinois. She was one of eight children. Her father had been involved with politics and was a personal friend of Abraham Lincoln.

As a child Jane had a spinal defect that was corrected by surgery. She graduated from college and then studied medicine, but plagued by poor health, she gave up her studies. Throughout her life she was never completely healthy, but what she lacked in stamina she made up for with determination and a deep conviction in what she thought was right.

While she was studying in Europe, she and her friend Ellen G. Starr visited a settlement house in London. Jane decided that this social experiment could be duplicated in Chicago. She and Ellen leased a large home built by Charles Hull on the corner of Halsted and Polk streets. The two friends moved into the house and began to use it as a center for the neighborhood. They raised money and told the story of their neighborhood and its people to wealthy women, who began to volunteer at Hull House. Kindergarten classes were held there, as well as classes for adults. By its second year, Hull House was the neighborhood home to over 2,000 people. It expanded with an art gallery and community kitchen. Soon the staff were providing art, music, and drama lessons. People came to them asking advice, seeking medical help, and just wanting to talk to someone who would listen and understand. Hull House expanded with a gym, a swimming pool, a library, and an employment agency. It even housed a labor museum.

As Jane's vision and accomplishments began to get noticed, she was asked more and more to take a leading role in Chicago. In 1905 she was asked to be on the Chicago School Board. She made herself available to the people not only of her neighborhood, but all over the city, to fight poverty, crime, and ignorance. In 1910 she was awarded the first honorary degree ever awarded to a woman by Yale University.

Jane believed in the equality of women and that they should have the right to vote and be completely involved in their communities and the politics of their country and the world beyond. She lived what she preached. After serving on several committees to foster peace throughout the world, Jane Addams was elected president of the International Congress of Women. Later that group founded the Women's International League for Peace and Freedom, with Jane as their president until 1929. Jane opposed America's entry into World War I. She served as an assistant to Herbert Hoover to provide food and medicine to the women and children of our enemies.

In 1931 Jane Addams suffered a heart attack. She was admitted to the hospital on the same day that the Nobel Prize was awarded her in Oslo, Norway. She never fully recovered, and she died of cancer in 1935.

Jane Addams's legacy was a life dedicated to others, to making their lives better, putting an end to senseless wars, and creating a better world.

The Gypsy Wagon
(a True Story by Dan Keding)

In the 1950s, when I was a boy growing up on the South Side of Chicago, Tuesday morning in the summer was a special time. The kids on my block would all gather at the end of the alley and look over to the block next to ours. There we could see the gypsy wagon, loaded down with fruits and vegetables, coming toward us. Now it was an unwritten law that you had to wait on your side of the street before you could get close to the wagon, and once that wagon crossed to your side it left the children from the other block behind.

We called it the gypsy wagon because our parents and grandparents always referred to the men who sold the produce from the wagon as gypsies. They were wonderful people who told us fantastic stories and would put our names into the tales as they weighed out green beans and tomatoes and strawberries for our mothers and grandmothers. They seemed to know every language and would talk to my grandmother in Croatian and to the lady across the alley in Italian and to the lady at the end of the block in Polish. They carried long folding knives that would flick open as they tossed an orange or apple into the air, and as it fell they would cut it into halves or sometimes even quarters and give the pieces to us kids. Several of them wore silk bandannas on their heads and had long mustaches or goatees.

These men were wonderful, but the most wonderful thing about the gypsy wagon was that a horse pulled it. It was an old horse that wore a straw hat with holes cut into it so the horse's ears could stick out, but it was still a real live horse. Living in a big city, most of us had only seen horses on television or photos in books. All week we saved apple cores and sugar cubes for the horse. My grandmother would tell me that the horse had all the apples he wanted, but that didn't stop me. She still kept finding sugar and apple cores in my blue jeans pockets when she did the wash.

Often the gypsies would lift the little kids up onto the back of the horse as they walked along the alley. The horse was a draft horse and was huge to us kids. It seemed more a horse for a giant than a person. If there was a story to be told of a knight charging into battle, the men would always point to the wagon horse and say, "It was just like our horse," and nod knowingly.

When we got a bit older, say eight or nine years old, they would let us sit on the seat of the wagon and hold the reins in our hands; and they'd teach us how to make the horse stop and walk. We could smell the saddle soap they used to keep the reins supple. It was like magic to be in control of the big horse, making it walk from one end of the alley to the other, making it stop at the back fences so the gypsies could sell their produce, and then making it walk again. I still remember the first time I was allowed to hold the reins. I looked at my grandmother and I felt so proud, as if I were one step closer to growing up.

One summer the gypsies came down the alley driving an old Ford flatbed truck. I still went to see them sometimes and listen to their stories, but not often. Without the horse, it seemed the magic was gone, and we just couldn't get it back.

Illinois Glossary

Gypsy: A term used for the Romany people of Eastern Europe. They were a traveling people who made their living as horse traders and handy men and by selling the beautiful hand sown shirts and blouses made by the women. They lived on the road and moved from community to community.

Illinois: A state that takes its name from the Illini people. The capital is Springfield.

Miami and Illini people: Native American peoples who share a very similar language. They were found in the Illinois and Indiana area.

Nobel Prize: A prize awarded every year since 1901 for achievements in physics, chemistry, physiology or medicine, literature, and peace. The Nobel Prize is an international award administered by the Nobel Foundation in Stockholm, Sweden. Alfred Nobel, the inventor of dynamite, was its founder.

Story Sources

American Folktales from the Collections of the Library of Congress, Volume 1

American Folktales from the Collections of the Library of Congress, Volume 2

American Myths & Legends, Volumes 1 & 2

Buying the Wind

Folk Songs & Singing Games of the Illinois Ozarks

Ghost Stories of Illinois

The Greenwood Library of American Folktales, Volume 1

Illinois: A History of the Prairie State

Legends & Lore of Southern Illinois

Myths & Legends of Our Own Land, Volumes 1 & 2

Nobelprize.org ("A Life Worth Living")

Sand in the Bag

Songs of the Great Lakes

Stagecoach & Tavern Tales of the Old Northwest

Tales & Songs of Southern Illinois

A Treasury of Mississippi River Folklore

Indiana

Indiana became the nineteenth state to enter the union, in 1816. In this chapter, Native Americans are represented by a story from the Shawnee people, who lived in the area.

Storyteller Bob Sander, whose family has lived in Indiana for generations, shares a story about a man he met while doing a storytelling project in a retirement center. Your ideas about traveling by train may change forever after reading it.

Indiana people like a good tall tale, and the one found here actually has a tail. In each state you can find stories about fools and wise men, and Indiana is no exception. The story "The Hoosier and the Yankee" illustrates this perfectly.

The Hoosier and the Yankee

"Well now, stranger," said the Yankee trader, "suppose you tell us about your own part of the country. You may be the only man I ever seen from West. I hear that most die of fever or are eaten by wild animals."

"Well, my old Yankee, I'll just tell you all about it. If a farmer in our part of the country plants his ground with corn and takes first rate care of it, he'll get a hundred bushels to the acre; if he's a bit less careful with how he takes care of it he'll get seventy-five bushels to the acre; and if he doesn't plant one seed at all he'll still get fifty bushels.

"In Indiana the beets grow so large it takes three yoke of oxen to pull a full-sized one out of the ground, and then it leaves a hole so large, that I once saw a herd of deer who all tumbled in a beet hole before it got filled up, and the earth caved in upon them and they all died.

"The trees grow so large that I once knew a man who commenced cutting one down, and when he had cut away on one side for about ten days, he thought he'd just take a look around the tree. When he got to the other side, he found a man there who had been cutting at it for three weeks—and they never heard one another's axes.

"I have heard tell, yet somewhat doubt *this* story, that the Ohio parsnips have sometimes grown clean through the earth, and have been pulled through by the people on the other side of the world. But Ohio folks are known for exaggerating."

"Well now," says the Yankee, "I rather guess I've heard enough, stranger, for the present. How'd you like to trade for some clocks to sell out west?"

"Never use them in Indiana. We keep time altogether with pumpkin-vines. You know they grow five feet an hour, and that's an inch a minute. We don't use clocks at all. It's no use, my Yankee friend, we can't trade today."

The Yankee trader gave up. A beaten man, he just packed up and left.

The Dog Who Went to College

There once was a wealthy farmer who had the most fertile land in all of Indiana. He was always laughing when he sowed his corn because it grew so fast that it tickled the back of his legs as he walked past the newly planted seeds. One stalk of his corn gave as much corn as an acre anywhere else.

Now this farmer had a son who was very smart and very quick. There are smart people and there are quick people, but it's rare and a bit dangerous to be both. This young man was his father's pride and joy, so when it came time for the boy to either work on the farm or go off to the university, there was no choice. Off to college he went. The young man had a pet bulldog that he was really fond of, and he took the dog to Earlham College when he left for his first year. A month or two later his father got a letter from his son with the most extraordinary news.

> Dear Father,
>
> You won't believe what has happened. My bulldog, Max has started to talk! He has begun to have conversations with my fellow classmates and me and seems to have an incredible mind. I would like to enroll him in the college. Just think, after four years we would have the most educated dog in the whole world and be able to send him all over the world, charging people admission to sit and talk with the world's only talking dog on any subject they choose. I think we could make a lot of money. If you agree just send me double the amount each month for tuition, books, fees, food, and any veterinary bills that might just come up.
>
> Sincerely,
>
> Your Son

The farmer knew how bright his son was, and if he thought it was a good investment, then it must be worth the risk. The farmer started to send his son double the money every month. Every month or two the young man would send a progress report on his own education and that of Max, the talking bulldog. After four years the farmer received word from his son that he had received his degree and so had the bulldog. They would be taking the train to Vincennes and then come by boat to the farm.

The old farmer was so excited on the day they were to arrive. All his friends had come down to the dock to welcome the boy and Max the wonder dog back to their small community.

When the boat landed the young man jumped off and ran into his father's arms and gave him a huge hug.

"Where's that educated bulldog of ours?" asked the farmer.

"Father, I hate to tell this story to you, but I'm afraid there's been an accident of sorts. Max and I took the train to Vincennes and we hired a boat to take us down the river. As we neared the town I turned to the dog and said, 'Won't it be great Max? In an hour or so we'll be back on the farm with father and all the other animals.'

"Max just looked at me and said, 'What? We're going back to that dirty, old farm? I hate it there with all those stupid animals and your father is just as stubborn and stupid as that old mule he keeps.'

"I was so mad that I threw Max right over the side of the boat, and with those short little legs of his he just couldn't swim all the way to shore and he drowned."

The father wrapped his arms around his son's shoulders and said, "Thanks for standing up for me, son." The two of them got in the wagon and headed for home. Folks all around came by for the homecoming party, and when they heard the story of the ungrateful dog and his sorry fate, you can be sure they all thought he got what he deserved.

Mr. Clark and His Train Ride (by Bob Sander)

Mr. Clark was ninety-two and living in a retirement center. When he told me that nothing had ever happened in his whole life, so he had no stories to tell . . . I was shocked, incredulous, and saddened all at the same time.

The stunned silence formed by that remark was like a big, white, blank canvas, onto which any image could be painted. Of course, this was exactly what Mr. Clark was after. Into the silence Mr. Clark murmured: "I did know Edison."

"The inventor? That Edison?"

"Yup. Knew Frank Capra too."

"Frank Capra!?"

"Yup. The film director. Sold him Cadillacs. Five of 'em. Not all at once, though."

"You're kidding!"

"Nope." A long pause followed.

Mr. Clark gazed at his dumb-founded and entirely "hooked" audience and said: "If you were on a public conveyance, traveling from one place to another . . . and a vague feeling came over you that you should bring that conveyance to sudden stop . . . and the power to do so presented itself, would you go ahead and do it?"

Now I ask you, have you ever heard a better lead-in to a story?

For three months I'd come to this retirement facility to meet residents interested in hearing and telling stories. I'd show up, tell a story or two to grease the wheels, and let the small group of elders take over. It didn't take much prompting. They began to tell and hear and learn things about one another that just never came up any other time. It was a marvelous, close sharing, and soon we all looked forward to the small, quiet story-circle on second and fourth Sundays.

It seemed odd to me that women came, but never any men. I asked about it.

"We don't know," said one of the women. "We've asked them. Maybe they're afraid."

"Afraid of what?"

"Talking in front of other people? We don't know for sure."

"Well, do your darnedest, will you? Bring a man next time."

On the next meet date the usual women filed in dutifully, followed by a man in a wheelchair being pushed by a staff worker. He was very small, frail looking and withered, not much left to fill out his clothes. He wore a brimless welder's cap and his sky-blue eyes were sunken in his gaunt face. He was introduced as Mr. Clark, a fellow resident. None of the women remembered inviting him.

When his turn came, we struggled mightily to understand him. He had a speech defect that made his words hard to follow until you became accustomed. When he reasoned we'd had time to unravel his comment, "ninety-two years and nothing worth remembering . . . ," he lowered the boom on us, as you now know. Then he said:

"In 1933 or 1934 I traveled from Indianapolis to Louisville and back by train. It was business. I wouldn't be gone but two days. While we were speeding down the rails, I was sitting in my seat, looking out the window. As we passed a big stretch of water, a lake, I noticed something unusual: Little burps of water rising up from the lake. Just shooting up like tiny geysers. Right then a strange feeling came over me, and I felt like I had to stop that speeding train. Immediately.

"That's when I looked up and saw the long cord that runs near the ceiling inside the train compartment. It was the emergency brake. I stood right up and stared at it."

Mr. Clark pinned us with another silence and his water-blue eyes and said:

"Would you have reached out your hand and pulled on that cord, over nothing more than some little water spouts and a feeling?"

We all said probably not, but what happed next?

"Next was . . . I reached my hand up toward that cord, determined to pull it, when the conductor walked over and grabbed my wrist and said, 'Just what in the world do you think you're doing?' And I said, 'I'm fixing to pull this emergency cord and bring this train to a halt right now.' To which he said 'You will do no such a thing.' We started in to scuffling and I don't know if it was him or me that got tangled in that cord, but one of us pulled it.

"Bags flew through the air, people fell onto the floor, and it was a grand commotion entirely. The conductor's face turned an amazing shade of red. He told me to get in my seat and not move an inch. Then he got off and walked up to the engine to tell the engineer what had happened."

More silence, and then: "Would you have stayed in your seat, or would you have gotten off to look around?"

We would have stayed put, we assured him, but we guessed that he did not.

"Exactly right," said Mr. Clark, now using his speech impediment with obvious purpose and skill. "I followed that conductor clear up to the front of the train. And that's when I saw it: a twenty-foot-long, hewn-timber beam, not a tree—jammed up under the front of the train. One end was digging down into the gravel railroad bed, spewing rocks into the air. Likely some were cast out into the lake we passed, and that's what made those little jets of water I'd seen. The engineer said if we'd gone much further the timber would probably have derailed the train. We all might have been killed.

"Everybody wondered where such a thing could have come from. The engineer said the only way to know was to back up and have a look around, so that's what we did. Five miles outside a small town, a crowd was gathered around the train crossing; a flat-bed lumber truck was smashed all to pieces; the man who drove it was alive but insensible; and his wife, who'd been riding with him, was laid out on the ground, stone dead.

"The townsfolk said the driver was all the time trying to race and beat the train through the crossing. They'd told him not to do it many times, but he never listened. They said the accident was tragic, but no one was surprised.

"Things were wound up as best as could be, we continued on, and I saw to my business in Louisville. On the trip back home, who should I see? It was the engineer from the trip down, sitting in the seat in front of me. He wasn't' working, just riding as a passenger. So I asked him, 'Why didn't you stop when you hit that truck?'

"'Didn't know we'd hit it.'

"'Didn't know? How could you not know?'

"'Shoot, I was back with the fireman having lunch at the time.'

"'Having lunch! Having lunch! You mean . . . no one was running the train?'

"'Look, buddy, it's not like driving a car. You don't steer it. It's on tracks, right? Only got one way to go. Once we got through town, we cranked her up and let her rip. There wasn't going to be another major crossing for forty miles. We were running flat out when that fella tried to make that country crossing. At that speed you don't feel a thing. A jiggle, maybe. A train lurches around all the time anyway. We didn't notice anything unusual.'

"'Well you must be going awfully fast not to even feel an impact like that. How fast is the train going when it's flat-out?'

"'I can't tell you that! That's official railroad business. You best get on back to your seat.'"

The by-now-expected Mr. Clark silent stare followed, after which he asked us:

"Now if he told you that . . . would you just give up on finding out how fast the train was going . . . or not?"

Likely we'd give up, we said, but surely you did not.

"Correct," said Mr. Clark. "Had a friend in Indianapolis who worked for the railroad. Told me I could ride with him up in the engine to Illinois and back. But first he made me sign a piece of paper that said if didn't do exactly as he instructed, he could stop the train, anywhere, and put me off."

Mr. Clark grinned and said, "Somewhere he'd got the notion I had trouble following orders."

So a few days later he was traveling along in the engine of another train with this friend of his, and the friend showed him they were hitting seventy miles an hour, running flat-out.

"See that gauge?" Mr. Clark's friend asked him. "That's a pressure gauge. When the needle gets into the red area, we either pull this cord for the whistle or we yank on this lever here that sends heat back to the passengers. Either way it relieves some pressure, and that's what you want. Don't want an explosion from pressure build-up. Understand?"

"I get it," said Mr. Clark. "Hey, where are you going?"

"Back to have lunch with the brakeman. You just keep your eye on that gauge and if it goes into the red, you know what to do."

"You're leaving me here?!! Alone?!!"

"Sure. There's nothing between here and Urbana. I'll be back in ten minutes anyway. I just wanna eat. Might as well earn your keep."

And then he was gone. Mr. Clark told us he kept looking at the gauge, and pulling the cord to sound the whistle, and sending heat back to the passengers.

"After a while," said Mr. Clark, "I started to relax and enjoy it a bit. But that all changed when I looked out the window. In the distance a light was coming toward us. There was another train on the track. We were going to hit it head-on.

"I couldn't leave the compartment to fetch the engineer—we'd build up too much pressure and blow up. I screamed his name as loud as I could, but the noise in the engine room was fearsome. No one could hear me. Finally I laid on the whistle and didn't stop, hoping someone would come forward. No one did."

Mr. Clark pinned us with his look, but we all said, "For God's Sake, Mr. Clark, just tell us what happened next!"

"Well," he said, clearly enjoying our discomfort, "what happened next was I took a last glance out the window, so as to look my doom square in the face. The little light was quite large now, as the onrushing train was nearly upon us. They were blowing their whistle, too. It was all up. There was no stopping now. Too fast and too close.

"At the last second I ducked my head inside, why I don't know, it wouldn't make any difference. 'Whoose,' went the wind from the other train as it passed us by no more than six feet away, for it was on another track, invisible to me in the darkness."

Mr. Clark, the man with no stories to tell, made a suitable pause, and then ended with this:

"You know, if the passengers on that train had known who was up in the engine that night, I believe they all would have pulled that emergency brake. And I wouldn't blame them."

How Wildcat Got His Spots (Shawnee)

A long time ago Wildcat was always chasing Rabbit. If he caught him, Rabbit became his dinner. Rabbit was fast and usually could outrun Wildcat. One day Wildcat caught Rabbit off guard and chased him until Rabbit leapt into a hollow tree. Wildcat was too big to follow, so he just sat down and waited.

"You can't escape," said Wildcat. "I am going to stay here until you come out. You'll get hungry sooner or later, and when you do, you'll come out and I'll be here waiting."

"You've beaten me," cried Rabbit. "But would it be possible for you not to eat me raw? I would like you to roast me over a fire. If you make a fire here in front of this hollow tree, I'll come out when the coals are ready and I'll let you cook me and eat me."

Wildcat agreed and built a big fire in front of the entrance to the hollow tree. Soon the wood had burned down to glowing coals.

"You can come out now, Rabbit," said Wildcat. "The fire is perfect for roasting you for my dinner."

Rabbit had been waiting for that moment. With his powerful back legs he sprang into the air and landed on the coals, scattering them all over Wildcat's chest. With another leap Rabbit was over Wildcat's head and had made his escape. The hair on Wildcat's chest was seriously burned. When it grew out, he had white spots where once his fur was brown. That is why to this day Wildcat has those spots on his chest and why he keeps chasing Rabbit.

Used with the permission of the Ridgetop Shawnee Tribe.

An Honest Man

Vincennes is one of the oldest towns in Indiana. It was a melting pot of all kinds of people from all over: French settlers from Canada, Southerners from Kentucky and Tennessee, Jews from Germany, immigrants from Ireland, and many, many more. They all trusted one another and they lived in friendship.

There was one man that everyone liked, and that was Adam Gimbel. Adam was known both for his kindness and his honesty. He owned the general store in town, so most folks had dealings with him, and they all praised his honest prices and his fine character. Now there was no bank in those days, so if folks had a little money in the house and they were afraid that it might get stolen, they took it to Adam's store. He would keep it safe for them. When they needed it, he handed it over.

Now Simon Brute was the bishop of that part of the country, and he was always asking people for donations to help the poor and sick and needy of his diocese. He always brought the money to Adam, and the merchant kept it safe for the bishop until a need was found that the money could fill.

Adam was always happy to see the old priest. "Monsieur Adam, I have brought more money that I have collected for God's work," said Simon.

"You know, my friend, people are good because that is the way God made them. I will keep your money safe until it's needed," said the merchant.

The years passed on until one evening when the old priest dropped in at Adam's store with a small bag of money he had collected. Adam invited the old bishop to dine with him in the back of his store. As the two friends ate, the merchant looked at the bishop and said, "You know you always bring the money to me but you never count it. Aren't you afraid I might take a little for myself once in a while?"

The old bishop smiled at Adam and replied, "My friend, you are known far and wide as one of the most honest men on God's earth. I know that when I leave my money with you there will always be more when I come and collect it. Your honesty and kindness to the people of Vincennes are like what rain and sunshine are to flowers."

The two men smiled at each other. For you see the old priest was right, because Adam always added some of his own money to the collection that was used for the poor and sick. He was that kind of man, and that was the honesty and friendship that was the rock of Vincennes.

Indiana Glossary

Hoosier: The nickname given to the people of Indiana. Its origins are a mystery.

Indiana: A state whose name is a form of "Land of the Indiana." The capital is Indianapolis.

Shawnee people: A Native American tribe that spoke the Algonquian dialect. They were one of the few tribes that had a tradition of female chiefs.

Yankee trader: A nickname for a trader or peddler from New England. Yankee traders were given the name once used for Continental soldiers.

Story Sources

American Folktales from the Collections of the Library of Congress, Volume 1

American Folktales from the Collections of the Library of Congress, Volume 2

American Myths & Legends, Volumes 1 & 2

Bob Sander

The Greenwood Library of American Folktales, Volume 1

Haunted Hoosier Trails

Hoosier Folk Legends

Indiana Folklore 1, no. 1

Indiana Folklore: A Reader

Jokelore: Humorous Folktales from Indiana

Land of the Millrats

Myths & Legends of Our Own Land, Volumes 1 & 2

Ridgetop Shawnee Tribe

Sand in the Bag

Singing About It: Folk Songs in Southern Indiana

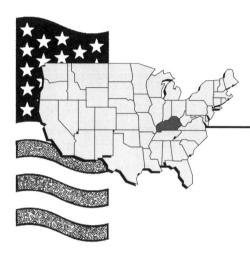

Kentucky

Kentucky, the fifteenth state to enter the union (1792), was the favorite hunting ground of the Shawnee for many years before the westward migration of European settlers, most of whom traced their ancestors back to English colonists. The Shawnee are represented in this chapter by the story "Why the Deer Has a Short Tail."

The early European settlers are represented by two stories, one of which features the most famous of all the pioneer hunters and marksmen, Daniel Boone. In this story we learn how the young Boone first met Rebecca, the girl he married. The ballad "The Hunters of Kentucky" celebrates those pioneer sharpshooters who became famous in the early history of the state. Mike Fink, an adventurer who spent many a day along the Ohio River and in the river towns of Kentucky, is a well-loved American folk hero. Here you will read the amazing tale of his first shooting contest.

How Daniel Met Rebecca
(Based on True Events)

When Daniel Boone was a young man, he and a friend went out on a "fire hunt." Carrying their muskets and a burning lantern into the dark night, they headed for the woods. Soon they found themselves in a heavily timbered area by a small stream that bordered the land of a very respectable farmer, a man named Morgan Bryan. Daniel's friend led the way with the lantern, while both of the hunters watched for its light to reflect in the eyes of a deer or raccoon. When this happened the light would hold the startled animal's attention long enough for Daniel, the better shot, to aim and bring down the game.

Suddenly Daniel quietly gave the signal to stop. He thought he had seen the eyes of a deer. Cautiously he crept forward and crouched behind a bunch of hazel and plum bushes. Sure enough, there again were two eyes, looking straight at him. Boone raised his musket slowly, ready to fire. Then, just as he took aim, he felt something he had never felt before. He was an experienced hunter, but something mysteriously caused his hand to shake and, with that, the animal bolted and ran away. Boone jumped up and took off, chasing the deer. It was so dark that he could barely see the fleeing animal, but he chased it by sound and shadow. They came to a fence, and the deer jumped over it in an oddly human way. Daniel clambered after it as best he could, burdened with his musket and hunting gear. As he cleared the fence, he saw the home and barn of Morgan Bryan outlined against the night sky. As he neared the house, he had to fight his way through a pack of dogs that guarded the homestead.

Daniel rushed onto the porch and knocked loudly at the door. He was admitted and welcomed by a surprised farmer Bryan. The young hunter, panting from his recent chase, scarcely had time to throw his eyes about the room before a boy of ten came rushing in. Behind him ran a flushed and breathless girl of sixteen, with ruddy cheeks, flaxen hair, and the softest blue eyes that Boone had ever seen.

"Father! Father!" cried the boy. "Sis was down at the creek to help me set my lines and a panther or bear or something chased her all the way home. She's too scared to talk."

The "panther" and the "deer" were now exchanging glances. Daniel Boone looked into those blue eyes and knew at once that they were the eyes he had seen down the sights of his rifle. To make a long story short, that is how Rebecca Bryan became Rebecca Boone.

The Spindle, the Shuttle, and the Needle (Anglo-American)

Immigrants from the British Isles brought this traditional tale to the new country.

A girl's granny took her to bring her up when all her other folks died. Her granny was good to her and raised her to have nice manners and be modest and not too brash and not too bold. From her granny she learned how to spin and weave better than any woman in the whole country.

The girl was about sixteen years old—you might say a young woman—when her granny was dying. From some hiding place, her granny brought out three keepsakes a fairy had given her when she was young: a spindle, a shuttle, and a needle, all made out of gold. Granny never had used the golden things. She had always used just her common everyday spindle, shuttle, and needle, and saved the golden ones as keepsakes. She had always thought they might be magic, but she never had tried them out to see for sure. Now she gave them to the girl and told her to use them and earn her living by selling the pretty goods she could spin and weave. Then she laid back and died.

After her granny died, the girl lived by herself. She wove such pretty goods that she made a nice living and earned a good reputation. Modest and shy, she never did show the golden things that she worked with, not wanting to seem proud. None of the local young men came to court her, but she figured they would come someday, and that day wouldn't come any sooner by worrying about it.

One day a king's son was out traveling, looking for a bride. He said his wife had to be the poorest and the richest. It sounded like a riddle, but what it meant was plain to his mind. He was sure he would know the right girl, the girl who would suit his wishes, when he found her.

The prince came riding past this girl's house and saw through the window and the door that was open to the springtime air that she was spinning thread. The girl blushed, and looked away from the window until the young man rode off. She was just that modest and shy not to stare at a stranger. As he rode off, she looked out of her window until he was out of sight. Then she said to her golden spindle some words she had learned from her granny.

"Spindle, haste away,

Bring my lover here today."

Her words worked magic, and the golden spindle left her hands, spinning a golden thread as it went. The golden spindle caught up with the king's son, and he followed the golden thread back to the girl's house. He could see that she was weaving cloth now. She blushed and looked away from the window until he rode off again.

Then she said to her golden shuttle some more words she had learned from her granny:

"Shuttle, weave for me today,

Show my lover along his way."

These words worked magic too. The golden shuttle jumped out of her hands. Without a loom to weave on, the shuttle started weaving a golden carpet with silver flower blooms.

The weaving just hung there in the air. The golden shuttle wove the golden carpet all the way till it caught up with the king's son. He followed the golden carpet back to the girl's house and looked in at her door and window. He could see her stitching some kind of cloth. She blushed and looked away from the window until he rode off again.

Then she said to her golden needle some more words she had learned from her granny:

"Needle that stitches all so fine,

Get my house ready for lover mine."

These words worked magic just like the other words. The golden needle started to work, stitching new curtains for the window, new coverlets to spread on the beds, new tablecloths, and other housekeeping things—all golden. The girl put the golden carpet that her golden shuttle wove on her floor. When the girl had her house all fixed fine enough for a queen, she sat down to work again and wait for her lover.

That time the king's son didn't need anything to lead him back to the girl's house. He just got to thinking about her, and his thoughts led him right back to her door. He looked in and saw her sitting in her house, all glittering with golden curtains and golden coverlets and all things golden. It looked to him fine enough for a queen. But the girl was wearing her old clothes and working away to earn her living. She was just the girl that he was looking for, "the poorest and the richest." He loved her with all his heart and mind, and he asked her if she would be his bride and live with him in the king's castle.

She said she would, and so they had a big wedding, and she went to live in the king's castle. She took with her the golden spindle, shuttle, and needle that her granny gave her, not just for keepsakes, though. She used them to spin and weave and sew, not to earn her living anymore, but just for the pleasure of making something beautiful.

The Hunters of Kentucky

Note: This ballad was written in 1822 to honor Andrew Jackson and the men who fought at the Battle of New Orleans during the War of 1812. It was also used as a campaign song for Jackson when he ran for president. The lines about Kentucky rifles and Kentucky hunters are in reference to the powerful long rifles of these remarkable marksmen.

You gentlemen and ladies fair,
That grace this famous city,
Come listen if you've time to spare,
While I rehearse this ditty.
And for the opportunity consider yourselves lucky.
It is not often that you see a hunter from Kentucky.
Oh Kentucky, the hunters of Kentucky.

Now, you all did read in public print
How Packenham attempted
To make our Hickory Jackson wince
But soon his scheme repented.
For Jackson he was wide-awake
And wasn't scared at trifles,
And well he knew what aim we take
With our Kentucky rifles.
Oh Kentucky, the hunters of Kentucky.

Well, a bank was raised to hide our chests,
Not that we thought of dying,
But that we always like to rest
Unless our game was a flying.
Behind it stood our little band,
None wished it to be greater.
Every man was half a horse
And half an alligator.
Oh Kentucky, the hunters of Kentucky.

Well the British found it was vain to fight
Where lead was all their booty.
And so they wisely took to flight
And left us all this beauty.
But now if danger ever annoys,
Remember what our trade is.
Send for us Kentucky boys
And we'll protect you gents and ladies.
Oh Kentucky, the hunters of Kentucky.

Why the Deer Has a Short Tail (Shawnee)

Once there were a brother and sister who lived alone in the woods in their lodge. One day the brother decided to go hunting.

"Sister, we need meat; it's time for me to go hunting. There is a shell in the corner of the lodge with some water in it. Do not drink the water. If I am killed while I am hunting, the water will turn red and warn you. Also, do not cook the little ear of corn that hangs in the corner above the shell." With those words he left his sister and started off on his hunting trip.

After her brother had been gone a few days, the girl began to wonder about the little ear of corn that was hanging from the roof in the corner of their lodge. She asked herself why it was special and why she shouldn't cook it. She shelled the kernels off the cob and put the kernels into a pot. They began to pop and pop and became large and white and tasted so good. But they wouldn't stop, and soon the lodge was so filled with the white, popped corn that the girl was pushed back against the wall.

Then she heard steps outside the lodge and the sniffing of many noses. The deer had smelled the corn and come to see what it was all about. They came to the door and began to eat; they thought the corn was delicious, too. More deer came, and they ate and ate and ate. The little ones came and the old ones came and the bucks and does all came to eat the corn. When the corn was all gone, they looked around for something else to eat, but there was nothing left. The girl had hidden under some hides, and they found her and told her that she must go with them. They put her on the antlers of a huge buck, and they took her away with them into the woods.

When the brother came back, he saw what the sister had done. He called up two black snakes to help him find his sister. One snake took the other's tail in his mouth and the other did the same, and they formed a wheel where the brother could stand as a warrior in the middle, while they carried him toward the deer and his sister. The snakes were actually evil spirits, and they knew the way the deer had gone. They followed day and night without ever getting tired. Finally the brother caught sight of the deer, but when the deer saw him following, they got frightened and stuck their heads into the ground. The brother grabbed his sister and then kicked the tails off every deer that had eaten his corn. That was their punishment, and to this day all deer have short tails.

Because his sister had disobeyed him, the brother painted her legs red. When he did this she turned into a duck and swam away down the creek. He turned himself into a wolf, and he hunts the forest to this day. They never became people again.

Used with the permission of the Ridgetop Shawnee Tribe.

Mike Fink and the Shooting Contest

When the keelboat *Half Moon* was tying up at the dock in Louisville, Mike Fink and his friends saw a notice tacked up on a nearby wall.

> *There will be a shooting contest at Thomas Crabtree's farm on Sunday, May the 6th. There will be a separate match for each quarter of the steer and one for its hide. One dollar to enter.*

Mike and the crew read that notice, and they all decided to ask their captain if it was okay to enter the contest while the keelboat's cargo was being assembled on the wharf.

Sunday came, and Mike and the rest of the crew walked to Crabtree's farm. The place was full of men, from ex-soldiers to frontiersmen to professional hunters. Mike found Crabtree, standing as straight as an oak, selling tickets to shoot in the match.

"You're awful young to be shooting against these fellows," Crabtree commented. "These are some of the best shots in all of Kentucky."

"Well sir," replied Mike, "I am young, but I can shoot and I'm here to prove it."

"Fair enough, son," replied Crabtree.

Mike wrote his name down and gave Crabtree the fee to enter all five of the contests.

"Mike Fink?" said Crabtree. "Not familiar with that name. Where you from, son?"

"Fort Pitt," replied Mike. "But I'm on a keelboat and I'm out to make my mark in the world."

"Well, I'm glad to see a young man with some confidence in himself," said Crabtree with a chuckle.

Simeon Maitland, a famous scout, was standing close by and said to Crabtree, "Don't be too hard on the boy. When I was Mike's age, I was a great marksman. I was able to shoot the eye out of a wild turkey almost every time. Wish I was that good now."

"Thank you, sir, for the kind words," said Mike.

The contest was set to begin, and the men who had put their money down now saw to their long rifles. The targets were pieces of white oak with a handmade nail set in the middle. The men had to hit the nail on the head and drive it into the wood. After the first round only eight men were left; Mike was one of them.

One by one the remaining shooters took their turns. Every one of the first seven nicked or came close to the nail, but none had driven it in. Mike walked up to the line last and calmly loaded his long rifle. He had named his rifle Bang All, and sure enough it did as Mike drove that nail into the wood with his shot. He won the first round and the first quarter of that steer.

Some of the older men declared it was beginner's luck, but when Mike won the second match as well that talk ended. After Mike won the third match, the other men just watched in awe as the young shooter calmly put every shot right onto the nail. The silence was complete as well as the admiration that was building for the young keelboat man as he won the fourth match.

Now some of the frontiersmen were saying in hushed tones that they had never seen anyone win that many matches in a row. Some said that not even the great Daniel Boone was that good. The fifth and final match came down to Simeon Maitland and his long rifle Merry Weather against Mike Fink and Bang All. Each man took his shot, and they both hit their targets perfectly. The match ended in a tie. The judges decided that they would have the two men shoot again to see who was the overall winner of the final match.

Mike shot first and once more hit the nail square on the head. When Simeon shot, the old scout missed just by a hair. Mike had won all five of the shooting contests that day.

The crowd erupted with shouts of both amazement and support. Mike quieted the crowd and turned to Simeon.

"Well, you sure shot fine today, sir, and I reckon if old Bang All wasn't as hot as he was, you might have beaten me. You know since we tied in the last match I would like you to have this hide." The crowd erupted again at Mike's generosity.

Simeon looked hard at the younger man and said, "You won fair and square today son, with the best shooting I've ever seen on this frontier. My sister lost her husband last spring, and this hide will help her and her little ones with leather for shoes. I thank you."

Mike turned to the judges and said, "I'm on a keelboat, and this one hind quarter is all I need or even can carry, so why don't you draw lots to see who gets the other three quarters?" Another roar of approval accompanied Mike's generous offer. Mike shouldered his hindquarter of beef and calmly walked down the path toward the *Half Moon* and into legend.

Kentucky Glossary

Hickory Jackson: General Andrew Jackson ("Old Hickory"), the commander of the American forces at the Battle of New Orleans.

Keelboat: A boat used on American rivers to haul cargo, usually by the use of oars or long poles. Lewis and Clark used keelboats for part of their exploration of the west. Keelboats were usually between fifty and eighty feet long and about fifteen feet wide and were very hard to navigate upriver.

Kentucky: A state whose name comes from the Iroquois word "Ken-tah-ten," which means Land of Tomorrow. The capital is Frankfort.

Packenham: General Edward Pakenham, the British commander at the Battle of New Orleans.

Shawnee people: A Native American tribe that spoke the Algonquian dialect. They were one of the few tribes that had a tradition of female chiefs.

Spindle and shuttle: Tools used in weaving. The spindle is a large pin that is used for twisting and winding the thread. The shuttle is a piece that is pointed at both ends and is used to carry the weft thread across and between the warp threads when weaving on a loom.

Story Sources

American Folktales from the Collections of the Library of Congress, Volume 1

American Folktales from the Collections of the Library of Congress, Volume 2

American Myths & Legends, Volumes 1 & 2

Ballad Makin' in the Mountains of Kentucky

Buying the Wind

The Greenwood Library of American Folktales, Volume 2

Half Horse Half Alligator

In the Pine: Selected Kentucky Folk Songs

Mike Fink

Myths & Legends of Our Own Land, Volumes 1 & 2

Old Greasybeard: Tales from the Cumberland Gap

South from Hell-fer-Sartin: Kentucky Mountain Folk Tales

Southern Indian Myths & Legends

Stockings of Buttermilk

Tales from the Cloud Walking Country

A Treasury of Mississippi River Folklore

A Treasury of Southern Folklore

Up Cutshin & Down Greasy

Yankee Doodle's Cousins

Louisiana

Louisiana was admitted as the eighteenth state in 1812. It is a state with great history and wonderful diversity that is seen through its stories.

The Natchez people lived in the land of Louisiana before any of the European settlers came, and they are represented by the story "Whose Children?" Tricksters are usually the kind of characters that get into trouble, but here we have a story from the Cajun people, that has a happy ending for Lapin. The Creole story "The Talking Eggs" gives us all the magic and wonder we expect from these old tales.

Annie Christmas, the legendary folk heroine of Louisiana, is remembered in a story about her and Mike Fink. Immigrants have always been drawn to New Orleans and Louisiana.

Whose Children? (Natchez)

Once, a long time ago in the very early days, Moon, Sun, Wind, Thunder, Rainbow, Fire, and Water were walking together. As they walked they met an old man. This man was the leader of all the Sky Spirits.

Thunder asked him, "Can you make the people of the world my children?"

The Wise Old Man replied, "No, that cannot be, but they can be your grandchildren."

Sun asked the Old Man, "Can you make the people of the world my children?"

"No, they cannot be your children, but they will be your friends and grandchildren. You are the one who will give them light," replied the Wise Old Man.

Moon then asked, "Can the people of the world be my children?"

"No, I cannot do that, but they will be your nieces and nephews and your friends."

Fire then asked the Old Man, "Can the people of the world be my children?"

Wise Old Man replied, "No, I cannot give them to you, but they can be your grandchildren. You will give them warmth and a way to cook their food."

Wind asked if the people could be his children. Wise Old Man said, "No, but they will be your grandchildren also. You can clean the air around them and scour the earth of disease and keep them healthy."

Rainbow wanted the people of the world to be his children. "No," said the Old Man. "You will be busy protecting them from floods and rain. You will always be their friend and they yours."

Water asked if human beings could be his children. The Wise Old Man answered, "No, but they will be your friends. When they get dirty you will clean them. When they get thirsty you will refresh them. You shall give them long life."

The Wise Old Man continued, "I have given you the ways that you can help human beings and be there to guide them. They are in need of your help and will always be in need of your friendship. You must remember that these people of the world are my children."

Used with permission from the Natchez Tribal Nation.

The Talking Eggs (Creole)

A long time ago there was a woman who had two daughters, named Rose and Blanche. Now Rose was mean and lazy and never had a good word to say about anyone. Blanche, on the other hand, was sweet and kind and never complained. The mother favored Rose because she was most like her, and she gave all the household chores to Blanche, while Rose just sat next to her mother in her rocking chair and did nothing.

One day her mother sent Blanche to the well to get some water in a bucket. When she arrived at the well there was an old woman who asked her, "Pray, little one, I am so thirsty. Can you get me some water from this well?"

"Yes, auntie," said Blanche. She washed out the bucket and dipped into the well and gave the old woman some clean water to drink. The old woman drank her fill and thanked the girl.

A few days later, Blanche's mother was so mean to her that she ran away into the woods.

The girl cried as she ran and was soon lost. She didn't want to return home, so she wandered in the woods until she saw the old woman she had met at the well, walking on the path in front of her.

"My child," said the old woman. "Why are you crying?"

"Auntie," replied Blanche, "My mother has scolded and beaten me and I've run away from home. I'm afraid to go back, and I'm lost here in the woods."

"Well you come with me, child. I'll give you supper and a bed for the night. But you must promise me not to laugh at anything that you will see."

Blanche promised, and they walked hand in hand through the woods. As they walked a bush of thorns opened in front of them and closed behind them as they passed. A little farther on, Blanche saw two axes fighting; she found that very strange but she didn't say a word. They walked farther and saw two arms fighting, then two legs, and at last two heads fighting. The heads looked at her and said, "Blanche, good morning child. God will help you."

At last they arrived at the old woman's cabin. The old woman turned to Blanche and said, "Make the fire, child, so we can cook our supper." Then the old woman sat down near the fireplace and took off her head. She placed it on her knees and began to comb out the tangles in her hair. Blanche was afraid, but she said nothing. The old woman put her head back on her shoulders and gave Blanche a bone to put into the pot. Blanche put the bone into the pot and suddenly it was full of fresh meat.

She gave Blanche one grain of rice to pound with the pestle, and as she did so the mortar became full of rice. Blanche put the rice into the pot with the meat, and soon their supper was ready.

After supper the old woman turned to Blanche and said, "My child, could you scratch my back?" But when she did so her hand was cut and began to bleed because the old woman's back was covered with broken glass. When the old woman saw that the girl's hand was bleeding she blew on it, and it healed instantly.

When Blanche woke up the next day the old woman said to her, "Child, you must go home this morning, but because you are such a good girl I want to make you a present of my talking eggs. Go to the henhouse and take all the eggs that say 'Take me, take me' but leave all the eggs that say 'don't take me, don't take me.' When you reach the road, throw the eggs behind your back and break them."

Blanche went to the henhouse and only took the eggs that said, "Take me." She left the others. As she walked down the road she broke the eggs. As each egg broke beautiful things tumbled out of the eggs. Diamonds and gold, beautiful clothes, and a fine carriage with beautiful horses all appeared from the broken eggshells. When she arrived the house was full of all the wealth that Blanche had brought back with her from the old woman's cottage. Now that she was rich, her mother was glad to see her back and was kind to her.

"Where did you get all these wonderful things, my daughter?"

Blanche told her about the old woman and how kind she had been to her and how she had sent her home with her talking eggs.

The next day the mother told Rose to go into the woods and bring back more wealth.

Rose walked into the woods, and she found the old woman walking down the path in front of her. The old woman invited her to stay with her that night but told her not to laugh at anything she saw. But Rose couldn't help herself. She laughed at the fighting axes and the fighting arms. She laughed at the fighting legs and the fighting heads. She laughed hardest when the old woman took off her head and started to comb out the tangles in her hair. When she asked Rose to scratch her back, Rose refused.

The old woman said to her, "You are not a very good girl, and I am afraid that someday you will be punished."

The next day the old woman spoke to Rose, "I don't want to send you back empty handed, so go into my henhouse and take the eggs that say 'Don't take me, don't take me."

Rose went into the henhouse and all the eggs started to cry out "Take me, take me." But she ignored them and only took the eggs that said "Don't take me, don't take me."

As she walked down the road she began to break the eggs, but instead of diamonds and gold and fine dresses, out poured snakes and toads and frogs that started to chase her. Some eggs even had whips come out of them, and the whips began to hit Rose as she ran.

When she arrived at her mother's house she was so tired she couldn't say a word. When her mother saw all the snakes and toads and the whips chasing Rose, she tried to bar the door, but Rose and her tormentors came in, and they chased Rose and her mother around the cottage and out the door. They chased them into the woods, and they were never seen again. Blanche lived a long and happy life because she was so kind.

Annie Christmas and Mike Fink
(African American)

Annie Christmas was one of the most extraordinary people to have walked the roads or paddled the rivers of Louisiana. She was a woman of few words. She worked on her own keelboat and worked hauling goods from the riverboats to the warehouses with her wagon team. She was stronger than any two men and worked as hard as any four men. She stood almost seven feet tall.

One day she was working on the docks of New Orleans, unloading huge bales of cotton off of a riverboat and onto her wagon. Mike Fink, who had heard of Annie Christmas but had never met her, was talking to some loafers who were sitting around the docks.

One of the men claimed that Annie Christmas was the strongest, best worker on the docks. This did not sit right with Fink.

"I tell you now that women should be home taking care of the house and the children, not working on the docks. Besides, how strong can a woman be anyway? She wouldn't be near as half as strong as I am. No, Annie Christmas should be at home being a lady and leave men's work to me. I'll tell that to her face if I ever meet her."

The men on the docks, both the loafers and the men working beside Annie, got very quiet.

Annie, bent over a bale of cotton on the riverboat, was only a few feet away from Fink as he stood in the bow of his keelboat. Slowly Annie took hold of that half a ton bale of cotton and started to straighten up. Mike Fink turned and watched, his eyes almost popping out of his head as he watched this giant straighten up and up and up with that huge bale over her head. She looked right at him and said, "I'm Annie Christmas, and it seems to me, sir, that you have an awful narrow opinion of what a woman should do and where a woman belongs."

Annie stared right at Fink and threw the bale straight down into the river. The force of that bale being thrown by that woman caused a tidal wave that sent Mike Fink and his keelboat all the way to Natchez. He never did return to New Orleans.

Annie looked around at the men on the dock and on the riverboats around her who had witnessed the exchange and said, "So that was Mike Fink. Not too much to him." The men couldn't agree more.

The Smokehouse (Cajun)

One day Bouqui went to Lapin's house to eat supper. As they ate Bouqui said, "You make wonderful gumbo Lapin. The meat is so tasty. Where do you get it from?"

At first Lapin didn't want to tell his friend where he got the meat, but he finally said, "It is smoked. Now you have to keep this a secret. There is a farmer down the road, an old Frenchman who has a smokehouse. Inside he has sausages and hams and all sorts of smoked meat. I steal the meat from him."

Now Bouqui was very poor and always hungry. "Please Lapin, show me where it is. I really need to have some of this meat for myself."

"No," said Lapin, "I know you too well. You'll get stupid and greedy and you'll get caught."

"No, no," cried Bouqui. "I'll do just what you say. Please let me come with you."

Eventually Lapin agreed, even though he knew it was a mistake. He told Bouqui to come over the next evening and spend the night. "We'll get up when the rooster crows, and visit the smokehouse."

The next evening Bouqui came by Lapin's house and was carrying a blanket. After a small meal they went to sleep, Lapin in his bed and Bouqui on his blanket.

About midnight Lapin woke up to noises from his henhouse. When he looked out the window there was Bouqui, poking at the chickens and rooster, trying to get the old man to crow.

"Stop that, Bouqui," cried Lapin. "Come back to bed. Let the old rooster and the chickens alone. Dawn will come soon enough."

But Bouqui was so hungry, and he couldn't stop dreaming of that smokehouse, so a couple hours later he was poking at the rooster again. Lapin woke up and yelled out the window, "Bouqui, stop that racket. The rooster knows when to crow. Leave him alone and come back to sleep."

Finally dawn came, and the old rooster crowed. The two friends started off in the grey light of early morning for the smokehouse. Lapin noticed that Bouqui was carrying something. "What is that?" he asked.

"My blanket," said Bouqui.

"Why are you carrying it to the smokehouse?"

"To carry all my sausages and hams back in," said Bouqui.

"You are too greedy," said Lapin. "Just take what you can carry in your hands. You're going to get caught."

They came to the smokehouse and uncovered the hidden hole. Lapin crawled in first, followed by his friend. Bouqui spread out his blanket and looked around. The smokehouse was filled with hams and sausages and chickens and turkeys, all hanging from the roof of the smokehouse, seasoning in the smoke.

Lapin took one sausage and was ready to go, but Bouqui was taking hams and sausages and any meat he could grab and putting them on his blanket. Lapin whispered to him, "We must go now. The farmer will be up and about soon."

"Yes, yes," said Bouqui, "just a few more."

"Hurry, Bouqui," whispered Lapin. "I think I hear the farmer coming."

Lapin crawled through the hole to the outside, but Bouqui couldn't get his bundle through the hole. He tried pushing it, but it got stuck halfway through. Even with Lapin pulling from the other side, it just wouldn't get free. Suddenly the smokehouse door opened, and there stood the old Frenchman, a stick in his hand.

"So it's you that has been stealing my meat," he cried. He raised his stick and started to hit poor Bouqui. Bouqui couldn't get past the old farmer in the doorway, and the bundle was stuck fast in the hole so he couldn't get out that way. Finally, he ran between the farmer's legs and made his escape, with nothing to show for his greed but a few lumps and the memory of the smell of that smokehouse.

Louisiana Glossary

Bouqui: A traditional character in Cajun folktales. He is usually referred to as a wolf.

Cajun: The descendants of the French Acadians from Canada, who came to settle in Louisiana. The Acadians were deported by the English governor of Canada in 1755 and were scattered throughout Canada, Europe, the West Indies, and Louisiana. Acadia is now known as Nova Scotia.

Creole: Americans of French descent. This includes both European and African speakers of French.

Gumbo: A spicy Cajun stew that is world famous for its flavor.

Lapin: "Rabbit" in French. Another traditional Cajun character. He is a trickster rabbit.

Louisiana: A state that was originally part of New France but was later named "Louisiana," the Land of Louis, in honor of King Louis XIV of France. The capital is Baton Rouge.

Natchez people: Native American people who lived in Louisiana and Mississippi. They arranged their thatched-roof adobe houses around a square that was used for gatherings and ceremonies.

Story Sources

American Folktales from the Collections of the Library of Congress, Volume 1

American Folktales from the Collections of the Library of Congress, Volume 2

American Myths & Legends, Volumes 1 & 2

Buying the Wind

Cajun & Creole Folktales

Every Tongue Got to Confess: Negro Folktales from the Gulf States

Folk Stories of the South

The Greenwood Library of American Folktales, Volume 2

Gumbo Ya-Ya: A Collection of Louisiana Folktales

Mules and Men

Myths & Legends of Our Own Land, Volumes 1 & 2

Natchez Tribal Nation

The Parade of Heroes

Southern Indian Myths & Legends

Stockings of Buttermilk

Swapping Stories: Folktales from Louisiana

A Treasury of Mississippi River Folklore

A Treasury of Southern Folklore

Why the Possum's Tail Is Bare & Other Classic Southern Stories

Maine

In 1820 Maine became the twenty-third state to join the union. Before the arrival of European settlers, the Passamaquoddy people occupied Maine.

Known as the Pine Tree State, Maine is home to a lumbering industry that has spawned its share of folktale characters. The moose may be the state animal, but the most famous Maine creature is Babe the Blue Ox, whose story is found here in a Paul Bunyan tale.

The first woman to win the Pulitzer Prize for poetry, Edna St. Vincent Millay, was a Maine native; her story is included here. Hunting and trapping have a long tradition in Maine and are represented here at their tall tale best. Maine sits just on the other side of French Canada and families on both sides of the border claim their French heritage; these people too are represented in story.

The Cat with the Wooden Leg

A long time ago there was a trapper who used to live deep in the woods. Every winter, when the coats on the beavers and otters and foxes were at their thickest, he would set dozens of traps. His only companion was a big tiger-striped cat that used to follow him around all day. Now that cat got to be such a good hunter that he was able to get all his food out in the woods, and the trapper never had to feed him.

One evening the cat didn't come back to the cabin, and the hunter got worried about his friend. The next morning he went out looking for the cat and found that his poor companion had gotten his front right paw caught in one of the traps the hunter had set along a nearby stream. When the trapper found him the paw was half chewed off. He got the cat out of the trap and took him home. That paw was so bad that the man had to amputate it to save the cat's life. The paw healed all right, but the cat kept on getting thinner. The big tomcat didn't enjoy the food the trapper gave him. The cat missed hunting and catching his own meals.

By and by the man said, "I'll have to do something, or I'll lose that cat sure," so he got a little piece of cedar and whittled out a wooden leg for the cat. He tacked some leather on the little piece of wood to make a socket to fit on the stump of the cat's leg, and he made leather straps to go around the cat's body to hold the leg in place. Well, when the cat first got that wooden leg on, he used to shake his paw trying to get the thing off, but by and by he got used to it and could prance around in great style, thumping around the cabin on his new wooden limb. As soon as he could run and keep his balance, the cat started going out into the woods again to look for his meals. After a couple weeks the trapper knew the cat was back to hunting successfully, because he started to fatten up. Knowing the cat wasn't near as fast as he used to be, the man got interested in how he was hunting with his new leg. One day he followed the cat out to see how he managed, and he saw the cat creep up on a mouse and grab it with one paw and hit it over the head with that wooden leg. Necessity is the mother of invention.

Babe the Blue Ox

There are many stories about people and the animals that share their lives, but none are as popular as the story of Paul Bunyan and his constant companion Babe, the Blue Ox. Stories about Paul Bunyan can be heard from coast to coast; they traveled with the men who worked in the lumber industry.

Now Paul was working way up north in the thick pine forests of Maine. It was the worst winter that anyone could ever remember. It was called "The Winter of the Blue Snow" because it got so cold that the snow itself turned sapphire blue. The snow fell and fell and cabins were buried, valleys were buried, whole towns lay under a thick blanket of snow, waiting hopefully for an early thaw. Paul was walking through the forest one day to see if the tops of the trees could be seen as yet from under the snow banks when he heard a little moaning sound. He thrust his huge hand into the snow, and way down at the bottom of the snowdrift he found a half frozen baby ox calf. Well Paul looked down at the little thing and saw that he was blue with the cold. He took the calf and put him under his coat so he could get warm, and he brought the calf back to his logging camp. The men took to the little calf as if he were their pet, but the little ox was always with Paul. He never left his sight, just following the giant logger around like a dog. The strangest thing happened, though: the little ox never did turn back to his natural color. He stayed a pale blue.

The little ox was fine for a few days, but then he started to grow. Sometimes Paul would swear that if he looked down at Babe (that's what he called the calf), and then looked away for a minute and looked back, the blue ox had grown a couple of inches. He just kept growing; and like all little ones that start that growing phase, he started eating everything in sight. One day Paul made Babe his own barn to sleep in, but when he woke up the next morning Babe and the barn were gone. He followed Babe's tracks and found him eating some early spring grass, the barn sitting right on his back. Babe had outgrown the barn over night. Now Paul could appreciate this kind of growing, because that was just the way he grew as a boy.

When Babe finally reached his full size, he was forty-two ax handles from the tip of one horn to the tip of the other. He ate over a ton of hay and then a couple wagonloads of turnips or rutabagas for dessert. He was so strong that only Paul could handle him, but Babe was as gentle as a kitten with all the lumberjacks. It was as if he knew how big and strong he was, so he was always really careful when he was around normal size people. But he and Paul would often wrestle, and when they did you could hear it for miles— the folks down in New York and Boston thought it was an earthquake.

Babe also had a wicked sense of humor. He used to stand outside the cook shack and wait until they were making bread and then poke his nose through the window and sneeze, sending flour all over the state of Maine. Many folks thought it was snowing in June when the flour fell from the sky. He also would like to go upstream of the river and drink it until it was totally dry, leaving the logs just sitting on the bottom of the dry riverbed.

Babe loved to work beside Paul hauling logs out of the forest to the river, where they could be floated down to the sawmills. One problem they had was that the road to Paul's camp was so windy it took forever to get to the river. One day Paul attached a log chain to Babe's neck and the other end of the chain to the end of the road. That great blue ox pulled and strained and pulled that old road until it was straight as an arrow. Of course the log chain had become so hot from Babe pulling it that it became a solid piece of iron. Speaking of iron, whenever Babe needed new shoes they had to open another iron mine up in Minnesota or Michigan to find enough ore to make them.

Paul and Babe were inseparable all their working years. Babe went all over the country with Paul, from Maine to the West Coast, and helped dig out Puget Sound, but that's another story for another state.

The Poet (a True Story)

A young woman sat at the piano and played, and then she turned to the audience and began to recite her poems. The poems were beautiful, and the audience was stunned, especially a wealthy woman named Caroline B. Dow. She approached the young woman, and they talked. Later Caroline Dow paid for the girl to go to Vassar College. The young woman was Edna St. Vincent Millay.

Edna was born in Rockland, Maine, in 1892. She was given the unusual middle name of St. Vincent to honor St. Vincent's Hospital in New York, where her uncle's life had been saved just before she was born. Her parents were separated, and she and her two sisters and her mother moved often. Though they were poor, her mother read to her daughters most nights from a trunk full of classic books that they always had with them. She and her sisters grew up listening to Shakespeare and the other great writers. Edna entered the prestigious Lyric Year poetry contest and took fourth place. The winner said that he felt horrible knowing that her poem was so much better than his entry.

After college Edna moved to New York; she also lived in Europe for a while. In 1923 she became the first woman to win the Pulitzer Prize for poetry. The famous poet from Maine died after a fall in 1950.

The Doctor and His Servant (French)

Some of the first Europeans to settle in Maine were of French ancestry. This tale, dating back to the times of kings and queens, comes from their tradition.

Once there was a poor farmer who had a son. He told his son that he needed to find work to help the family. The boy went out that very day wearing the coat his mother had made for him. The coat had a white front and a red back. Now he happened to walk past a castle where there lived a doctor. He saw the boy walking down the road and called out to him, "What are you looking for, young man?"

The boy replied, "I'm out to make a living and help my family. Do you have any work?"

Now the doctor did need a servant and called out to the boy, "Do you know how to read?"

"Yes sir. I've been to school and can read."

"Then you won't do, lad," replied the doctor.

The boy went away, but the next day he walked past the doctor's castle again, and this time he was wearing his coat backwards. The doctor called out, "Boy, what are you looking for?"

"Well sir, I'm looking for work," said the young man.

"Can you read?" asked the doctor.

"Sorry sir, I can't read a word. I've never been to school."

"Perfect," said the doctor. "I'll hire you and give one hundred francs a year plus your room and board."

Now this doctor was a powerful wizard. He took the boy into his library and showed him his book of ancient secrets. He told the boy that he must very carefully dust that book and all the books in the library every day. He must keep the castle tidy and take care of everything for the doctor whenever he left on his many journeys. The duties were light, and the boy was happy to have a job with so few duties.

Not long after the boy started his work, the doctor left for a long trip and was gone a whole year. The young man took advantage of the doctor's absence and read his book of secrets every day. He learned many of his master's skills.

When the doctor returned, he was very happy with his new servant and felt that he had someone he could trust to take care of his castle when he traveled. He left for another journey that lasted another year. During that year the young man learned most of the first half of the book of secrets by heart.

When the doctor returned, he was so pleased with his servant that he raised his wages. Soon he departed for another year of travel. During this time the young servant learned the other half of the book by heart. He was now confident in his magical skills.

When the doctor returned, the young man left his position and returned to his family. Even with the money he had sent home, they were still as poor as ever.

The night before the village fair, the young man had an idea. He said to his father, "Tomorrow go into the stable and there you will find a beautiful horse. Take the horse to the fair and sell it, but be sure to keep the halter. Under no circumstances do you sell or lose that halter."

The next day the father found the horse in the stable. He took the horse to the fair and sold it for a good price, following his son's instructions to keep the halter. He left the village with the halter and a pocketful of gold. He heard a voice behind him, and when he looked around there was his son walking toward him. The young man had transformed himself into a horse, and then while the new owner was celebrating in the tavern he transformed himself back into his normal shape and left the village. The father and son were both delighted at their new adventure.

When the money was gone the son told the father to go to the stable and get the steer that would be waiting for him and to take it to the fair and sell it. "Make sure you keep the rope you use to lead the steer," he told his father.

Just like before the man sold the steer, and the young man turned himself back into his own shape as soon as the new owner's back was turned.

Now the doctor thought it was odd that his young servant should leave his employment. He also heard rumors at the fairs in the towns around his castle of disappearing animals that had been bought and then were gone as if by magic.

He consulted his book and found that the young man had learned all the spells and secrets from the book. Now he knew that he was using those secrets of magic to cheat people and make money. The doctor was angry that the boy had lied to him and was now using his magic without his permission or knowledge.

At the next fair the father sold a horse, but he didn't know that the man who bought it was indeed the doctor. The wizard took the young man's father to the local tavern and bought him drink after drink, until the old man walked home unaware that he had left the halter behind.

He took the horse to the blacksmith and told him to give the horse a good shoeing. He thought that the pain of being shod would teach his ex-servant a lesson.

The blacksmith tied the horse to the door, and as some schoolchildren walked home, one of them heard the horse talk. "Untie me."

The child was shocked and was on the verge of running home when it said in a soft voice, "Please child, untie me." The child untied it. The horse transformed itself into a hare and ran away.

The doctor saw what had happened and turned the boys into hunting dogs, and they started to chase the hare. The young man then came to a lake and dove in, turning into a fish. The doctor bought the lake and had it fished out. The last fish out of the lake turned into a lark and flew into the sky. The doctor turned into an eagle and chased it. The lark flew over a palace and flew into the chimney, and as it neared the bottom it turned into a grain of wheat and rolled under the table in a young girl's bedroom.

In the evening the young man spoke from under the table, "Mademoiselle, if you would be so kind . . . ."

The young girl screamed and called for her parents. They came and searched the room, but found nothing.

He tried the next night, but again she became scared and called for her parents. Again they searched the room and found nothing.

On the third night he talked to her and convinced her not to be afraid. He told her that if she would let him stay in her room and hide, he would turn himself into a beautiful ring that she could wear all day long. She agreed and soon was wearing a beautiful jeweled ring on her finger.

When the doctor learned of this, he caused her father to become ill. They sent for the doctor and he told them that he could not cure the father for any price except the ring on his daughter's finger. The father promised, but the young man overheard the bargain that was made between them.

"The doctor is going to ask you for your ring, but don't hand it to him. Instead let it drop on the floor," he told the girl. She did as she was told, and as the ring dropped to the ground the young man turned into hundreds of grains of wheat. The doctor turned into a rooster and started to peck and eat the grain. The young man swiftly turned into a fox and ate the rooster up.

In the end, the young man became the doctor, and he and the girl lived happily for a long, long time.

Maine Glossary

Maine: A state named to honor Queen Mary, the wife of King Charles I, who came from the French Province of Mayne. The name might also have come from explorers trying to distinguish the "mainland" from the coastal islands. The capital is Augusta.

Passamaquoddy people: A tribe of Native Americans who at one time were found both in Maine and in the Canadian Maritime Provinces. They were part of the Wabanaki Confederacy. They lived in round buildings called wigwams and traveled using birch bark canoes along Maine's extensive waterways.

Pulitzer Prize: A literary prize named after Joseph Pulitzer, the owner of the *New York World* and *St. Louis Post-Dispatch*. Pulitzer was the first to call for the training of journalists at the university level in a school of journalism. In his will he left the money that is used to this day to award prizes to American writers in various types of literature.

Story Sources:

The Algonquin Legends of New England: Myth & Folk Lore of the Micmac, Passamaquoddy & Penobscot Tribes

American Folktales from the Collections of the Library of Congress, Volume 1

American Folktales from the Collections of the Library of Congress, Volume 2

American Myths & Legends, Volumes 1 & 2

The Borzoi Book of French Folktales

British Ballads from Maine

Buying the Wind

The Faithful Hunter: Abenaki Stories

The Greenwood Library of American Folktales, Volume 1

Jonathan Draws the Long Bow

Myths & Legends of Our Own Land, Volumes 1 & 2

New England Bean-Pot

New England Legends & Folklore

Of Kings and Fools: Stories of French Tradition in North America

Paul Bunyan

Paul Bunyan Swings His Axe

Songs & Ballads of the Maine Lumberjacks

Spirit of the New England Tribes: Indian History & Folklore

Tall Timber Tales: More Paul Bunyan Stories

A Treasury of New England Folklore

Maryland

Maryland, located on the Atlantic coast, was one of the thirteen original colonies, officially becoming a state in 1788 when it ratified the Constitution. Before Europeans arrived to explore and colonize the lands along the coast, and for many years afterward, a rich diversity of Native American cultures thrived in the lands along the coast, including the confederacy of the Powhatan, whose chief was the father of Pocahontas.

"A Ride for a Bride," a story of personal triumph, was told along the Maryland coast during the days of the Revolutionary War. "The Singing Geese" is a timeless tale reflecting the hunting tradition of the state in the tale of a remarkable goose and the couple who just can't get it to accept its fate.

Storytelling is an important part of the African American heritage, and Maryland's history includes a rich tradition of storytelling, represented here by "One for Me, One for You." Jack tales are found in many cultures in the United States, and here we see one of Jack's many sides in "The Tablecloth, the Donkey, and the Club," a story that belongs to both Anglo and African American folk literature.

A Ride for a Bride (Based on True Events)

Albert De Courcy sat on his horse and looked down into the eyes of the woman he loved. Helen Carmichael, his fiancée, looked back at him with eyes that were both sad and proud. Albert was going north to find General Washington's army and fight the British. Albert's brother Ernest, who stood nearby, was staying behind to take care of the family farm and raise the rebel cause through speeches.

Time passed slowly after Albert left home. Letters passed back and forth between Washington's Continental Army and Bohemia Hall, the home of the De Courcy family in Cecil County, Maryland. Then, abruptly, the letters from Albert stopped. Soon the news of a disastrous rebel defeat by the British army reached Helen and Ernest. It was almost a year later that a ragged soldier passing through the county stopped at the Hall for food and lodging. He told of the battle and the death of the young officer, Albert De Courcy, who had been shot as he and his men tried to swim across a river to safety. Helen was devastated.

Stories like this one were common in those days. How could anyone know that this poor soldier was wrong? Albert was alive. He had been bogged down in the mud on the riverbank, where he was captured and placed on a prison ship anchored offshore. Lying in the hold of the prison ship, he sometimes wished for death. He lived in the darkness with barely enough to eat and never any clean water to slake his thirst. At night he heard the cries of his fellow prisoners as they died. Day after day their bodies were taken up on the deck and thrown overboard. Day after day the tide carried the dead to the shore, where the birds and beasts picked their bones clean.

Then one day Albert was dragged up into daylight. He and a dozen other officers were being transferred to another prison along the Delaware River. In no time he regained his strength and became a favorite among the British soldiers. Even though he always spoke against the king, his captors admired his frankness. They liked his honest ways and easy manner, and soon he was allowed to walk freely around the inner yard of the prison.

What Albert's captors did not know, however, was that this prison was just twenty miles from the young officer's home and his love. It didn't take long for Albert to discover where the prison wall was lowest and the ditch narrowest. Then one day, as Albert walked in the yard, a soldier led a handsome horse through the gate. Suddenly the animal snorted and reared, breaking away from the startled soldier. It galloped straight to Albert, who laughed as the big bay nuzzled him and rubbed its nose against his chest. "Why, look who it is!" exclaimed Albert. "It's Cecil, my old horse. There's not a better hunter in all of Maryland."

"We just took this horse from your brother," replied one of the British officers. "He's been stirring up trouble, talking out against the king. He escaped, but we know where he is. He's going to be married today, and we have scouts riding out to arrest him at the altar."

"Married? My brother?" laughed Albert. "I never thought he would marry. He's just a dry lawyer and orator. That's a hard way to break up a wedding, boys, with muskets and soldiers."

"It may be hard for your brother, but I hear the lady has no great love for him," said one British officer. "I've heard he is marrying her out of duty since the man she loved is dead."

Albert's expression changed. "What is the lady's name?" he asked.

"Helen, Helen Carmichael, I believe."

For just a moment Albert De Courcy could see her face as clearly as if she were there beside him. Time stood still. Then he spoke quickly. "Well, an unhappy wedding you'll make for him this day. Now, if he had old Cecil here, he could outride you all. You know, when Cecil and I rode I could snatch a pebble off the ground while he ran at a full gallop. We never missed a step."

"Do you think you could you do that now?" asked one soldier.

"Maybe not a pebble, for your prisons have made me a bit stiff, but I think I could snatch a handkerchief from off the ground."

"Well, I have half a crown that says you can't do it," said the prison commandant.

"Well, I'll place my money on our rebel friend," said another officer, as he reached into his pocket.

Without a moment's hesitation, De Courcy climbed into the saddle slowly and started to cross the grounds at a canter. His bearing on the horse was so noble, and he sat so easy in the saddle, that the soldiers cheered as he rode by. Then Albert and Cecil picked up speed. When they neared the handkerchief, the bold young officer leaned far over the side of the horse, picked the white flag up off the ground, and waved it high over his head as a farewell. He galloped straight at the lowest part of the wall and, sailing through a hail of musket balls, jumped it with one tremendous leap.

Albert's shout of triumph told all the men inside the prison—captors and prisoners alike—that he had reached the road and was galloping away, free at last. He knew most of the shortcuts in the area, and he took them all until he came to the turnpike. There, riding down the road ahead of him, were the scouts who had been sent to arrest his brother. Quickly Albert reined Cecil off the road and onto an old path that ran straight through the woods to the back of the church. He knew that the British soldiers would be there in no time.

When the startled wedding party turned around, all they could see was a wild rider beating toward them and screaming, "The British are coming! The British are coming! To your horses! Make for the manor!"

Then one man called out in amazement, "Albert has risen from the dead."

Riding straight through the doors of the church, Albert headed for the altar, leaned down to Helen, and pulled her up onto the saddle behind him. "Save yourselves. The British are coming! To your horses!" he called once more.

As Albert rode out the door of the church, Helen clung to him, crying tears of joy, while Ernest and all the wedding guests ran for their horses. By the time the British scouts arrived, most of the guests had vanished. The next morning Ernest was captured by the British and took his brother's place in the prison. Still, preparations had been made for a wedding, so there was one. And a happy wedding it was, with Albert as the groom!

One for Me, One for You (African American)

One day two friends went out fishing. They fished all day long, and at the end of the day they had a big basket full of fish. It was getting dark and cold, and the men decided to go back home.

"Where shall we divide our catch?" asked one man.

"We'll find a place out of the wind on the way back to town," replied the other.

They walked for a while and started to get tired carrying that big basket filled with fish. They passed the graveyard and then stopped.

"Let's climb over the graveyard wall and divide our catch. We'll be out of the wind on the other side of the wall." So the two men struggled to get the basket over the wall. While they were trying to get their catch over, two fish slipped out of the basket just as they crossed to the other side of the wall.

"We'll get those later," said one of the friends.

The two men started to divide the fish. "Here's one for me and one for you, one for me and one for you, one for me and one for you"; they just kept on that way as they divided their catch.

One of the elders in the church and a good friend of the local preacher heard them as he passed by the graveyard. "One for me and one for you . . . ."

He thought for sure that it was God and the devil dividing souls right there in the cemetery. He ran around the corner to the preacher's house and told him to follow him quickly to the graveyard. "The devil and the Lord are dividing souls in the cemetery," he told the minister.

"How do you know?" asked the preacher.

"You just come and listen for yourself," he said.

The two men walked quietly up to the graveyard wall and crouched down low and listened.

"One for me and one for you," said one of the friends counting fish. "That's about all of them."

"Wait a minute," said his partner. "Let's not forget the two on the other side of the wall. Let's get them now."

The preacher and the elder stood up and screamed and ran as fast as they could for their homes.

The Singing Geese

One day a man went out hunting. He wanted to bring back something special for his family for their supper. As he walked along the shore of a nearby lake he heard a flock of geese squawking.

"Squawk, squawk, quee, quee," one of them sang as it flew along. The hunter raised his gun, took aim, and shot. The bird fell to the ground. He threw it into his bag and as he walked home he heard the goose still singing. "Squawk, squawk, quee, quee."

He took it home and gave it to his wife to cook for their supper. As she cooked it she could hear singing softly coming from the oven. "Squawk, squawk, quee, quee."

When the goose was cooked the family sat down at the table, and they could still faintly hear it singing. "Squawk, squawk, quee, quee."

The hunter took up a fork and a huge carving knife and was just about to stick them in the goose and carve it up for his family's dinner when he heard, "Squawk, squawk, quee, quee." This time it was very loud and seemed to come from everywhere at once. Suddenly a whole flock of geese flew through the window. As they flew by the table, each one plucked out a feather from its back or wing or tail and stuck it into their cooked brother. As they placed the feathers on the goose each one sang, "Squawk, squawk, quee, quee."

As soon as the cooked bird was covered in feathers, it flew up from the table and out through the window and joined the other geese as they flew off into the evening sky.

The Tablecloth, the Donkey, and the Club
(Anglo-American)

Jack tales, common in the British Isles, date back centuries. They traveled to America with British immigrants who settled here. Here is a favorite British import.

Once there lived a boy named Jack and his mother in a small rundown house. Now Jack's mother had planted some barley, and after a great deal of coaxing Jack went out to harvest the grain. When he finally had gathered all the barley together, a great wind rose up and took the barley away. It went flying up into the sky and disappeared. Jack was so angry that he picked up a branch and started whipping it around and around. As he was beating the air with his stick an old man walked up and asked, "Son, what are you doing?"

Jack stopped and turned to the man and said, "The wind took all the barley that I had just harvested and blew it all away. I'm beating the wind with this stick to get my barley back."

The old man smiled and took out a cloth from the pocket of his coat. He opened it and said, "Spread, tablecloth, spread." As the tablecloth opened and spread itself out a grand supper spread out on the tablecloth. It was a feast.

"Take this tablecloth home to your mother and it will keep you both well fed and happy."

The old man smiled and walked on down the road.

Now instead of going home Jack went to the nearby inn, and talked and sang with his friends. He placed the cloth on the table in front of him and said, "Spread, tablecloth, spread." A feast appeared in front of them and they ate a wonderful meal. Soon Jack fell asleep, and the people who owned the inn took his cloth and replaced it with one of their own tablecloths. When Jack woke up he took the tablecloth home and gave it to his mother. When she told the tablecloth to spread it just lay there on the table. She told Jack that he shouldn't make up stories like that. And he ran out of the house and back to the empty barley field, where he picked up that stick and began to beat the air with it.

The old man was standing by the road and he called out, "What's the problem, Jack?"

Jack told him about going to the inn and how when he gave his mother the tablecloth it wouldn't work at all.

The old man was leading a donkey and he said to Jack, "Son, take this donkey, and when you need some money just tell the donkey to shake."

Jack took the donkey's halter and said, "Shake." The donkey lifted one foot and gold coins came tumbling out. He lifted another and silver coins came tumbling out.

"Now go home and give this to your mother," said the old man, and he walked away and disappeared down the road.

Once again Jack went to the inn instead of going home. He told his donkey to shake, and when it did he took the money and bought supper for everyone in the inn. They laughed and sang and told stories deep into the night until Jack fell asleep. While he was asleep the owners of the inn went into the barn and exchanged their donkey for Jack's.

The next morning Jack took the donkey home and called his mother out into the yard and said, "Watch this. Shake." The donkey just stood there and nothing happened. His mother just looked at him and shook her head and went back into the house and closed the door.

Jack ran to the barley field again and once more started to beat the air with his stick, crying, "I'm going to beat you wind. If it wasn't for you, none of this would have happened." Then he heard a familiar voice.

"Jack, what are you doing now?" There stood the old man who had given him the two gifts.

Jack told him everything that had happened. The old man gave him a club and told him that if he told the club to beat, it would keep beating someone until Jack told it to stop. The he told Jack what to do with it.

Jack went to the inn and sat down and had some supper and started to talk to his friends, and sing and dance. He told the owners of the inn that he had just gotten a magic club. He told them all he had to do was say, "beat club" and the magic would happen. Later, after Jack had fallen asleep, the owners of the inn took his club into the kitchen and said, "beat club." The club jumped up into the air and began to beat the two people until they cried for help.

Jack heard the cries and ran into the kitchen, and there was his club chasing the owners around and around the kitchen table, beating them on the back and shoulders.

"Jack, make it stop," they cried.

"Where are my tablecloth and my donkey?" Jack demanded. They took the tablecloth out of a drawer and threw it at him. Then they told him where they had hidden the donkey in the barn. Jack said, "stop club." The club fell to the floor, and Jack picked it up and went into the barn and got his donkey. He got home just about dawn and showed his mother the wonderful gifts he had gotten from the old man. They lived happily through the magic of the tablecloth, the donkey, and the club.

Maryland Glossary

Continental Army: The name given the army of the thirteen colonies that fought against England for their independence.

Graveyard: Another name for a cemetery.

Maryland: The state named after Queen Mary. Its capital is Annapolis.

Powhatan people: The powerful Native American tribe that lived in parts of what is now Maryland and tidewater Virginia when the first English settlers came to the New World. The Powhatan were farmers and hunters who lived in villages made up of round houses called wigwams. Their chief was Powhatan, ruler of the Powhatan confederacy of tribes, father of Pocahontas.

Story Sources

American Folktales from the Collections of the Library of Congress, Volume 1

American Folktales from the Collections of the Library of Congress, Volume 2

American Myths & Legends, Volumes 1 & 2

The Greenwood Library of American Folktales, Volume 1

Maryland Folk Legends & Folk Songs

Myths & Legends of Our Own Land, Volumes 1 & 2

A Treasury of Southern Folklore

Upstate Downstate

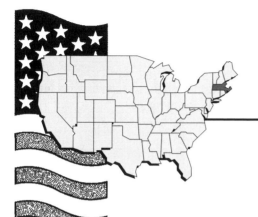

Massachusetts

Massachusetts was one of the original thirteen colonies that fought in the American Revolution; it officially became a state in 1788, when it ratified the U.S. Constitution. From that period in Massachusetts's history come two stories, one about Esther Dudley, an unreformed loyalist, and the other about Josiah Breeze, a young man of uncommon bravery. The Pequot people were among the tribes who lived in Massachusetts before the arrival of Europeans. The English heritage of the state is found in the story "Rose," a lovely version of "Beauty and the Beast."

Boston has always opened its arms to immigrants who have come to America from around the world, and those countless travelers are represented here by an Irish story.

Esther Dudley's House (Based on True Events)

The armies of the new nation had forced the surrender of Boston, and General Washington was at the outskirts of the city. The American cannons were aimed at the British army, and the city was in chaos. Sir William Howe, the royal governor of Boston, walked through the doors of Province House, the last of the royal governors to ever do so, and cursed the rebels for their insolence. As he walked down the steps he saw an older woman curtseying to him as he passed by and turned and spoke to her, "Esther, what are you doing here? Why haven't you left with the rest of the household staff?"

Esther Dudley stood up straight and replied, "I am the housekeeper to the King's governors, and I shall never leave this house. This has been the only home I've ever known, and I will stay here until you return and take Boston back from the rebels."

Governor Howe smiled thinly and said, "I hope I can return, Esther, with more troops and drive these rebels into the wilderness. Until then, here is the key to Province House and money to maintain it until the King's men return." He handed her the key and a small bag of gold coins. Then Sir William Howe got into his carriage and drove off, never to return to Boston again.

When the American army entered Boston they needed homes to place their troops in, but they left the old governor's mansion alone. Esther Dudley and her unshakable devotion to the king and his cause amused them, and deep down they even respected her for her unwavering loyalty to a cause that was losing ground daily.

Esther took great care of Province House. The flowerbeds were always neat and the windows were always clean as she looked out on an ever-changing world. She swept the walk, and the Union Jack always flew from the flagpole. No one seemed to care if she occasionally had a few other aging unrepentant Tories over for dinner, where they hoisted a toast to King George and prayed for Sir William's safe return. Rumors started that she even had the ghosts of past royal governors over for a quick supper and a glass of sherry. The stories of her ghostly parties probably also kept the prying eyes away from her window.

As the war dragged on Esther withdrew into her own world of the past. She refused to listen to stories of American victories and instead began to change them into Tory and Royalist gains. She always lit candles on the king's birthday and watched for the British fleet from the cupola that topped the great house. People just smiled and shook their heads, remembering an old prophecy that said that the English governor would return when the golden Indian on Province House would shoot his arrow and the rooster on the spire of the South Church would crow. The weather vanes kept still and quiet.

When word spread that the new governor was coming to Province House, Esther Dudley thought it was the new royal governor. She cleaned the house from top to bottom, though with all her care through the years it hardly needed it. She dressed herself in her best silk gown when the day of his arrival finally came. Esther saw a man of importance walking through the courtyard surrounded by a staff of men and followed by a company of soldiers. She threw open the door, fell to her knees, and shouted, "This is the hour for which I've waited. God save the king!"

The new governor took off his hat and helped the old woman to her feet. "A strange greeting, I'm sure, but we will echo it in our own way. For the good of the realm that still owns him to be their ruler, God save King George."

Esther looked into the face of the new governor and now recognized him for who he was, John Hancock, the rebel leader of Massachusetts. Esther cried out, "Have I welcomed a traitor? Let me die."

"Mistress Dudley," said Hancock, "the world has changed, and America no longer has a king." He offered her his arm, but she sank to the ground and the great key that Howe had given her when he left fell to the cobblestones. With her dying breath she sighed, "I have been faithful. God save the king."

Hancock and the other men took off their hats and were silent. The new American governor of the state of Massachusetts spoke softly, "When we stand at her grave we will say farewell to the past forever. A new day has come for us all." Indeed it had.

Rose (Anglo-American)

Traditional British tales, which date back centuries, arrived in America on the lips of British immigrants. Here is an old favorite.

Once upon a time there was a widower with one daughter, named Rose. He married a widow who had two daughters of her own, both older than Rose. Now the two stepdaughters were fond of parties and dances, and they expected young Rose to help them get ready, brushing their hair and ironing their dresses and making sure they looked as beautiful as they could look. Rose was not allowed to go to the parties, for she had her chores to do, like cleaning the house and cooking and taking care of her father. Though she had to do all the work by herself, she never complained.

One day the father had to go on a business trip, and he asked each of his three daughters what they wanted him to bring back for them. The oldest girls wanted dresses and silks and jewelry.

He turned to Rose and asked, "And what does my little Rose want her father to bring her?"

Rose smiled and replied, "All I want is a rose." Her father was so pleased that her request was simple and lovely that he promised her that he would bring her the finest rose he could find.

On his return journey the father stopped to ask for lodging at a palace, but there was no one in sight. The doors were open and a room was made up for him, but not a soul stirred in the great house. The next morning his breakfast was waiting in the dining room, but no host or servants were to be found anywhere.

He walked out into the beautiful garden that grew next to the house, and there he saw the most beautiful rose bush covered with roses, perfect roses that he knew his own Rose would love. He plucked a rose to bring to her, but when he turned a huge Lion stood in his path and roared out at him, "For picking this rose you must die."

The terrified man told the Lion that he had picked the rose as a promised present for his youngest daughter, whose name was Rose. He pleaded with the Lion, "If you let me go home to say my farewell to my daughter, I promise I will return."

The Lion allowed him to go home on the condition that he would return. As he came down the road, Rose saw her father and ran to meet him.

"Why do you look so sad?" she asked.

At first her father said nothing, but eventually he told her about the palace, the rose, the Lion, and his promise to return and face his fate.

Rose stood and looked at her father and said, "You will not go back to die. I will go back instead and plead for your life."

Rose walked to the palace. When she entered, everywhere she looked the words "Welcome, Beauty, here" appeared, on her cup and saucer, on the furniture in her bedroom, on everything she looked at in the great house.

Rose went looking for the Lion. When she found him she told him that her father had plucked the rose for her to keep a promise he had made to her. The Lion didn't care at all about her father's promise. He said that he would let her father live if she married him. Though her father was dear to her, Rose was not eager to marry the Lion, and so she would not give him an answer.

The Lion then gave her a gold ring and told her that if she wanted to see her father she only had to lay the ring on the table next to her bed at night, and then wish to see her father. When she woke up she would be at home with her father. Now her father was getting old, and after a few days Rose decided to visit him. She followed the Lion's instructions and woke the next day in her father's house. Her father's hair had turned white with worry over his youngest daughter. She comforted him and told him how well the Lion had treated her.

That night she placed the ring on the table next to her bed and wished to be back at the palace. The next morning she was there, and it was more beautiful than ever. The breakfast table was set and each plate had the words "Welcome, Beauty, here" on it.

She went outside, and there in the garden she found the Lion, lying on the ground, weak and sick, barely able to raise his great head. Rose knelt by him and said, "I cannot bear to see my Lion so sick. What can I do?" Finally she called out, "I will be your wife."

In a moment the Lion was gone and a handsome prince now stood before her. She had broken the spell that had trapped him in the body of a lion. They were married and sent for her father to come and live with them in their palace home. The stepsisters came too and were made servants to stand at the gate before the palace. The prince and Rose were happy and lived that way forever.

The Bravery of Josiah Breeze
(Based on True Events)

Cape Cod was at the mercy of the British navy during much of the American Revolution. Over 2,000 men from the Cape had gone off to join the Continental Army and had left the island almost defenseless. The island had been so terrorized by the king's sailors that there was not a man, woman, or child who did not hate the British. When the frigate *The Sommerset* was wrecked off the Cape, the crew was helped as they came ashore exhausted after battling the storm, but they were marched to the prison and locked up there awaiting the judgment of the American courts. Her battered hull, wrecked on the offshore sand dunes, seemed like a warning to other British men of war ships to keep clear of Cape Cod.

It was November when one of those powerful storms that often come in late fall to remind us that winter is coming hit the Cape. The people on the shore saw a three-decker man of war flying the red naval flag of King George's fleet, which had been tacking offshore, start to drift toward the sandbars. The crew fought to keep her on course, but the wind and the tide were combining to bring the huge ship to certain destruction. The people just stood and watched as the ship neared the dangerous reefs. No one lifted a hand to rescue the crew. No one lit a fire to warn them of the danger. They saw the ship lower its anchors and bring in the sail in an attempt to avoid whatever danger the storm might conceal.

Ezekiel and Josiah Breeze watched the ship as it floundered in the storm. The father and son watched as the cables strained and the crew called out to each other in terror as the storm increased in violence.

The young man turned to his father and said, "I can't stand by and watch this happen. I'm going to try to help."

"If you go help them, then you are no son of mine," said Ezekiel Breeze.

"But she's in danger of sinking."

"As she should. By morning she'll be wrecked on the reefs and sand dunes, and she'll be a wreck like *The Sommerset* before her. There won't be a mast or spar that will hold a sail, and the water will fill her hull and drag her down."

"But what of the men who crew her?" asked Josiah.

"Judgment," was all his father replied.

Josiah remembered when the captain of *The Ajax* had sent his sailors and marines ashore to steal the people's food and burn their homes. He remembered how his friends and neighbors were cut down if they tried to resist. Josiah had even been slashed by a sailor's cutlass as he tried to help a family get out of their burning home. He had vowed revenge when that attack was over. But this was different. There were hundreds of men on that ship, fighting for their lives. Sitting back and doing nothing wasn't revenge; it was being a coward.

"I'm sorry, father, but I have to try to do something to help. Tomorrow there will be 500 bodies along the shore, covered with ice and staring lifeless at the sky, and in England there will be 500 mothers wondering if they will ever see their sons again. If I saw those men, if I looked into their lifeless eyes and knew that I could have helped but did nothing, I would never get the sight of them out of my mind and they would haunt me forever. Tomorrow is Thanksgiving, and what would I be thankful for, father? I have to go, and I will." With those words young Josiah ran toward the beach and was swallowed by the night.

Ezekiel stared after his son and swallowed hard. As the boy rain into the night he called out, "You're right, son, and I'll go with you." But the storm was so loud that Josiah could not hear him. As Ezekiel came to the shore, he could see a small boat cresting the first wave. He watched as it climbed the second and third waves and then disappeared into the storm. Ezekiel waited a half hour or more, and then he saw something coming toward the beach. He ran and found Josiah's boat overturned and lying on the sand. There was no sign of his son.

The next day the storm was over and a blanket of new snow covered the ground. Captain Breeze, father of Ezekiel and grandfather of Josiah, walked around his Provincetown home, helping to prepare for the celebration he had planned for all his family and friends who had not joined General Washington at the front. There were turkeys and breads and squash and cake all waiting for the gathering.

The guests started to arrive and talk happily about the beautiful snow and the coming of winter. In the middle of their conversation Ezekiel staggered into the room, haggard and soaked to the skin, teeth chattering, with the look of a wild man in his eyes. He leaned his face against the fireplace and whispered only one word, "Josiah," before collapsing to the floor. Most of the folks there were sailors of one type or another; they knew what the sudden loss of a loved one meant and knew the grief that one word held. Captain Breeze held his son tight, and they all shared the grief that had suddenly walked through the door with Ezekiel. Suddenly a cry was heard that a ship encased in ice was coming up the channel to the harbor. When the people gathered at the harbor they saw a strange sight. A ship so weighted down with ice that it floated deep in the water was slowly making its way up the harbor. British sailors in blue were trying to beat the thick ice from the spars and masts and rigging. It was plain by the way the ship handled that an experienced hand was at its helm, one that knew the way.

"What ship are you?" someone called out from shore.

"As I am a sinner, we are *The Ajax*," came the reply. The people gathered at the wharf, angered that their old enemy was back to spoil their celebration. Some men talked of getting their guns, while others said there were too many of them to fight. A boat was launched and they saw an officer, his naval cloak barely hiding the gold braid that told of his rank as captain, with a young man sitting near him.

The boat touched the dock and Josiah Breeze jumped from the boat into the waiting arms of his father, who made no attempt to stop the tears that filled his eyes. The officer followed and spoke softly. "This is a son to be proud of. He came to us out of the dark in a little boat during a storm that had most of my crew frightened to death. He helped us steer away from the reefs and sandbars and brought us to a safe place to ride out the storm and then piloted us here this morning. He risked his life to save the lives of his enemy. I could do no less than bring him back to you." There was a silence for a moment and then a cheer went up from the people on shore for Ezekiel's brave son, and the cheer was raised on *The Ajax* as well. That night many a sailor and officer had supper in a warm house with a family that welcomed them, and at Captain Breeze's table the commander of H.M.S. *Ajax* was the most grateful guest of all.

The Field of Boliauns (Irish)

In the mid-nineteenth century, when the deadly potato famine hit Ireland, many Irish families began immigrating to the United States. Many settled in Massachusetts, particularly in the Boston area. Although they had little but the clothes on their backs, they brought their stories of leprechauns and magic.

One sunny Lady Day in the harvest season, Tom Fitzpatrick was taking a walk through the woods alongside the hedge. All of a sudden he heard a clacking sound on the other side of the hedge. He thought that the stone chatters were singing a bit late in the season and decided he would try to get a look at what was making the noise. He stood up on his toes and looked over the hedge, but then the noise stopped. Tom looked down through the bushes and saw a brown pitcher that might hold a gallon or so of liquor. Next to the pitcher was the tiniest little man he had ever seen, an old fellow with a cocked hat stuck on his head and a leather apron around his waist standing on a tiny wooden stool and drinking from the brown jug with a straw. Tom watched as the little man drank all the liquor in the jug and then sat down on the stool and started working on the heelpiece of a small shoe he was making that would just fit him.

Tom said to himself, "Well, I often have heard stories about Leprechauns from my granny, but I never really believed them until now. Here's the real thing right on the other side of this hedge. If I don't take advantage of this I'd be a mad man. They say you must never take your eyes off them or they'll disappear into thin air."

Tom crept through the hedge as quiet as he could and then came upon the little man. When he was very close he said, "Good morning to you sir, and God bless your work. Isn't it a fine day?"

The little man looked up and replied, "Thank you sir, and indeed it is a fine day."

"I was wondering why you'd be working on a fine holiday such as this?"

"That's my own business and not yours," came the reply.

"Well said," replied Tom. "Would you tell me what you have in the pitcher there?"

"That, my friend, is golden beer," replied the tiny man.

"Beer!" cried Tom. "Where did you get it from?"

"I made it myself," came the reply. "Do you know what I made it from?"

Tom said, "Well I suppose malt and barley."

"Really? No I made it from the heath." The little man smiled triumphantly.

"Heath? You can't make beer from heath."

"Did you ever hear of the Danes, my lad?"

"I've heard a bit about them," said Tom.

"All you need to know is that they taught my family how to brew beer from heath, and we've been doing it ever since. It's a family secret," he said with a smile.

"Could I have a taste?" said Tom. "I've never had beer made from heath before."

"Well my lad, I think you should be tending to your own business and not into mine. I think that your father's cows have gotten into the oats and corn and are trampling them away. You better be off and take care of your own farm."

Tom was so taken aback by this that he almost turned around to head home, but then he remembered that Leprechauns disappear if you don't keep them in your sight. He leaned down and grabbed the little man by the front of his coat and said, "Instead of all this talk, why don't you show me your store of gold."

Tom looked serious and intent on getting the little man's treasure. "Come along with me to a field not far off and I'll show you my crock of gold," he said to Tom.

Tom and the tiny man crossed over fields and through hedges and ditches and finally across a bog until they came to an enormous field full of boliauns. The Leprechaun pointed to a big boliaun and said, "Dig under that boliaun and you get a great crock filled with gold guineas."

Tom had never thought about digging the gold up and hadn't thought about bringing a shovel along with him. He took off one of his red garters and tied it around the plant.

"Swear to me that you'll not take that garter off the boliaun." The little man swore that he would not touch it.

"I suppose you'll have no further use for me?" asked the little man.

"No, I am finished with you," said Tom. "You can go now, and I hope that good luck attends you in your travels and in whatever you may do."

"Well thank you, Tom Fitzpatrick," said the Leprechaun. "I hope much good will come from the gold once you get it."

The Leprechaun disappeared and Tom ran for his dear life until he came to his barn. He grabbed a spade and ran back to the field as fast as his legs could carry him. But when he got back to that field of boliauns, what did he see? Every single boliaun had a red garter tied to it. There must have been forty acres of red garters floating in the autumn breeze. He could never dig it all up. He went home with his spade on his shoulder, a much wiser man than when he had started out that day. He even smiled when he thought about the trick the Leprechaun had played on him.

Massachusetts Glossary

Boliauns: A flowering weed in Ireland similar to ragwort.

H.M.S.: His Majesty's Ship if a king rules England or Her Majesty's Ship if a queen rules. The British navy uses these initials before the name of the ship, as in the story about Josiah Breeze, in which the British ship is called H.M.S. *Ajax*.

Ireland: An island country in Europe west of England. Great numbers of Irish people immigrated to America, and Boston was a favorite spot for settling down.

John Hancock: A leader in the American revolt against King George and one of the writers of the Constitution and the Declaration of Independence. He was the first American governor of the Commonwealth of Massachusetts.

Leprechaun: One of the fairy people of Ireland. They are tiny and magical but also mischievous.

Massachusetts: A state named after the Native American tribe by the same name. The capital is Boston.

Pilot: Someone who would go out to a ship and bring it safely into harbor past all the dangers like shoals and rocks.

Tory: An American loyalist to King George during the Revolutionary War.

Union Jack: The nickname for the flag of Great Britain.

Weather vanes: A metal object placed on top of houses and other buildings to let people know which way the wind is blowing and help them guess what the coming weather will be.

Story Sources

American Folktales from the Collections of the Library of Congress, Volume 1

American Folktales from the Collections of the Library of Congress, Volume 2

American Myths & Legends, Volumes 1 & 2

The Greenwood Library of American Folktales, Volume 1

Jonathan Draws the Long Bow

Myths & Legends of Our Own Land, Volumes 1 & 2

New England Bean-Pot

New England Legends & Folklore

Spirit of the New England Tribes: Indian History & Folklore

Stockings of Buttermilk

Tall Tales of Cape Cod

A Treasury of New England Folklore

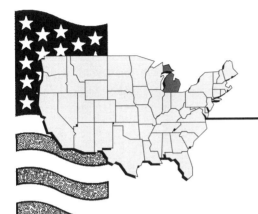

Michigan

Michigan became the twenty-sixth state in 1837. The mining region of the Upper Peninsula of Michigan brought a diverse immigrant population to the northern part of the state, whose stories like the ones included here helped create a rich folklore. African Americans came north to work in the industrial trades of the automotive industry and brought their folktales with them, including the story "Straighten Up and Fly Right."

Michigan has one of the largest Arab populations in the country, and the story "The Impossible Tale" comes from that tradition. Michigan has many fine storytellers, and one of them, Jenifer Strauss gives us a personal story about the Upper Peninsula. Before the coming of European settlers the Chippewa people hunted and fished in Michigan.

Konsti Makes Money (Finnish)

In the late nineteenth and early twentieth centuries, many Finns immigrated to the United States and specifically to Michigan's Upper Peninsula, seeking work in the copper and iron mines there. Here is one of their traditional tales.

Once a long time ago there was a farmer who was deep in debt to a very rich man. He could not pay the wealthy man the $30,000 he owed him, so he was taken to court. It was decided to have an auction of all the man's possessions. They would sell off his farm and house, his cattle and horse, his chickens and even his clothes.

On the day the auction was to begin, the sheriff was there to begin the sale. Among the people who were there was Konsti Koponen. Konsti walked into the farmhouse and found the farmer sitting at his kitchen table almost in tears over the loss of his farm.

"Do you have any newspapers?" asked Konsti. The farmer went into the next room and came back with an armload of old newspapers. Konsti took the newspapers and tore them into strips. Then he walked out into the farmyard and in full sight of everyone he handed the sheriff $30,000.

"Is the debt paid?" asked Konsti.

"It is," said the sheriff, and paid the wealthy man the money the farmer owed him. He gave the deed to the farm back to the farmer.

"Your debt is paid," he told the farmer.

The sheriff turned to the rich man and said, "Go home now. You've got your money."

But when the rich man got home he found that his pockets were not stuffed with $30,000, but with torn strips of old newspapers.

Konsti the trickster had struck again.

The Storylamp (a True Story by Jenifer Strauss)

Many years ago, when I was still a classroom teacher, I had something very precious in those days called summer vacation. On the first morning of vacation, I would wake up early, put the chairs on the front porch, and just before eight o'clock in the morning, I would sit down with a big cup of coffee and watch my neighbors go to work, because I didn't have to. When it was quiet on the road out in front of my house, I would start to plan my summer vacation.

Growing up in Michigan, summers were filled with adventures that almost always involved a trip north, across the Mackinaw Bridge and into the Upper Peninsula, otherwise known as the U.P. If you are from the Upper Peninsula of Michigan, you are affectionately known as a "Yooper." I am what the Yoopers refer to as a "Troll" because I live under the Mackinaw Bridge, but in my heart, I have always secretly wished I was a Yooper.

One year, on the first morning of summer vacation, I was sitting on the front porch, waving to my neighbors as they headed off to work. That day I decided that I would spend the entire summer traveling in the Upper Peninsula of Michigan. My goal was to spend each day traveling, learning as much as I could about Michigan history, and to camp in a different location each night. I loaded my truck with camping gear, supplies, and a set of Michigan county maps, and on a cool June morning, I headed north.

By early afternoon, I crossed over the Mackinaw Bridge. A five-mile-long, total suspension bridge, it is the longest of its kind in the world. Since November 1, 1957, the "Mighty Mac" has connected the Lower Peninsula of Michigan with the Upper Peninsula. I still get excited every time I drive over that bridge. I always drive slower than I need to, so I can take in the views over the Straights of Mackinaw: the intense sparkles on the waters where Lake Michigan and Lake Huron meet, the green, pointy pine trees of the north, and the fast ferry boats heading back and forth between the mainland and Mackinaw Island. I always hope I will see one of the impressive Great Lake ore boats pass under the bridge while I'm driving over it.

Once over the bridge, I headed west on Highway 2, so that I could follow the Lake Michigan shoreline, before taking the most direct route north, to Michigan Highway 28, to continue west along the Lake Superior shore. When I got to the town of L'Anse, the road divided. I saw a sign that said, "Keeweenaw Peninsula . . . Copper Country." I had not been to that part of Michigan in years, so I turned north. I passed through the towns of Houghton and Hancock, across the Portage canal, on to the historic mining town of Calumet. I spent hours touring the town and the Copper Mining Museum. I had taken a tour of the Quincy copper mine to see what it was like for the copper miners years ago, who worked long hours under ground.

It was late one afternoon when I finally headed north again. I was planning to camp that night at historic Fort Wilkins State Park, on the tip of the Keeweenaw Peninsula. I came to the small town of Ameek. Like so many other small towns in the U.P., Ameek is a mining ghost town. When the copper was gone, people left behind abandoned towns from a time long past in Michigan's history.

There wasn't much left in Ameek, but on the north end of town, at the base of Five-Mile Point Road, was an old antique store. I took one look at the place and knew that I had to go inside and see what they had.

Once inside, I realized that it was more of a Michigan museum than an antique store. I found remnants of Michigan history there, on the walls and the shelves: old tools, snowshoes, red and black plaid woolen hunting clothes, long cross-cut saws, miners' helmets, and metal lunchboxes. I came around the corner into one of the booths, and there I saw a simple, wooden and glass lantern hanging on the wall. Only about a foot tall, and square in shape, it was like other lanterns I had seen. But there was something about the lamp that made me walk over to it, reach up, and carefully remove it from the iron hook where it hung by a simple wire handle.

I was holding the lantern in my hands, wondering where it had come from and how old it was. I must have looked at the lamp a bit too long, because the storeowner headed my way. Standing in front of me, and just about my height, was a friendly, older man who reminded me of my grandfather. He had beautiful, white wispy hair sticking out, haphazardly, from the sides of his head, but there was no hair on the top of his head. Because the ceiling and store lights were low, there was a gentle reflection coming from his bald spot.

He had a pair of reading glasses perched on the tip of his nose, and he was looking at me over them with cheerful blue eyes. He had on a pair of old blue-jean work pants that were hanging down so low on his hips, it made me a little nervous. I wondered why his pants were hanging down so low. It was long before it was fashionable to wear your pants sagging down in the back, and that style has generally been worn by the younger generation. Then I realized that he had spent many years in that store, visiting with all those who came in, and in that time, he had acquired a very endearing potbelly that only stuck out in front. I figured that he bought the work pants long before he had acquired the belly and just couldn't get the waist up any higher. The only thing holding up his pants were a pair of wide, red suspenders. I knew they were the only thing holding up his pants, because at one point he turned around to get something off the table behind us. That's when I was greeted by what I affectionately refer to as a vertical smile down the other side. I was a bit embarrassed and relieved when he turned to face me again.

We talked for a while and did the usual "Where ya from?" and "Where ya headed?" when he finally put his hands on his hips, looked at me over his glasses, and said, "So, you really like my lyhty (pronounced lewfta), don't you?" I said, "I like your what?" He repeated, "The lyhty, you really like it, don't you?" I said, "Are you talking about this lamp?" He replied, "Oh yes!" I asked, "Can you tell me anything about it?" and he said, "Oooh, yes!"

He gently took the lantern out of my hands and set it down on a table nearby. He told me he couldn't speak about the lamp until he lit the candle that was still inside. I watched as he pulled up on a wooden dowel that protruded from the top of the lamp, raising the candle up through a hole in the top of the lamp. He lit the candle and then placed the holder gently back inside the glass walls. Once the candle was lit, he started telling me where the lantern had come from.

There was a family by the name of Koivela, who had come from Finland to Michigan over a hundred years before, to work in the mines. Someone in the family had made the lamp a long time ago. When they came to Michigan, it was one of the things they brought with them. When I asked why it was so important, he told me that there had been a long-standing tradition in the family that originated in Finland. On cold winter nights, when darkness came early in the north, the family would turn all the other lights out and gather around the lantern after dinner to tell stories. The family tradition continued when they came to Michigan, with new stories being added to the ones they had always told.

I asked the storeowner why they weren't still doing that, and how the lamp ended up for sale in his store. That is when he told me the sad ending to this tale. There came a time when the last two boys in the family left home. They moved to lower Michigan, and only returned to the Upper Peninsula to visit. After their parents died, the house sat empty. The lantern was placed in a box in the attic. The candle had not been lit for years, and they were not telling stories around it any longer.

The brothers realized that no one in the family wanted to live in the house, and they were making that trip north less and less. One summer they sold the house and all the contents they no longer wanted. The lantern, along with many other items from the house, was sold in an auction. The storeowner told me he won the bid on some of those household items, including the lantern. When he inquired about the lantern, he learned the story behind it.

When I heard that over one hundred years of stories had been told around that lantern in Finland and in Michigan, I said, "Will you let me let me buy that lamp?" A bit protective of it, I suppose, he said, "And what are you going to do with it?" I smiled and said, "I am going to tell stories around it again, the way that family use to." He smiled and softly said, "I think that's a good idea."

As I was leaving the store, I turned and asked the storeowner what he had called the lantern earlier. He said, "You mean lyhty?" I said, "What is that?" He told me it was a word in Finnish that meant lantern. He asked me to try to say it, but since I was not used to speaking Finnish, it came out all wrong. That's when he stepped a bit closer to me and said, "You need some help." He reached over and squeezed my cheeks with his hand. He said, "Now try to say it." I said, "lewfta." He said, "Now you're talkin' like a Finn."

I left the store with the lyhty that day and made myself a promise to light the candle each time I told stories, in honor of a tradition too rich to lose.

© Jenifer Strauss. Used with permission.

Straighten Up and Fly Right
(African American)

In African folklore, Monkey plays the role of the great trickster. He takes center stage in this tale, which came to the state of Michigan with African Americans who settled there seeking employment in the automobile industry during the twentieth century.

It was hot. It was really hot, and buzzard was flying slowly in the sky looking for something to eat. It was so hot that most animals were in their burrows or in the shade, and buzzard couldn't find any food. Suddenly he saw rabbit. Rabbit was trying to find some cool shade. He had never been this hot before. Buzzard he landed near rabbit and spoke to him, "How are you doing today?"

"I'm so hot. I can't remember being this hot before," said rabbit.

Buzzard told rabbit that it was cool up in the sky. He suggested that he should join buzzard for a ride up in the cool air.

Now rabbit thought that it should be hotter up in the sky because it was so much closer to the sun, but buzzard looked awful cool and relaxed, so he finally accepted. Rabbit climbed up on buzzard's back and away they flew. They sailed through the sky, higher and higher. It was cool and rabbit felt so refreshed. Finally, when buzzard knew that rabbit was cooled off, he went into a power dive. He dove straight down and then he veered off at the last minute and rabbit fell off and hit the ground with a sickening thud. Buzzard had rabbit for his dinner.

Monkey was watching the whole thing from his hiding place in the trees.

The next day buzzard went looking for food again, and this time he saw squirrel running from one tree to the other. Buzzard landed near the tree and spoke to squirrel, "How are you doing today, squirrel?"

"I'm hot," said squirrel. "I can't remember it ever being this hot before. How are you doing?"

"I'm just fine," said buzzard. "When I get too hot I just fly up where the air is cool. Would you like to take a ride and cool off for a bit?"

Now squirrel knew that the higher you climbed in a tree the cooler it got, so he thought that it must be just fine up in the sky, so he accepted buzzard's offer and climbed up on his back. Up they flew, higher and higher, until it was wonderfully cool. Squirrel felt better than he had in days. He closed his eyes and enjoyed the ride. Buzzard looked over his shoulder and saw that squirrel was cool and comfortable. Suddenly he went into a power dive, faster and faster, straight down and then at the last minute he veered off and squirrel fell off just like rabbit had the day before. Buzzard had squirrel for his dinner.

Monkey watched the whole thing from his hiding place in the trees.

The next day monkey watched the sky, looking for buzzard as he flew in lazy circles. When he saw buzzard monkey walked out from under the shade of his tree so buzzard could see him. Monkey just sat down on the ground pretending to be hot.

Buzzard landed near monkey and said, "How are you today, monkey?"

"I'm hot, buzzard. I've never been so hot in my whole life. How are you doing?" replied the monkey.

"Well monkey, I feel fine. You see the air up where I fly is cool and sweet, just the thing for a hot summer day like this. Would you like to join me and have a ride up in the sky where it's cool?"

Monkey didn't need to be asked twice. He jumped up on buzzard's back, and they flew off into the air. They flew higher and higher and the air got cooler and cooler and monkey was feeling great. Buzzard was right; it was wonderfully cool up here in the sky. Buzzard looked over his shoulder and saw that monkey was cool and comfortable, leaning back with his eyes closed. Buzzard started to head down, going into a power dive, when suddenly monkey wrapped his long tail around buzzard's neck and pulled tight.

"What are you doing, monkey? You're choking me," cried buzzard.

"That's right, buzzard. Now you straighten up and fly right, because you are not having monkey for your dinner tonight."

Buzzard stopped his dive and kept flying straight as an arrow. Monkey had buzzard fly him around all day until monkey was cool enough to sleep well in his tree that night. Buzzard rubbed his sore neck and thought twice about giving any more rides to the earthbound animals.

The Impossible Tale (Arab)

The state of Michigan boasts one of the largest Arab American populations in the United States. Here is one of their traditional tales, which dates back many centuries.

Once it came to the ears of the Caliph that there was a storyteller in his city of remarkable talents who could entertain his audiences with countless tales. He could tell stories from sundown to sunrise and never repeat himself. The Caliph sent his court attendants to find this man.

When the storyteller stood before the Caliph the ruler said, "They say that you are the greatest storyteller in the city, perhaps in the entire kingdom. Why is it that I never heard of you before?"

"I am merely a teller of tales," said the man modestly. "I weave a few stories for my friends in the coffeehouse."

"I do not like false modesty," said the Caliph sternly. "It is said that you can tell every kind of tale, one that makes your audience laugh or cry or fills them with terror or memories of their youth or dreams of love. They say you can tell the old tales of the heroes of long ago or spin a new story about a few words that were said in the marketplace just yesterday. You are my guest here. Please refresh yourself with food and then I will listen to one of your stories."

The storyteller was taken to a private dining room and fed the best of foods from the Caliph's kitchen. When he was finished, he was brought back before the ruler.

"There are so many stories that a man like you can tell. If I wanted a true story, I'm sure you could tell it. If I wanted a story from the legends and myths of our people, I'm sure you could do that as well. If I wanted a story that would last until dawn or even longer, I know it is within your art. But what I want is a story that is not too long, but that everything you say in it must be false, not a word of truth. If I hear anything that is not a lie, you will become my slave and all your family with you."

The storyteller waited for a moment before beginning. It is hard to tell a story where truth doesn't hide somewhere in the words. But finally he smiled, bowed to the Caliph, and started to weave his tale.

"Oh Great Caliph, I was my father's oldest brother. I was about eight years old when he was born. My grandmother put him in my arms and told me to keep him from crying. Nothing I did would stop his howling. Finally, he told me to carry him to the bazaar. There he seemed happy because he could argue with old men in the coffeehouse about the finer points of the Koran. Before we left the bazaar, he asked me to buy him some eggs, but before we got home a chicken pecked its way out of one of the eggs. Since the chicken was very large and we were very tired, we rode the chicken home. By the time we arrived home the chicken had grown to the size of a large camel. I had to hand my father down to my grandfather, who since my father was my brother was also my father."

The Caliph nodded and waved the storyteller to continue.

"The chicken had a huge appetite. It ate so much that soon we were all on the edge of starvation. We decided to put the chicken to work. Every morning my father who was my brother took the chicken out into wilderness and collected firewood that he piled on the chicken's back and soon we were selling firewood from our yard. The problem was that the firewood rubbed the feathers off the chicken's back and the chicken developed sores that made him sick. My father's great grandmother advised him to make a poultice out of ground walnut seed and place it on the sores. He did. The next morning the chicken was well again, but a walnut tree was growing from its back. Within three days the tree was so big that it swayed as the chicken moved. Within a week a huge crop of walnuts was hanging in the branches. It took twelve men from Saturday to Thursday to climb up on the chicken's back and pick all those walnuts. The branches were spread so far apart that if a man started picking in the early morning and worked his way across a branch it would be sundown before he got to the other side."

The Caliph nodded again and waved the storyteller to continue with his story.

"When the work was done, I walked around the tree to make sure that all the nuts had been picked and it took me all day to make that journey. Just as I was about to leave, I saw a bird nesting in one of the branches so I took a piece of earth and threw it at the bird. But the clod of earth never fell back down. It spread and spread and soon we had forty acres of rich soil up above the branches of the walnut tree that grew on the back of our enormous chicken. We decided to graze our cattle up there. The next season we got our new forty acres ready for planting. My grandfather and I planted forty acres of sesame seeds, but after a month we saw that nothing was growing. Our neighbor told my grandfather that sesame would not grow on freshly turned sod and that only melons would grow there. Grandfather sent my father who is also my brother up the tree to pick all the sesame seeds we had planted and bring them down. We found that one seed was missing so we searched and searched until we saw an ant with the seed on his back carrying it to his hill. I seized the seed but the ant would not let go and we had a furious tug of war. Neither one of us would let go and finally the seed broke in half and so much oil ran from that seed that it became a river and our neighbors were able to float their crops to the city in their boats on a river of sesame oil."

The Caliph nodded to continue.

"My grandfather, who was my father and my father who was my brother were planting the melon seeds up on those forty acres in the sky when a terrible storm came upon us. There was no shelter of any kind, so my grandfather and I jumped into my father's hollow tooth. After catching a sheep that was grazing nearby, my father jumped in and joined us. The storm lasted forty-seven days and we would have starved to death had it not been for the fat sheep my father had brought along. Finally we peeked out of the tooth and saw that the sun was shining. But we also saw that the storm had washed away the forty acres and now we were trapped in mid air. Fortunately my father had a rope and we tied it securely and let it down to earth. We slid down one at a time and were saved."

The storyteller nodded to the Caliph that the story was over.

"That was a remarkable adventure you have told me today, storyteller. But I have one question for you, was it true?"

"Great Caliph," said the teller of tales, "of course it is true. Every word from beginning to end."

""If it is true then you have failed and are now my slave, for I ordered you to tell me a story without a word of truth in it."

"My Great Caliph," said the man, smiling. "I have followed your instructions to the letter, for when I said the story was true I was merely telling anther lie to round out the tale."

The Caliph laughed long and hard and finally said, "The stories I have heard about your art are also true. You are a wonderful weaver of tales."

The storyteller was given a bag of gold and sent on his way. But don't you think that he returned to tell another tale or two?

Michigan Glossary

Buzzard: A carrion-eating bird that eats animals that have already died. Buzzards are not hunters. They have very large wingspans that allow them to soar slowly while looking for food.

Chippewa people: Another name for the Ojibwa people. They lived in wigwams in small villages. Wild rice was one of their staples, which they harvested in birch bark canoes, men poling the boat while women knocked the grain off the plants and into the canoe.

Finn/Finnish: An inhabitant of Finland in Northern Europe/the language spoken in Finland.

Michigan: A state whose name comes from the Native American word "Michigana," meaning "great lake." The capital is Lansing.

Story Sources

American Folktales from the Collections of the Library of Congress, Volume 1

American Folktales from the Collections of the Library of Congress, Volume 2

American Myths & Legends, Volumes 1 & 2

Arab Folktales

Ballads and Songs of Southern Michigan

Bloodstoppers & Bearwalkers: Folk Traditions of the Upper Peninsula

Daylight in the Swamp

The Greenwood Library of American Folktales, Volume 1

Jenifer Strauss

Lore of Wolverine Country

Mythical Creatures of the North Country

Myths & Legends of Our Own Land, Volumes 1 & 2

Negro Folktales in Michigan

The Parade of Heroes

Paul Bunyan

Paul Bunyan Swings His Axe

Pioneering Michigan

Songs of the Great Lakes

Stockings of Buttermilk

Tall Timber Tales: More Paul Bunyan Stories

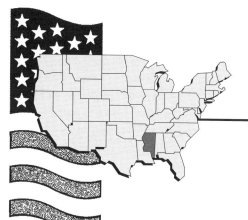

Mississippi

Mississippi became the twentieth state in 1812. The state is home to several Native American tribes, including the Natchez and the Choctaw. In this chapter we have a Choctaw story called "The Hunter and the Alligator."

Every state has a hero or two, and Mississippi is no exception, as shown in the story and ballad of Casey Jones, the fearless train engineer. "The Hunting Dog of the Tombigbee Bottoms" comes to us from the rural hunting tradition. It might be a tall tale, or it might just be one smart dog.

The river played a big role in Mississippi's history, and the story of a very protective riverboat captain gives us an insight into life on the river. There is also an old story about a lonely telegraph operator and his unusual pet. And finally, the African American culture is represented here by a story about one of the most beloved tricksters in African American folk literature, Rabbit.

Casey Jones: A Hero in Song and Story
(Based on True Events)

The folks near Vaughan, Mississippi, could hear the whistle of the train as it sped along the tracks. They knew just from listening that it was the Illinois Central, and they knew who the engineer was at the throttle. It was Casey Jones. A long time ago trains didn't have the same whistles. Each train had its own unique sound that was put on the train by the engineer. Folks who lived along the train tracks could tell which train it was and who the engineer at the throttle was just by listening to the whistle of the train as it passed by.

Casey Jones had heard those whistles as a boy and had dreamed of becoming an engineer.

His dream had come true.

On Sunday, April 29, Casey and his fireman, Sim Webb, took the southbound mail train, called the Cannonball, out of the Memphis depot. The train was late getting into Memphis, so Casey was already over an hour and a half behind schedule as he was leaving the station. Now Casey had a reputation as a fine engineer and was greatly admired by all the folks who worked with him. He also had a reputation as a man who stayed on schedule.

The season had been rainy and that night it was cloudy, but Casey kept his train speeding along and was nearly back on schedule by the time he got to Vaughn.

The station at Vaughn had four freight trains that had been taken off the main track and put on sidetracks to let other trains like the Cannonball go by. Because of delays caused by the recent floods, there wasn't enough room that night for all the freight trains in the sidings, and a caboose and three cars stuck out onto the main track. Men had gone down the track with warning flags and flares had been set out, but the night was dark and cloudy and the lights couldn't be seen by the engineer as the Cannonball rounded the bend in the track. Casey and Sim never saw the warnings until it was too late. Sim jumped from the cab of the locomotive, but Casey stayed on, applying the brake and trying to avoid a disaster. He was found dead in the wreckage of his engine; he lives on in legend and in the following ballad.

Casey Jones

Come all you rounders for I want you to hear

The story of a brave engineer.

Casey Jones was the rounder's name,

On a big eight wheeler of mighty fame.

Caller called Casey about half past four.

Casey kissed his wife at the station door.

Climbed to the cab with orders in his hand,

He says, "This is my ticket to the holy land."

The rain been coming down five or six weeks.
The railroad track was like the bed of a creek.
They slowed her down to a thirty mile-gait,
And the south-bound mail was eight hours late.

Fireman says, "Casey you're running too fast.
We barely saw the last station you passed."
Casey says, "I believe we'll make it though,
For the train's steaming better than I ever know."

Casey says, "Fireman, don't you fret.
Keep piling on the coal don't give up yet.
I'm going to run her til she leaves the rail
Or make it on time with the south-bound mail."

Around the curve and down the dump
Two locomotives are bound to bump.
Fireman hollered, "Casey there's a train ahead.
We need to jump or we'll both be dead."

Around the curve come a passenger train.
Casey blows his whistle and says, "Ring the bell."
Fireman jumps and cries, "Good-bye,
Casey Jones you're bound to die."

Headaches and heartaches and all kind of pain.
That's all part of a railroad train.
Stories of brave men, noble and grand
Belong to the life of a railroad man.

The Hunting Dog of the Tombigbee Bottoms

Now there are dogs that are good at hunting, and there are dogs that love to hunt. Then there are the dogs that live for the chase. Down in Monroe County in Mississippi there was a dog that would rather hunt than eat. Raccoons, possums, and squirrels—this dog would hunt anything that moved. The problem was the man who owned him was a busy man and didn't have the time to go hunting with his dog as often as the dog would have liked.

Sometimes when they did go hunting, the man would flag down Erbie Lee's train in the Tombigbee Bottoms between Amory and Fulton. The two of them would ride the train until they came to a spot where they wanted to hunt. The man would ask the engineer to stop, and the two of them would hunt until they heard the train whistle on its run back. The man would flag the train down again, and the man and his dog would ride back to town.

As the man grew busier the dog became depressed. He wouldn't eat and barely moved around the house, just sleeping and growling and running in his dreams. One day, though, the dog went out the door and didn't come back for several hours. This happened again the next day, and again the next day. Suddenly the dog was his old self, playful, alert, and full of life. You see the dog found a way to do the one thing he loved to do.

The dog realized that the train would stop when his master waved the signal flag. So when his master couldn't go hunting, the dog would go down to the railroad track, stand in the middle of the track, and wag his tail as hard as he could as the engine approached. The engineer would stop and the dog would get on board. He'd bark at the engineer when they reached the Tombigbee Bottoms, which suited the dog for his day of hunting.

When the dog had caught an animal he would just wait by the tracks until he heard the train whistle and then flag it down with his tail again and get a ride home.

There are dogs who like to hunt and dogs that love to hunt, and then there are dogs who live for the chase.

The Hunter and the Alligator (Choctaw)

Long ago in the land of the Choctaws lived Tushka Chaha, or Tall Warrior, who most certainly was *not* a great hunter. He was the strongest of all Choctaw hunters, but he had the worst luck. Every time he went hunting, he came home empty handed. It hurt Tushka Chaha that his family went hungry.

Determined to change his luck, he decided, "This time I will not come back until I have found us meat."

Tushka Chaha went deeper into the swampy forest than anyone had ever gone before. It was said that if a hunter was brave enough to enter this dark forest, deer were plentiful. But all sorts of horrors stalked the thick-green tangles and lurked just beneath the murky bayou.

Tushka Chaha followed the dried creek bed, seeking deer tracks. All of a sudden, two big eyes popped out of the sand. Tushka Chaha jumped back. Then a long mouth with sharp teeth appeared. He watched as one humongous alligator slid free and shook itself off.

"Brother," said the alligator, "can you help me? The water here is gone and I am close to death. Is there any water nearby?"

"Just beyond that stand of trees is a spring-fed pool that will never dry up. If you can make it there you will live."

"Brother, I am too weak. Can you carry me? If you help me, I will tell you the secret of great hunters."

"I am sorry. I cannot help you, though I want to. But I am a man and you are an alligator. You might decide to eat me."

"It is true that I am quite hungry, but I will not hurt you. And that is a promise."

Tushka Chaha thought hard. "I will help you. But you must let me tie up your legs and your mouth."

"But you are also a hunter," said the alligator, "and a man, the most frightening of all hunters. And *you* are hungry too. How do I know that I won't be *your* dinner?

The hunter realized that the alligator had an excellent point. "I am willing to help. I will not hurt you, and that is *my* promise."

"Do as you must," the alligator said, rolling onto his back.

Taking strips of leather from his pouch, Tushka Chaha tied the alligator's legs and quickly bound its powerful jaws. He lifted the alligator to his shoulders and trod through the forest.

Seeing the pool through the trees, Tushka Chaha was reminded of his hunger. *The alligator is weak,* he thought. *He is tied up, and, well, alligator stew is* not *so bad.* Then he also remembered: *I made a promise.*

Meanwhile, the alligator thought, *I could easily break these straps, and chewed up Choctaw hunter is* not *so bad.* But he too remembered: *I made a promise.*

Coming to the edge of the water, Tushka Chaha lowered the alligator from his back and untied his legs. But when he moved to untie the alligator's mouth, he saw that the strips had come untied. At any moment the alligator could have snapped his head right off. But he had not, because he had made a promise.

The alligator rolled into the pool, disappearing for a long time. Finally, the alligator stuck his head out of the water and spoke.

"*Yakoke*. Thank-you, brother. You have saved me. Now I will tell you the secret of truly great hunters. When you leave here, you will eventually come across a young doe. You must not shoot her. She is young and will be the mother of many more deer to come.

"Next you will see a young buck. You must not shoot this deer either. He will be the father of many deer. Then you will come across an old doe. But still you must not shoot. She is not done being a mother and still has much to give. Finally, you will come to an old buck. He will give himself to you so that you can feed your family. Then give thanks to the deer's spirit. If you follow this way you will become a great hunter."

For a long time Tushka Chaha walked. He wondered if he would see any deer at all, much less four.

Then suddenly, at the edge of a clearing, he saw a young doe. He raised his arrow and aimed. But then he remembered the alligator's words. *You must not shoot her. She is young and will be the mother of many more deer.*

"I can't believe I'm doing this," he sighed as he lowered the bow and walked away from the doe. "That would have fed my family for a long time."

As the sun reached its highest point of the day, Tushka Chaha stopped to drink from a small stream. As he cupped the water, he looked up to see a young buck not far downstream. This deer was much bigger than the last and would certainly make his family happy. Again the alligator's words came to mind: *You must not shoot this deer either. He will be the father of many.* Tushka Chaha dropped his bow and the buck darted away.

Angry with himself for letting a second chance pass, Tushka Chaha crashed into the forest. "I am not likely to get another chance like that today," he spoke out. "I should have taken the deer when I had it. My family is hungry. Next time, I am making the shot."

The hunter turned to continue his trip, but stopped dead in his tracks. Not thirty feet in front of him stood a doe. She was big and old and staring right at him. He lifted his bow and reached for an arrow. The doe remained still. The doe was an easy target. But again, the alligator's voice rasped in his thoughts, *she is not done being a mother and still has much to give.*

"But she is right here, right now," he argued with himself. "She will feed us good." He blinked twice to clear his vision and sucked in a deep breath.

If you follow this way of hunting, then you will become a great hunter.

The muscles in his arm began to twitch.

Tushka Chaha lowered his bow and sank to the ground, praying that the alligator was right, that there would be a fourth deer.

He continued through the trees, each step adding to his doubt. When the afternoon sun was at its hottest, he found a shady place to rest. With his back against a tree, Tushka Chaha closed his eyes. Soon he was snoring loud enough to wake the moon.

The sound of snapping twigs startled him awake. The biggest and oldest buck he had ever seen stood in front of him. Tushka Chaha reached for his bow, expecting the buck to jump. It stood firm, frozen.

The Choctaw bowed his head. He had learned the power of patience and now respected the alligator's wisdom. With a new understanding of nature's gift and the promise of life, he whispered, "*Yakoke*, brother deer. *Thank-you*! Your gift will give life to me and my family." Then he let loose the arrow. After cleaning the old buck, he lifted it to his shoulders and carried the gift home.

And so Tushka Chaha, who was *not* a great hunter, became the greatest Choctaw hunter of all. Soon all of the men followed the alligator's ways, and the Choctaws became a nation of great and wise hunters.

Used with permission of Greg Rodgers, Choctaw/Chickasaw storyteller.

The Talking Snake

In the old days, before telephones and computers, messages were sent via telegraph. Telegraphing was a real art, and it took time to be able to send the dots and dashes that represented words over the wire quickly and without error.

Now one young man was trained as a telegraph operator and sent by the Illinois Central Railroad to be the night shift operator in Way, Mississippi. Way is located down in the Big Black River Bottoms. It was a lonely job, and the young man worked all alone and often had to fight to stay awake. His job was to report the trains as they passed by, giving times and locations. It was important because a fatal mistake could cause an accident that could be disastrous.

The young man tried different ways to stay awake and note the passing of trains. He placed a string across the track and attached it to a "coal hod," which is a pail that held the coal for the potbellied stove. If he fell asleep, the train would hit the string and rattle the coal hod. It also meant that if a cow or raccoon or any other animal hit the string, it would also rattle the pail.

The young man also placed coal cinders on the track, so the train would crunch them and wake him with the sound, but if the night turned windy or rainy, the cinders would be swept from the tracks.

One night as he was reading a detective story and trying to stay awake, he glanced up and saw a large rattlesnake crawl through the door of his telegraph office. The snake curled up and began to sway back and forth, looking around and taking in the office. At first the young man was frightened, but then he saw that the snake just stayed there and didn't seem to even notice him. The snake looked just like the porter who worked the day shift, long and lean and very alert. The porter's name was Leander. The young man rose very slowly and poured some milk into a saucer and pushed it carefully toward the rattlesnake.

The snake eyed the young man and then looked at the milk and slithered over and lapped it up hungrily. After the snake finished, the two of them just sat there looking at each other. The snake seemed calm and right at home; and the young man was actually grateful for the company. The young man then got a crazy idea. He walked over to his cabinet and took out his practice telegraph set. He sat down facing the snake and started to slowly tap out the alphabet in Morse code. The snake, which the man decided to call Leander, watched intently, seeming almost hypnotized by the series of dots and dashes. The snake crawled onto the table and watched carefully, its tongue flicking in and out rapidly, its eyes intently watching the hands of the young man. Soon the snake was trying to imitate the man. The telegraph operator would tap out a letter and then the snake would mimic it by shaking the rattles on his tail.

The snake would come every night and visit the young man, first having a saucer of milk and then sitting on the table learning Morse code. In a very short while, the rattler had learned the alphabet. Some of the letters were harder than others, like the "P," which was five dashes. That letter seemed to tire out his old tail, but soon he mastered it and was able to talk to the young man in Morse code. The young man and the snake would converse all night, and the once lonely hours of his night shift were soon filled with lively conversation.

The rattler told the young man that he had been born and raised right there in the Big Black River Bottoms and that he was one of twenty children. He told him about life in the swamps and the ways and tricks of staying alive in that hostile environment. He told him about escaping floods and staying out of the way of the men who hunted in the woods and bottomlands. The young man told the snake about growing up in a small town and how he always wanted to work on the railroad and travel around the country.

Leander became quite the helper around the office. He could grab the broom and use his strong tail to sweep out the office. He also kept the office totally free of mice and rats and any other annoying creatures. He even helped the young telegraph operator report the trains.

A snake's tongue really "hears" vibrations. Leander would crawl up on the telegraph table, lean his head out the window, and stick out his tongue, flicking it in and out. He could feel the vibrations of trains over thirty-five miles away. Then he would crawl over to the sleeping young man and gently touch his face with his tongue to wake him, so he could exchange signals and information with the crew of the oncoming train and report its passing farther up the track. This partnership lasted for a few years, and the man and the snake learned a great deal from each other and became good friends.

One day the telegraph operator got word that he was being transferred. He told Leander about his leaving, and thanked him for his help and his friendship. He asked if the big rattlesnake would like to come with him and see other parts of the country. Leander told him that his people had been in the Big Black River Bottom since creation, and that this was his home. He said he had learned about the outside world from his friend during their talks and was content to stay right here at home. He thanked the man for teaching him Morse code and started to slither out the door. The he stopped, curled up, and looked the young man in the eye and tapped out "73" with his rattles, which is a telegrapher's traditional way of saying good-bye.

The young man watched as the snake crawled away into the night, and he even shed a few tears, because he knew he would miss him and their nightly talks.

The Captain and the Robbers

Once, in the days of the great steamboats, a captain brought his boat to dock in Natchez. Walking through what they called the lower parts of town near the docks, one of his men was robbed of all his pay. Now the captain knew that this was an honest man who was always sending money home to his family; and he was distressed that his boatman had been robbed. The captain went ashore and being not only angry but also brave, he sought out the thieves in their house near the dock and told them to give the money back. The thieves didn't care if the man was hard working or if he had a family. They laughed at the captain and told him to get out of their house. So the captain left, but not for long.

He went back to the boat and came back with his crew and most of the 300 passengers he was carrying on the boat. All these folks were hauling a huge cable that they passed around the house a few times and then brought back to the boat. The captain walked over and stood in front of the house and called out to the robbers.

"You have fifteen minutes to come out and hand over that money to my boatman. If you do not I will bring my boat to a head of steam and drag that house of yours into the river."

The robbers came out of that house so quick you would have thought it was on fire, and gave the man back all his money. They knew by reputation that this was one captain who always kept his word, and that was scary enough for them.

Playing Godfather (African American)

Rabbit, Possum, and Fox decided to go in together and start a farm. They bought lots of groceries to see them through until the crops were harvested: butter, coffee, everything they would need. The butter was the most important and the one food they all really loved. Every day they wet into the fields to work.

Rabbit made a plan to leave Fox and Possum in the field and get some butter for himself while they worked. One day he let on that someone was calling him out of the field. "Yoo-hoo, yoo-hoo."

"Who's that?" asked Fox.

"Sorry, Fox, but these folks keep bothering me. I can't work until I settle this. I'll be back in awhile." Rabbit left Fox and Possum working while he went back to the house and ate some of the butter.

When he returned he pretended someone was calling him again. "Yoo-hoo, yoo-hoo."

"What do they want now?" asked Possum.

"The want me to help christen one of their babies. They're always bothering me. I'm not going."

"Well if it's a christening, you better go this time," said Fox.

Rabbit went back to the house and ate some more butter.

When he returned Possum asked, "What did they name the baby?"

Rabbit said, "They named him Just Begun."

The next time it happened Rabbit went to the house and ate some more butter. When he returned his friends asked what they named this baby. ""Pretty Well on the Way."

The next time it happened Rabbit ate more of the butter, and when he returned they asked him again what the baby was named. "About a Quarter Gone," replied Rabbit.

The next time Rabbit filled his belly with butter. When he returned they asked about the new baby's name. "They named this one Half Gone," said Rabbit.

It seemed that Rabbit was always being called out for a christening. He complained, but in the end he always went, swearing it would be the last time. Fox and Possum were always understanding of the interruptions since it was a christening and had to do with children. They never suspected.

The next time it happened Rabbit ate more of the butter. When he returned they asked what this baby had been christened. "They called this one Quarter Left," said Rabbit.

Rabbit pulled the trick on Fox and Possum one more time, and when he returned he told his friends that this child was named All Gone.

Later that month they decided to open the barrel of butter, and it was all gone.

"Who stole our butter?" they all asked. Rabbit was a little worried that the other two might suspect him, so he said, "Possum has been lying around the house an awful lot lately. It must be that Possum is the one who ate all the butter."

Possum declared his innocence. Then Rabbit said, "I have an idea. We'll build a big fire and we'll all sit around it. The guilty one will have butter coming out of the pores of his belly, and we'll know who the thief is once and for all."

They built a big fire and they all sat close around the flames. Soon the warmth of the fire made them all tired and they fell asleep. Rabbit opened his eyes and saw his chance. He rubbed grease all over Possum's belly and tail. He rubbed grease on Fox's belly too, but Fox woke up.

Rabbit started to holler, "I told you Possum was the thief. You too, Fox, took some of the butter. I can tell." Fox knew what game Rabbit was playing and took off after him. Rabbit was too quick and he got away from Fox. Fox turned to Possum and said, "We've both pretty stupid. Rabbit tricked us again." Then Fox slapped Possum and Possum fell right into the fire. The flames licked at the grease and Possum's tail caught fire. That's why to this day Possum's tail is bare.

Mississippi Glossary

Choctaw people: A Native American people who called themselves "Chahta" after a legendary leader. At one time they lived throughout Mississippi, Alabama, Louisiana, and Florida but they were removed during the Trail of Tears and resettled in Oklahoma. In the olden days they lived in settled villages with houses made of plaster and river cane.

Mississippi: A state named after the river that forms its western border. The word comes from the Ojibwa word "misi-ziib," which means Great River. The state capital is Jackson.

Natchez people: A Native American people found throughout Louisiana and Mississippi. They are still found in small communities but are not a federally recognized tribe and do not have their own reservation. They were defeated by the French and scattered to live with other tribes. They were the only tribe to have a king, called The Great Sun. The line of this king was passed down through the mother's family. Natchez is an English pronunciation of their name for themselves. The French *Notch-ay* is closer to the original. The city of Natchez is named after them.

Possum: A slang term for "opossum," a small to medium-sized marsupial that, although covered in fur, has a bare tail.

Story Sources

American Folktales from the Collections of the Library of Congress, Volume 1

American Folktales from the Collections of the Library of Congress, Volume 2

American Myths & Legends, Volumes 1 & 2

Folk Stories of the South

Folksongs of Mississippi and Their Background

The Greenwood Library of American Folktales, Volume 2

Greg Rodgers, Choctaw/Chickasaw storyteller

Myths & Legends of Our Own Land, Volumes 1 & 2

Southern Indian Myths & Legends

13 Mississippi Ghosts & Jeffrey

A Treasury of Mississippi River Folklore

A Treasury of Southern Folklore

Walking the Choctaw Road

You Live and Learn Then You Die and Forget It All: Ray Lum's Tales

New Hampshire

New Hampshire, one of the thirteen original colonies, was the first colony to declare its independence from Great Britain. The mountains and valleys of this state are home to many folktales, including one about a garden wish that is included here.

Before the Europeans settled the area, several different groups of Native Americans resided here, including the Abenaki. Hunting stories are common in this state, and the tall tale about one hunter's extremely lucky shot just about tells all we need to know about the truth found in those tales. The story "Ocean Born Mary and the Pirate" reminds us of the goodness in people and the romance of those early days in New Hampshire, while the story about Jonathan Moulton gives us a glimpse into the cleverness of its citizens, no matter who the foe.

Only One Shot

A hunter was returning home after a disappointing day in the woods. He had shot at just about every animal he saw and missed them all. He was coming home with no meat for the table and only one shot left in his gun.

When he got to the Connecticut River he saw that the boat that was always there to ferry people across was gone. He figured that it had been carried away by the spring floodwaters. This was only one more bit of bad luck on a bad luck day. He wasn't a very strong swimmer, but he knew that even during floods the river was never very deep, so he decided to wade across. He held his rifle with its one shot high over his head, and he started to walk across the river. His head bobbed under the water, but he kept his gun dry.

Now the hunter noticed that he had gotten very tired the last few yards wading across that river. When he reached the far side, he could barely climb up the bank. When he finally did, he discovered that his pockets and boots and pants legs were filled with fish. He took a line from his pocket and strung those fish together. He must have had at least thirty pounds of fresh fish. He hung his clothes up to dry on the branch of a tree, and as he did he noticed a field. In that field there was a haystack, and on the other side was a fence. Sitting on that fence were a dozen quail. He thought to himself, if only there was a way he could shoot all those quail with the one shot he had left in his gun. The fence was curved around that haystack, and shooting those quail would be a problem. Then he got an idea. He put the barrel of his gun under a rock and bent it into a half circle. He crept up next to that haystack and fired. Sure enough, his bullet went in a perfect curve and killed all of those quail. The problem was that the bullet went through the last one and almost hit the hunter. But at the last second he ducked, and the bullet went straight into a goose that was walking along the riverbank. The hunter took up his fish, the dozen quail, and the fat goose and headed home. It hadn't been such a bad day after all.

The Island Garden

A long time ago a rich man lived on a lake in the White Mountains. He had three daughters. The man owned the entire lake and all the land around it. The oldest daughter was beautiful, the second daughter was pretty and cute, and the youngest daughter was just sweet and nice and very shy. Of course, like most stories, what you saw on the outside wasn't the whole truth. The two oldest daughters were mean spirited, greedy, jealous, and lazy, while Becky, the youngest, was kind and had a natural goodness about her.

There lived nearby a young farmer. He had a fine farm, with cattle and horses. He was an honest young man and not bad looking, either. Every young woman who lived in the area had her eye on him, but he was in no hurry to marry. In fact, he had his eye on his neighbor's daughters, and the oldest and middle daughter had their eyes on him and didn't do a thing to hide it.

Now the young farmer was a frequent visitor to the rich man's home. He talked with all three of the girls and laughed many an hour away in their company. The problem was that he couldn't make up his mind which one to marry.

One evening he came to their home and they began to talk. As conversations sometimes go, the talk turned to the future. He asked them what they wanted most in the whole wide world.

The oldest smiled and said she wanted to live in a big city and wear expensive clothes and wear silken slippers and have a fine carriage and horses to take to plays and opera.

The second sister said she also wanted to live in the city in a fine house with servants and silver plates and golden goblets and beautiful jewels. When it was Becky's turn, she thought for a moment and said that she wanted a beautiful garden, more beautiful than the one she had now, that would be safe from the cows and goats who got into her garden all the time and would trample and eat her flowers. Becky loved flowers, and she loved her garden.

The young man left that night with their answers ringing in his head. He was still having trouble making up his mind among the three sisters.

After the young farmer left, the rich squire turned to Becky and said, "Child, do you really love flowers so much?"

"Yes, father, I do, but my garden is always being trampled by the farm animals, and it breaks my heart when I find my precious flowers ruined by the hooves."

"Now I can fix that," he said. "I have many islands on my lake, and you can choose any island you like and you can plant your garden there. No cows to trample them and no goats to eat them. It will be an island just for you and your garden."

The two oldest heard this and started to cry and pout. They said that Becky always got what she wanted because she was youngest. They wanted an island, too.

The father finally said, "You may have an island also, but because I offered it to Becky first she gets to pick first."

He turned to Becky and said, "Now I have twenty-one islands out on my lake and you can have the first pick."

The sisters were sure she would pick the biggest, but instead Becky picked a small island that was just perfect for a garden.

"Are you sure, Becky?" asked the father.

"The small one is just perfect for a garden. It's all I need."

The two oldest daughters were relieved. "Becky's a fool, but I'm not. I want the largest island, father," said the oldest.

"I want the next largest island," said the second daughter.

"You shall both have what you asked for," replied their father.

The story spread throughout the surrounding farms and villages of how the sisters got their islands, and how they made their choice.

Some folks thought Becky foolish for asking for the smaller island, but others thought she was wise. Her island had no big trees to cut down and no wild animals to forage in her garden and ruin it. They said that Becky was modest and sensible, and that she was a smart girl for the right man.

The young farmer heard about the island, Becky's Garden, as the folks now called the little island. He listened and smiled to himself, and it didn't take long for him to know which sister would make the best wife. So he went to Becky's father and asked for her hand in marriage. The two were married and lived, as they deserved, happily ever after.

The older sisters just grew meaner and more jealous every day. In the end, they were so mean and greedy and spiteful that no one would marry them.

Ocean Born Mary and the Pirate

The Wolf set sail from Ireland in 1720 with a ship full of immigrants headed to the New World. They were traveling to New Hampshire to join friends and family members who had gone on before them. The Wilson family was among those passengers, and as they neared the coast of the New World, two extremely different events happened, entwining themselves forever.

Mrs. Wilson was pregnant with a child, and on July 17 she went into labor as *The Wolf* neared Boston Harbor. Before the ship could gain the safety of the harbor, a pirate ship came into view and cut off *The Wolf*'s approach. The pirates boarded the ship and assembled all the passengers and crew on deck. The pirate captain, Don Pedro, walked onto the deck of the helpless ship. He was tall and dark, and although he had a Spanish name, he spoke perfect English. He announced that he was taking the ship and all its contents and that the passengers and crew would be put to death.

Suddenly there was a cry from beneath the decks. Don Pedro drew a pistol and headed down the main hatch. In a cabin below he came upon a mother and her newborn daughter.

The pirate captain became very quiet and his face softened when he looked upon the baby. "My dear lady, if you will allow me to name this child, I will spare the entire crew and all the passengers of this ship and leave you all in peace."

The new mother was only too happy to allow Don Pedro to name her daughter in exchange for all their lives and agreed immediately.

"The child shall be called Mary after my own dead mother who loved me so well," said Don Pedro.

The pirates left the ship, but soon Don Pedro reappeared. The people were afraid that he had changed his mind, but he simply walked down to the cabin where the baby was lying with its mother. He handed Mary's mother a bolt of the finest Chinese silk, a beautiful, deep grey green. "This is for her wedding dress when she becomes a woman and chooses a husband." Don Pedro simply left the cabin, returned to his own ship, and the pirates sailed away.

Not soon after the ship landed in Boston, Mary's father became ill and died. Her mother took her to New Hampshire where they could be closer to friends and family. The years passed and Ocean Born Mary, as she was called by friends and family, was now a wife and mother of four boys. She was a tall woman of six feet with shocking red hair and startling green eyes. People who met her always talked about her beauty. Her husband died when her sons were still quite young, and many people were saddened by her plight.

Don Pedro, who had never forgotten the baby named after his beloved mother, heard of her husband's death. The tall pirate captain was older now and longed for a more settled, peaceful life. He was the black sheep of a noble family in England. He decided to settle on an estate that he had along the Contoocook River in New Hampshire. He had his ship carpenters build him a fine house that was very much like the ships he had spent so much of his life on. He brought servants and fine furniture and silver plates and rare books to his new house. He then sought out Mary and asked her to come to his new home with her sons and be his housekeeper. She accepted and took over the running of his house and his estate. He helped her with her sons' educations and helped her raise them as fine young men. Mary lived as a grand lady and was often seen riding in a coach that Don Pedro gave her. She and her four tall sons were popular with the neighbors and on the farms around the estate.

Don Pedro was often gone on business trips, and upon his return one time his servants brought a huge seaman's chest into the house. Little was thought about it until some of his old crew visited, and there was a horrible argument in the garden beneath Mary's window. Mary heard a scream and then the sound of people running away. She rushed down into the garden and found Don Pedro dying from a stab wound to the chest. He asked her to bury him beneath the hearthstone, and then whispered the location of his treasure chest. He died in her arms.

True to his last request, Mary and his servants buried Don Pedro beneath the hearthstone. The pirate captain had left her everything, so she stayed there in the big house. She never dug up the treasure, but would occasionally visit it for whatever she needed to keep the estate and household going. It was a treasure so vast that she would never be able to use it all. Her sons all served in the Revolutionary War and returned to build homes of their own on the estate and raise their families. Ocean Born Mary lived alone in the big house until her death in 1814.

After her death, people began to notice strange things happening in and around the big house. Lights would appear in the windows of the now abandoned home, and some folks said that they could see a tall, beautiful woman walking in the garden. Others said they saw her walking down the broad staircase, coming down from the second floor. Some folks said they saw a beautiful coach pull up to the house and a tall, red-headed woman come out of it and walk through the front door, with the coach disappearing behind her. Groans could be heard from the garden, as if a man was in mortal agony and pain.

When the house was opened to the public, the rocking chair where Mary sat as an old woman would often rock by itself, as if welcoming the visitors to her home. Framed in the house was an old piece of China silk, grayish green and fading, the last mortal reminder of Ocean Born Mary and her adventure with the pirate captain.

Jonathan Moulton and the Devil

General Jonathan Moulton, the hero of legends in New Hampshire, was a man who craved wealth and possessions more than anything. One day while sitting in a public house with friends, he declared that he would sell his soul if he could become the richest man in New Hampshire. At that moment the fire in the room's fireplace sparked, and several men suggested that the devil himself, Old Nick, had heard Moulton's words.

When Moulton finally made his way back home, there was a guest seated in his parlor. He was dressed in black velvet and had the cool appearance of someone who knew who he was and how powerful he was and enjoyed it.

"Your servant, General Moulton," the stranger said as he rose from his chair by the fireplace and bowed to the master of the house. Then the man reached into the fire and with his bare hands took a red-hot coal between his fingers and used it to read his pocket watch. "We should conduct our business quickly, for I have other appointments in the capital in less than half an hour that demand my attention."

"Who are you?" asked the bewildered general. The capital was at least an hour away, and the sight of someone picking up a red-hot coal with bare hands without leaving a burn or a mark was unsettling.

"Well, I heard you call on me while you dined with your friends tonight, and I thought we could negotiate our deal before I make my way to my other business," replied the man. He smiled and in that cold and cruel smile, old General Moulton saw the Fallen Angel, Old Nick himself, standing in his parlor. He could barely stand because of the trembling of his legs.

"You must be the devil," said the frightened man.

"What's in a name? You can call me anything you want as long as we make the deal you offered not very long ago."

The general sat down in his favorite chair, and although he was scared, he took out his pocketknife and began to whittle on a piece of wood from the stack near the fireplace. At the mention of a deal, he had calmed down considerably. It was known throughout New Hampshire that no one had ever gotten the better of him in a bargain, and he was not going to let that streak end with Old Nick.

The devil sat opposite him and took out his own knife and began to trim his nails. Both the man and the devil acted almost bored, each trying to get the better of each other in a small war of nerves.

The general spoke first. "What proof do I have that you'll keep your end of the bargain?"

Old Nick ran his hand through his long black hair, and golden coins fell to the ground and rolled around the floor in every direction. Moulton tried to pick one up, but it was as hot as coal, so he dropped it at once.

Old Nick laughed and said, "Not so fast, my friend. Let it cool a bit. You can pick it up now if you like."

Jonathan Moulton reached down and took up the gold piece. It was real and quite cool now. He bent down and began to pick up the coins that had scattered across his parlor floor.

"Satisfied?" asked the devil.

"Completely, sir."

"Then let us drink on it, and sign our contract. Do you have any rum?"

Moulton poured two glasses of rum, and the devil drank his glass down with one gulp. Then Old Nick took out a piece of paper from his coat and held out a quill to Moulton. "Sign here and I will make you the richest man in all New England. Every month I will fill your two boots with gold coins from the toe to the top of the boot. But no tricks, Jonathan Moulton, because I know your reputation."

The general hesitated, and Old Nick sneered and said, "Have I made this trip for nothing?" The devil began to gather up the coins on the table and put them in his pocket. It was more than the greedy man could bear to see those coins leave his house. He took up his glass and swallowed the rum, and then he took up the quill and signed his name.

Old Nick smiled. "Keep the faith by me Moulton, and I will keep my end of the bargain. Just put your boots at the bottom of the chimney on the first day of each month, and I will pour the gold coins down and fill them. But remember, no tricks. I know you." With that Old Nick wrapped his cloak around him and in a flourish disappeared up the chimney and was gone.

The devil kept his bargain. Every month Moulton hung his boots on the iron cooking crane in the chimney. The next morning they would be filled with gold coins. He used his old riding boots that came up over the knees so he would get the most coins. Moulton soon became the richest man in New England, and everything he did prospered. Some of his friends, who actually remembered that evening conversation, wondered aloud if Moulton and the devil had an agreement.

One night on the first day of the month Old Nick came to Moulton's house and started to pour the coins down the chimney, but something strange happened. The boots didn't fill up as quickly as they had the month before. He kept pouring and pouring, but still the boots would not fill up. The devil became suspicious and said to himself, "Something is wrong here." He flew down the chimney and found that the parlor floor was covered with gold coins. He tore the boots from the crane and saw that the old general had cut the soles and heels off the boots, so that the gold just kept pouring through the boots onto the floor. Old Nick had to admit that the old man was a crafty one, but he had broken the bargain. That night Jonathan Moulton's house burned to the ground, and the old fellow only escaped with the clothes on his back.

As Moulton stood there in the glow of his burning house, he cursed his own greed. But he consoled himself that gold does not burn, and that his treasure was safe. Why, he could dig it up once the ashes had cooled. But the next day, search as he might, it seemed the gold was all gone. Mouton rebuilt his house around the old chimney, the only portion of the original house that still stood. He lived the rest of his life, a more contented man, knowing that although he was poor, the bargain was broken and salvation might still be within his grasp.

New Hampshire Glossary

Abenaki people: A Native American tribe whose lands covered much of what is now Vermont, New Hampshire, and Maine. They were part of the Wabanaki Confederacy, a group of several tribes that banded together. The Abenaki lived in birch bark houses called wigwams or lodges and were famous for their birch bark canoes.

New Hampshire: A state named after the English county of Hampshire. The capital is Concord.

Old Nick: One of the many names that the devil is known by in folk literature.

White Mountains: Part of the Appalachian Mountain range. They cover over one-quarter of the state of New Hampshire. They are considered the most rugged mountains in New England.

Story Sources

American Fairy Tales

American Folktales from the Collections of the Library of Congress, Volume 1

American Folktales from the Collections of the Library of Congress, Volume 2

American Myths & Legends, Volumes 1 & 2

The Faithful Hunter: Abenaki Stories

The Greenwood Library of American Folktales, Volume 1

Jonathan Draws the Long Bow

Legends of the New England Coast

More New Hampshire Folk Tales

Myths & Legends of Our Own Land, Volumes 1 & 2

New England Bean-Pot

New England Legends & Folklore

New Hampshire Folk Tales

Spirit of the New England Tribes: Indian History & Folklore

A Treasury of New England Folklore

New Jersey

New Jersey was one of the thirteen original colonies; it officially became a state in 1787 when it ratified the U.S. Constitution. The Lenape people, a Native American tribe, lived there long before the Europeans came to this country.

Like most states in the colonial and early days of this country, fiddle music was an important pastime that helped folks to forget the dangers and hardships of coming to a new land and provide some entertainment with music and dance. "The Fiddle Contest" tells us about an epic battle between two fiddlers. Throughout the colonial period, witch trials would scar communities and cause divisions that took generations to heal. Sometimes these trials ended in death, but one judge in New Jersey, in the story "The Double Trial," had a special way of handling these baseless claims.

The mosquito is said to be the unofficial bird of several states, but the story from New Jersey may top them all. Most states have their resident monster or creature that lurks in the woods or swamps or mountains, and New Jersey is no exception, with its own "Jersey Devil." Menlo Park was Thomas Edison's research center in New Jersey, and the inventions that were perfected there changed our lives.

The Double Trial (Based on True Events)

The mood in the courtroom was tense. Two women stood accused of witchcraft, but most of the town did not believe it at all. The two were well liked. Mistress Betty and Mistress Mary had been at the birth of half the people in the small town of Mount Holly. They had been there for people when they were sick or lonely or just needed to talk to someone. The two who accused them, the Cabots, were not nearly as well liked and had a reputation for being spiteful. They accused the two women of talking to animals and turning the weather bad, of making the milk go sour, and of making animals and people alike sick. They demanded that the two should hang.

The ladies pleaded their innocence. Most of the people in the courtroom cried out in their defense, but the judge said that the two women should be tried by water and bible. The two ladies held their chins up high and said that they were not afraid of any tests to prove their innocence, but since they had to endure the tests they felt it only fair that their accusers should also take the tests.

The judge almost smiled when he heard their request. "I see no reason that the accusers should not take the test alongside the accused. Since we know the Cabots are not witches, the test will not hurt them." No one had ever heard a judge rule like that before, and many thought it was strange. Betty and Mary's supporters thought this was a sure way to prove they were not guilty.

The judge ordered the town sheriff to examine the prisoners to make sure that they did not have any hidden weights in their clothing. They carried a huge bible belonging to the judge up to the gallows and placed it on one side of a great scale that had been brought to the square for the trial. The prisoners walked up the gallows' steps followed by the two accusers. Mr. Cabot sat on the other side of the scale. The entire town stretched their necks to see what would happen. Would the bible be heavier than Cabot, which proved innocence, or would he outweigh it? The crowd moaned as Mr. Cabot sat down and his side went down with a thud and the bible flew up into the air. The same thing happened for his wife and both of the accused women. Now there was real confusion in the town square. The people roared out for blood. Maybe they were all witches. The Cabots turned deathly white when the crowd cried for their deaths.

"Trial by water," they screamed.

The four were then taken to a nearby pond. All their clothes except a white shift were taken from them, and all four were thrown into the pond. The sheriff tried as he might, but every time they were dunked they came up again, spitting out water. All four, the accused and the accusers, just bobbed up to the surface. The crowd was silent and all eyes turned to the judge.

Calmly the judged addressed the crowd. "We all know that the Cabots are law-abiding citizens and not witches. Since they and Mistresses Betty and Mary have all tested the same, I declare them all innocent." The relieved crowd nodded their approval, and everyone walked home.

From that day forward Mount Holly never had another witch trial. I guess most people didn't want to take the chance that if they accused someone they might have to take the test with them. Wise judges are hard to come by.

The Fiddle Contest

Sammy Giberson was one of the best fiddle players in the Pine Barrens, and that was in the days when there were a lot of good fiddlers in that part of New Jersey. Everyone knew Sammy—he played for weddings, dances, parties, and just about any social get together. He and his fiddle were always welcome at the homes of the people in the Pines. After supper, Sammy would pull out his fiddle and soon everyone in the room would be tapping their feet and smiling as his fingers flew and the tunes rolled off his fiddle bow.

One night he and his good friend Bill Denn were having supper at a small inn. After their meal they started to drink a bit of New Jersey Lightning and swap a few stories about fiddle tunes and their adventures as traveling musicians. Soon the stories turned to bragging about their own talent, and they started to argue about who was the better dancer and fiddle player.

They decided to have a little contest, with the other patrons of the inn as the judges. They cleared some tables, then took turns playing for each other as they danced. First Sammy then Bill would dance while the other played, each one trying to play as difficult a tune as possible to throw off the other one's dancing. Soon they were exhausted, and their appreciative audience declared it a draw.

"A draw?" said Sammy. "Now you all know that's not right. There isn't a man in all the Pines that can outdance or outfiddle me. In fact the devil himself would be surprised to find that I could even beat him." Everyone laughed at his bragging. Sammy said his good nights and left the inn, a little worse the wear for his night of dancing, fiddling, and drinking.

As he came close to the bridge near his home a dark figure stepped out into the road and blocked his way.

"Sammy Giberson?" the stranger asked.

"I am."

The figure stepped onto the bridge and into the moonlight. "I hear you think you can beat me at dancing and fiddling."

"I've haven't met anyone who can beat me yet," replied Sammy bravely. "Who are you, stranger?"

"I'm the Devil, come to take up your challenge. Shall we start?"

Sammy took his fiddle and bow from his case, rosined the bow, and began to play a tune. The Devil started to dance. Soon it was the Devil's turn to play, and Sammy danced to the music. All night long they played and danced, until the music became wilder and wilder and it seemed that the night would break apart with the sound of their fiddles and the beat of their feet. Finally, just before dawn, the two fiddlers looked at each other and realized that neither of them could beat the other. The Devil so admired Sammy's playing that he taught him a few new tunes, including one called the "air tune" that no one had ever heard before. He promised Sammy that he would be the greatest fiddler to ever pick up a bow. Sammy in turn taught the Devil a couple of his tunes, and the two of them parted company.

Sammy continued to play for parties and weddings and christenings all over the Pine Barrens. He played behind his back and over his head, delighting his audiences with his skill and his music. He could play all night and never repeat himself. There were a few songs though that almost spooked his audiences with dark melodies and moody changes.

Then Sammy began to tell stories of his encounter with the Devil, and how they kept in touch. He told people about trading tunes with Old Nick, how they would meet at night and play together. On some dark nights travelers would hear two fiddles playing in the woods. The music was wild and fast. Sometimes when they played together Sammy would slip in a phrase from an old hymn, and the Devil's fiddle would fall silent until they came back to the dance tune.

Sammy continued to play for the folks in the Pines. Many fiddle players tried to match his style and speed, but none came close. The "air tune" became his signature piece. He seemed to just pick the tune right out of the air, and no matter how many times a fiddle player heard it, he could never come close to playing it.

Sammy eventually died. Some folks say he still walks the Pine Barrens, playing his fiddle. Others say that on dark nights you can hear the sound of two fiddles in the woods. They'll tell you that it's Sammy and the Devil still meeting out there, still trying to best each other as they dance and fiddle all night long. Other folks say that Sammy's family has his fiddle, and that on dark winter nights the violin sometimes starts to play a song all by itself.

Who knows what can happen when you have such a strange partner to play your tunes with as the Devil himself?

The Mosquitoes

All along the East Coast people talk about their mosquitoes and whose are the biggest, fiercest, and meanest and have the most deadly of stingers. Now it really doesn't matter what most people say out east, because most folks know that New Jersey has the most monstrous skeeters of all.

When the Dutch and the Swedes still held New Jersey under their rule, the mosquitoes were the size of sparrows and as fierce as hawks. Their bite was so poisonous that it could paralyze a cow and keep it from moving for at least ten minutes. They would travel in packs, diving out of the sky at their victims, sounding like the roar of the sea during a storm.

The Dutch and Swedes tried every means to get rid of the vampirelike creatures, and they failed. But the Native Americans were much wiser than the newcomers. They kept the mosquitoes in their lodges and trained them to hunt like the kings did in the old country with hawks. The mosquitoes would bite the animals and paralyze them, giving the Indians time to shoot their prey with their bows and arrows.

Now the Indians soon learned that the skeeters that fed on the white settlers had deadlier venom than the ones that fed on the Indians. They started using these skeeters for hunting, and prospered even more. These skeeters not only paralyzed their victims, but silenced them as well. The Indians trained their skeeters to go into the Dutch and Swedish settlements to feast on roosters, goats, and sheep, and while the animal was silenced, the mosquitoes would drag it back to the Indian villages.

Well the Dutch decided to retaliate by stealing the favorite horse of the chief. Now folks on both sides were out for blood. The Dutch and Swedes primed their muskets and sharpened their pikes and swords, and soon the battle commenced. But the Indians had a secret weapon. They released their hunting skeeters, letting them loose on the settlers. Soon not a soldier or farmer could move or speak. Eventually a peace was arranged. Everyone was hoping to forget the whole battle, especially the settlers. The soldiers of Sweden and the Netherlands were ashamed that they had been defeated by mosquitoes, but felt a lot better when they heard that their neighbors in Delaware had surrendered their finest fort after mosquitoes besieged it. They held a dinner celebrating the peace, and all agreed that they should be mighty proud of their mosquitoes and that no one should ever be ashamed of losing a battle to the fierce Jersey skeeters.

Bringing the Future to Light (a True Story)

The buildings stretched for two blocks, each one a place of discovery, a place of imagination, and a place where the future began. This was Menlo Park, the first industrial research laboratory in the United States. This was the place where dreams became reality—and the playground of the Wizard of Menlo Park, Thomas Alva Edison. Here Edison oversaw a group of engineers and scientists whose main objective was to find practical applications for the mechanical inventions that were either invented there or earlier ideas that they improved upon.

Edison, who patented 1,097 inventions during his lifetime, had little formal education and was actually thought stupid by one of his teachers. He was partially deaf due to a bout of scarlet fever; and as he grew older, his hearing became increasingly impaired.

Born into poverty, by the age of twelve he had quit school to work full time selling candy and newspapers on the railroad. After saving the life of the station master's son, Edison was given a job as an apprentice telegraph operator. This stroke of luck started his fascination and work with electricity. He began inventing full time and filed his first patent when he was twenty-one. He started a workshop in Newark, New Jersey, that eventually became The General Electric Company. Later he moved his workshops to Menlo Park. When he was nearing a breakthrough on an idea, Edison often worked twenty-hour days.

The electric lamp, the light bulb, the phonograph, the quadruplex telegraph that could send four messages at the same time, the Dictaphone, the electrical distribution system to send electricity into homes from a central power source, the fluoroscope (the X-ray machine,) the first successful overhead electric railway, and the motion picture camera and projector were just a few of the amazing inventions that were sparked by the imagination of Edison and the hard work of his staff.

The Jersey Devil

The storm raged as the traveler made his way down the lonely road through the woodsy swamps near Leeds Point. But suddenly the storm was overpowered by an unearthly scream. Out of the trees stalked a creature that could only be described as part horse, part snake, part bird, and all evil. The man's horse shied while the traveler drew his gun. The creature screamed once more in defiance, then disappeared once again into the hidden places that only it knew. Once again, the Jersey Devil had made its appearance.

It was a storm that brought the Jersey Devil into the world all those many years ago. Mrs. Leeds was in her cabin surrounded by the elder women in the community, who had come to help her give birth to yet another child. Although she was openly a Quaker, it was often whispered that Mrs. Leeds was a witch and had dealings with the dark arts. It had actually been said that someone had heard that when she found she was going to have her thirteenth child, the over burdened woman cried out, "I hope this time it's a devil!" The older women were relieved that the child born that night seemed to be a perfectly healthy, normal child.

But they watched in horror as the child began to change before their very eyes. First the human features started to melt away, then a long, serpentlike body transformed itself from the human trunk. Next the facial features faded and a bony, almost horselike head erupted from the child's skull, sprouting horns and wide, evil-looking eyes. Hooves replaced the feet and hands, and huge batlike wings sprouted from its shoulders. A long, whipping tail emerged and started to beat the older women and the rest of the Leeds family about the room, while the creature screamed an unearthly howl and then flew out the open door of the cabin into the swamp and forest. The Jersey Devil had been born.

Some say that the first victims were members of the Leeds family as they slept one night. Their evil sibling came through the unlocked door and devoured several of the younger children before being driven off by older members of the family. After this first meal, the creature seemed to avoid human contact except for the occasional visit to a farm to spoil the milk or scare the farm animals or make off with a pig or goat or sheep. People said you could see it outlined in the moonlight as it silently flew over the land, its huge wings beating soundlessly as it swept from place to place.

In 1740 the area of the Barrens had been so terrorized by the monster that a brave minister with a candle, book, and bell exorcised the Jersey Devil from the land for 100 years. It seemed to work, and most people fell into an uneasy peace. There would be sightings, but most folks thought they were the work of overactive imaginations. That peace lasted until 1840, 100 years after the creature was banished from the Pine Barrens. Once again the Devil started its flights over farms, terrorizing cows and horses and trying to snatch at children who strayed too far from their doorsteps in the evening.

Folks on the road often talked about the monster they encountered at night on the road, and whole groups of folks traveling by coach would swear to the horrors they saw as they bounced across those old roads in the dark. The Jersey Devil was working its own brand of magic once again.

Some say the Jersey Devil still roams the Pine Barrens, waiting to scare those who dare to roam at night in its world. Others say that now it is the evil omen that appears just before bad news or horrible tragedy strike. It was seen just before the Spanish American War and World Wars I and II. Is it still lurking at the edge of our imagination, ready to be the sign that evil is coming our way once again, or has the Jersey Devil finally left this world behind and found some peace somewhere in another swamp? Was it the devil child of old Mrs. Leeds or some unfortunate creature, deformed and misunderstood, brought into the world of legend and myth? We'll never know.

New Jersey Glossary

Lenape people: The Lenape or Delaware people were found throughout Delaware and New Jersey and parts of southeastern Pennsylvania and southern New York. They were part of the Algonquin Confederacy.

New Jersey: A state named after the Isle of Jersey in the English Channel. The capital is Trenton.

Pine Barrens: A region of forests, swamps, and streams that cover one-quarter of New Jersey. It is a wilderness area with many state forests and wildlife areas.

Witch trials: Trials held during the colonial period at which people who were accused of being witches had to undergo a series of physical tests. Sometimes these were a lose-lose proposition. One favorite test was to throw the person into a lake or pond with his or her hands and feet tied. If the accused floated to the surface, it proved he or she was a witch and the unfortunate person was executed. If the accused sank to the bottom and drowned, he or she was innocent but sadly still dead.

Story Sources

American Folktales from the Collections of the Library of Congress, Volume 1

American Folktales from the Collections of the Library of Congress, Volume 2

American Myths & Legends, Volumes 1 & 2

The Greenwood Library of American Folktales, Volume 1

The Jersey Devil

Legends of the Delaware Indians and Picture Writing

Myths & Legends of Our Own Land, Volumes 1 & 2

Pine Barrens Legends, Lore & Lies

Upstate Downstate

The White Deer & Other Stories Told by the Lenape

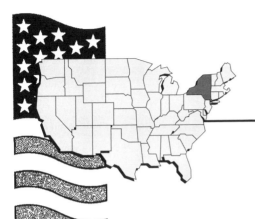

New York

New York was one of the original thirteen colonies, and it officially became a state in 1788. Today it is home to a diverse population and the biggest city in the United States, New York City. The first people to settle in this area were Native Americans, including Seneca, Iroquois, and Mohawk people. Once the Europeans arrived, the area became a Dutch colony, and the city was called New Amsterdam. That heritage can be found in the story "A Baker's Dozen." Since then, New York has been a harbor for those coming to America seeking a new life—Italians, Germans, Jews, Polish, and more recently Africans, Chinese, and Pakistanis.

As in any metropolis, urban legends are found on the sidewalks, subways, and diners all over the city, and one of the most famous, about an alligator, is recalled here. Two New York citizens who made a difference appear in the stories of the first woman doctor in America and the founder of the American Society for the Prevention of Cruelty to Animals. When the Great Depression hit America, money became scarce and many families faced ruin. Mayor LaGuardia's story of a little courtroom mercy softens the memory of that tragic period.

Elizabeth Blackwell, the First Woman Doctor in America (a True Story)

A strange silence greeted the dean of the medical school at Geneva College in Geneva, New York, when he spoke to the student body. He was there because a woman had sought admission into the medical school, and he didn't know how to handle this embarrassing situation. The problem was that the man who had recommended her and with whom she had studied was Dr. Joseph Warrington, a prominent physician and a financial supporter of the school of medicine. If the dean refused her admission, he would insult a well-known doctor and a friend to the school. But a woman doctor? How could he admit a woman? In 1847 there were no women doctors or nurses in the United States.

Then he and the faculty came up with the idea of letting the student body vote on her admission. If the students rejected her, as the faculty was sure they would, the dean and the administration would be blameless. The dean told the students that a young woman had applied for the medical school, and that it would be up to them to accept or reject her application. Did they think that women could or should be doctors? Did they want a woman with them in class? He told them that their decision would be final, and he would abide by it.

The dean left the group of medical students so they could make a decision. At first the students were against the idea, but realizing that a no vote was what the faculty wanted from them, they decided to turn the tables on them. If the faculty wanted a no vote, then the students, all 129 male medical students, would give them a yes vote. And that's how Elizabeth Blackwell became the first woman in America to enter a medical school to train as a doctor.

At first the students, faculty, and even the townspeople were shocked that she actually came to the school. At times she was asked not to attend anatomy class, and she was often pushed to the back of the class where she could barely see what was being demonstrated. But slowly most of the other students learned to respect her knowledge, ability, and perseverance. In January 1849 she graduated with her degree in medicine at the top of her class and became the first woman to graduate from medical school and become a doctor of medicine in the United States.

Elizabeth Blackwell had been born in England and came to America when she was ten years old. Her father, a businessman, was involved with issues of peace and justice in England, which he continued in the United States. After his death Elizabeth, her mother, and her two sisters started a private school in Cincinnati, where Elizabeth began her teaching career. All the while she had her mind set on becoming a doctor. She knew that many women would rather consult with another woman over health issues and were not comfortable being examined and treated by male doctors. She applied to many schools, but they all rejected her until the students at Geneva Medical College voted her in on a whim.

While studying in France after her graduation, she suffered a serious eye infection that left her blind in one eye. From Paris she went to London and worked at St. Bartholomew's

Hospital. It was during this trip that she met and formed a friendship with Florence Nightingale, the English nurse who became famous in the Crimean War.

In 1851 Elizabeth returned to America, but hospitals refused to hire her. She started a practice out of her home and lectured on health. Finally, in 1853 Elizabeth; her sister Emily, who had just gotten her medical degree; and Dr. Marie Zakrzewski, a Polish immigrant who had been encouraged by Elizabeth to pursue her medical dreams, opened a clinic for women and children in the slums of New York City. In 1857 the two Drs. Blackwell and Dr. Zakrezewski incorporated their clinic as the New York Infirmary for Women and Children.

During the American Civil War Elizabeth trained nurses. In 1868, with her sister Emily, she started the Women's Medical College at the Infirmary. The college operated for thirty-one years, but Elizabeth left the college and went back to England, where she founded the London School of Medicine for Women. In 1875 Dr. Elizabeth Blackwell was appointed professor of gynecology at the London School of Medicine for Children. She died in England in 1910.

A life spent in the service of health and medicine and service to others, a life spent proving over and over again that she and other women could be as good as any man in the medical profession, a lifetime of firsts in medicine, and it all began with what some medical students thought of as a joke.

A Voice for Those Who Can't Speak
(a True Story)

The crowd watched as the driver of a coal wagon got down from his seat and began to whip his tired, emaciated horse. Out of the throng walked a man, elegantly dressed. He grabbed the driver's arm and quietly but firmly explained to him that it was now against the law to beat an animal, even if it belonged to you. The wagon driver looked into the eyes of Henry Burgh, nodded, and went back to his seat.

Henry Burgh was born into a wealthy family in 1813. His father was a prominent shipbuilder, and young Henry spent his early adult years traveling around Europe. In 1863 he was appointed to the diplomatic corps, assigned to the court of the Russian tsar. It was while he was in Russia that he first became interested in trying to prevent cruelty to animals. On his way back to America he stopped in London and met and spoke with the Earl of Harrow, who was president of England's Royal Society for the Prevention of Cruelty to Animals.

When Burgh returned to New York he had become a man with a mission. He wanted to convince people that these servants and companions to humankind, who had no voice of their own, needed protection. He would be their voice. He spoke in halls and at meetings around New York City, giving graphic details about bull fighting in Spain and dog fighting here in America. In those days dogcatchers were a feared and dangerous group of men, who were paid per animal picked up. It was not uncommon for them to steal pets right out of people's backyards. The way the dogs were treated was horrific. As many as 300 dogs a day were rounded up in Manhattan, put into a large cage, and then lowered into the East River, where they drowned.

Bergh worked tirelessly, trying to convince people that preventing cruelty to animals was a moral obligation. His dream finally came true on April 10, 1866, when the charter for the American Society for the Prevention of Cruelty to Animals passed. A few days later an anticruelty law passed, and the ASPCA was given the power to enforce it.

Bergh's work didn't stop there. He worked alongside police officers and members of his staff, inspecting slaughterhouses and raiding dog-fighting pits. Once he even dropped through a skylight into a dog-fighting pit owned by a notorious gambler. He lectured passionately to any group that would listen, from ladies' society meetings to children in schools. In 1875 the ASPCA operated the first ambulance for sick and injured horses. Bergh supplied fresh drinking water to the horses that pulled the public streetcars and also had water fountains made that were visited by dogs and cats.

By the time of his death in 1888, thirty-seven of the thirty-eight states in the union had passed anticruelty laws. Chapters of the ASPCA had sprung up in cities across the country. Henry Bergh not only became the voice for animals during his lifetime, but through the organization he created he became the voice of animals in this country forever.

La Guardia Fines the Courtroom (a True Story)

When Fiorello La Guardia served as mayor of New York, he was also a magistrate and would often listen to cases in police court. This was during the Great Depression, and some of the cases the mayor heard did not always fall into the area of hardened criminals. One winter's day during the height of the Depression an old man was brought before La Guardia because he had stolen a loaf of bread. When asked if he had anything to say about his crime, the old man looked up and told the mayor that he had stolen the bread to feed his starving family.

La Guardia sat quietly for a moment and then said, "You broke the law and I have to punish you. I fine you ten dollars." Ten dollars during those days was an enormous amount of money. You could see in the old man's eyes that he had no way of paying.

La Guardia then reached into his own pocket and took out the ten dollars and placed it on the table in front of him. "Here is the ten dollars to pay your fine. Now I reverse my verdict and remit the fine." He threw the ten dollars into his hat and started to pass it around the courtroom. "And I fine everyone in this room except the prisoner fifty cents each for living in a town where a man has to steal in order to feed himself and his family."

The man walked out with $47.50 in his hand, and a look on his face like he finally saw the light at the end of a long dark tunnel. Kindness can do that to a man.

A Baker's Dozen (Dutch)

The Dutch were among the first European immigrants to settle in the new country, and during the first wave, many settled in New York. Here is one of their traditional tales.

It was the last day of the year, and the baker had kept his shop open later than usual. People had been coming in all day to buy his New Year's cakes and cookies. The next day folks in the towns along the Hudson River would be celebrating the holiday with mince pies and olie-kocks. It had been a good year, and the baker hoped that the new one would be even better.

Customers drifted in and out. The steady flow became a trickle, and soon no one was out on the streets. It was approaching midnight, and the baker, looking out the window into the dark gloomy night, became a little uneasy. It was the last night of the year. You never knew what creatures might be out on this night trying to make your life miserable one more time in the old year.

Just as the baker was about to close his shop, he heard a knock on the door. An old woman, bent over and toothless, hobbled through the door. She walked along with a cane and rapped it loudly on the counter. "Give me a dozen New Year's cakes," she yelled.

The baker looked startled and replied, "I can hear you, grandmother. No need to shout." He counted out twelve cakes, put them in a bag, and handed the bag to the old woman.

She peered into the bag, and looked up at him and said, "You're trying to cheat me. I want a dozen cakes and you have only given me twelve." She squinted at the baker with her cold blue eyes. Her long nose seemed to point at him accusingly.

"Twelve is a dozen," said the baker.

"But I want one more," she cried. "I want a dozen."

"The baker was tired from his long day at the ovens and at the counter and snapped back, "If you want another cake then go to the devil and get one."

The clock struck midnight as the old hag walked out of the shop leaning heavily on her cane.

As soon as she left, the baker felt bad about what he had said to her. But what happened next was even stranger than her visit and their argument. The baker's luck turned bad. That night all his mince pies were stolen. Every day brought another disaster. His bread was too light and people complained; or it was too heavy and they complained even more. His family was plagued by illness.

Spring came, and the people of the town were happy to see the end of winter. But the baker was hardly ever happy anymore. He sat in his shop and wondered at how slow business had become the last few months. Suddenly the sky opened up with a terrible thunderstorm. The lightning split the sky, and the rain came down like stones. The door to the shop flew open, and in walked the old woman, her cane tapping on the hard wood floor. She banged on the counter with her walking stick and demanded a dozen cookies.

The baker slowly and deliberately counted them out, "One, two, three, four, five, six, seven, eight, nine, and ten, eleven, twelve." He handed her the bag.

"I want a dozen," she screamed. "You have only given me twelve."

"Twelve is a dozen," he replied stubbornly.

"I want one more. I want a real dozen."

"Then go to the devil and get one more," the baker yelled. Just as the words left his mouth, the sky grew even darker and the old woman stomped out of the shop and into the storm.

If the baker's luck was bad before, it was terrible now. His oven fell down one day as he was baking, and all the bricks landed on him and left him bruised and battered. His children were always screaming with runny noses and itchy scabby skin, and his wife could not hear a sound. All his customers left and went to other bakers to buy their cakes and breads and cookies. Life was awful.

A year had passed when the old hag walked into the shop and demanded a dozen cookies. The baker slowly and sadly counted out the cookies and when he came to twelve he added one more.

The old woman smiled and spoke kindly, "Now the spell is broken. From now on a dozen will be thirteen, a baker's dozen."

The baker nodded and said, "I think you are right. A baker's dozen is what I'll sell from now on."

The baker and his family started to have their old luck again. The baker always was kind and generous. Now he knew the value of tenderness.

Be Careful What You Flush
(an Urban Legend)

Jimmy's family had not been crazy about the idea, but they finally went along with it to stop the constant nagging and whining. They bought him a baby alligator while they were vacationing in Florida. But baby alligators are like any other "baby" animal—they start to grow, and they keep on growing. One day while he was at school, his mother took the little alligator and flushed him down the toilet. Down he went, swirling and tumbling into the sewers of New York City. And what did he do down there? He kept on growing, that's what he did.

Years later, a sanitation worker was down in the sewers checking on a broken pipe. He heard something moving in the darkness just beyond the reach of his flashlight. Then it came into his sight, and his fellow workers topside heard his awful screams. When they hurried down the ladder they saw him being dragged away by an enormous white alligator. The creature was huge. It had turned white from the lack of sunlight in the sewers, and blind from the total darkness. Was this Jimmy's lost pet, or some other child's souvenir that had waited for someone to visit it in the sewers?

They say that alligators had bred down there in the dark, and although they had become blind, their other senses had more than compensated. They hunted rats and strays that venture too close to sewer openings. And they waited silently and deadly in the dark for their favorite treat, an unsuspecting sewer worker.

How many are down there, the remaining pets of once happy vacationers come back from a holiday in the South? Too many to even think about.

New York Glossary

Dutch: The people of the Netherlands.

Great Depression: A period in the 1930s during which the world was in a deep economic slump. Banks closed, and at one time one out of every four American workers was unemployed.

Iroquois: A league of several tribes that had a great council to decide policy that would affect all its members. Often tribes are referred to as Iroquois when they were part of this league.

Magistrate: A judge, someone who applies the law in a courtroom.

Mohawk people: A woodland Native American tribe that was part of the Iroquois League or Federation.

New York: A state named in honor of the Duke of York. The capital is Albany.

Seneca people: A woodland Native American tribe that was part of the Iroquois League or Federation.

Story Sources:

Adirondack Voices

Amazing American Women

American Folktales from the Collections of the Library of Congress, Volume 1

American Folktales from the Collections of the Library of Congress, Volume 2

American Myths & Legends, Volumes 1 & 2

Body, Boots & Britches

The Canaller's Songbook

Encyclopedia of Urban Legends

Folk Songs of the Catskills

Folklore from the Adirondack Foothills

The Ghost of Peg-Leg Peter & Other Folk Tales of Old New York

The Greenwood Library of American Folktales, Volume 1

Iroquois Stories

Myths & Legends of Our Own Land, Volumes 1 & 2

New York City Folklore

Seneca Myths & Folk Tales

Songs of the Great Lakes

Upstate Downstate

The Vanishing Hitchhiker: American Urban Legends & Their Meanings

North Carolina

Although not officially a state until 1789, North Carolina was one of the thirteen original colonies that fought against Great Britain in the American Revolution. "The Ride of Betsy Dowdy" comes from that period in history, handed down as the true story of a young colonial girl and the daring ride she made in the dark of night. True heroes come in all shapes and sizes and even species, as the remarkable story of "Hatteras Jack" well proves.

American storytelling brings to life some great characters. Among them, the indomitable Jack is one of the greatest, as you will see when you read about him and his amazing animal friends in "Jack and the Robbers." Finally, in "Laying Out Mrs. Fox," Donald Davis, an award-winning North Carolina storyteller and author, tells a personal story from his childhood. Here you will see how the special love of a boy for his grandmother allows him to realize how important "laying someone out" can truly be.

Jack and the Robbers

Jack tales, common in the British Isles, came to the United States with some of its first immigrants.

Jack was a lazy boy. He was about twelve, I reckon, when his mama started trying to make him help with the work around the place. But Jack, he didn't like working much. One day his mother told him that he had to start pulling his weight around the old farm, or he'd have to leave and make his own way in the world. Well, Jack decided to go out and seek his fortune, and the next morning he left the old farm..

He walked down the road a few miles and saw an old ox standing in a field by a rail fence, bellowing like this was the saddest day in its life.

"Hello!" says Jack. "What's the matter?"

"I'll just tell you," says the old ox. "I'm getting too old to pull the plow. I heard the men talking about how they were going to kill me tomorrow and get rid of me."

"Come on down here to this hole in the fence," says Jack, "and you can slip off with me."

So the old ox followed the fence to where there was a hole, and Jack helped pull the fence apart a bit more, and the old ox got out. So together they walked on down the public road.

Jack and the ox traveled on, and pretty soon they came where there was an old donkey standing with his head hanging down over the gate. His eyes were closed; he was just crying and moaning.

"Hello," says Jack. "What's troubling you?"

"There's no help for me!" says that old donkey. "The boys took me out to haul in wood this morning, but I'm getting so old and weak I couldn't pull the wagon. I heard them say they were going to kill me tomorrow and get rid of me."

"Come on, and go with us," says Jack.

So he let the old donkey out, and Jack and the ox and the donkey walked on down the public road. The old donkey told Jack to get up on his back and ride.

They walked until they came to a farm where an old hound dog was sitting in the yard. He was howling so pitifully, it would break your heart.

"Hello," says Jack. "What are you howling about so sadly?"

"Nothing can save me!" says the old dog. "The farmer's sons took me out hunting last night. They cut down a small tree where the raccoon had climbed up. When it came crashing down, I got hold of the raccoon all right, but so many of my teeth are gone and I'm not as strong as I used to be, and that raccoon got loose from me and ran away. They said they were going to kill me today and get rid of me."

"Come on, and go with us," says Jack.

So the old dog crawled under the gate and joined the strange group of friends.

The old donkey says to him, "If you're too tired, just get up on my back and ride."

Jack helped the old dog up behind him, and they all went on down the public road.

It wasn't long until they came to another farm, and here an old tomcat walked along the fence. He was crying and meowing to raise the dead.

"Hello!" says Jack. "What's the matter with you?"

"There's no hope!" says that old cat. "I caught a rat out in the barn this morning, but I'm getting old and my claws aren't as sharp as they used to be, so he got away. I heard the farmer and his wife talking about putting me in a sack and taking me to the river to drown me. I'm not worth my keep, they said, if I can't catch rats and mice."

"Come on, and go with us," says Jack.

So the old cat jumped down off the fence.

The old donkey says, "Hop up on my back and you can ride and rest your old bones."

The old cat jumped up, got behind Jack and the dog, and they all walked on down the public road.

They came to a farm where they saw an old rooster sitting on a fence post, crowing like it was midnight, making the saddest, most lonesome racket.

"Hello!" says Jack. "What's troubling you?"

"My life is over," said the old rooster. "the farmer and his wife have company coming over tomorrow, and I heard them say they were going to wring my neck and roast me for their dinner."

"Come on with us," says Jack.

Old rooster flew on down, got up on the back of the ox, and was ready to leave. So they all went right on down the highway. The six friends moved together, talking and thinking how lucky they were to have found each other. They traveled on until it got dark out. Now all these animals, even Jack, were born and raised on farms and didn't have a lot of knowledge about being out on the road alone, especially after dark.

"Well," says Jack, "we better get off the road and find a place to stay tonight."

They came to a little path that led off into the woods. They walked down the path, hoping they might find some shelter where they would be safe for the night. Then they came to a little house. There was no clearing around it, no vegetable garden, no barn, no animals, just a lonely house. Jack hollered hello at the fence, but nobody answered.

"Come on," says the old donkey. "Let's go investigate this place."

Well, nobody came to the door, and there was nobody around back of the house, so they went on in. Inside they found plenty of food to eat, and even piles of silver and gold coins in the corner of the room.

Jack says, "Now, who in the world do you reckon could be living out here in such a wilderness in a place like this?

"Well," says the old ox, "it's my opinion that a gang of robbers and thieves might live here."

So Jack says, "Then it looks to me that we might as well stay here. If they've stolen all this food and all that money, then we've got as much right to it as they have."

"Yes," says the old dog, "that's exactly what I think, too. But if we stay, I believe we better get ready for a fight. I expect they'll be coming back here later tonight."

"That's just what I was going to say," says the old cat. "I bet it's pretty close to midnight right now."

"It'll be midnight in about an hour," says the old rooster.

"Come on, then," says Jack. "We'd better get ready to fight them if we have to."

The ox said he was too big for the cabin, so he'd stay out in the yard and hide in the shadows. The old donkey said he'd take up his stand on the porch just outside the door. The old dog said he'd get in behind the door and fight from there. The old tomcat got down in the fireplace, and the old rooster flew up on the comb of the roof and said, "If you boys need any help now, just call on me, call on me!"

They all waited. Soon they heard somebody coming down the path, and who was it, but seven highway robbers. When they got pretty close to the house, they told the youngest one to go on ahead and make sure the coast was clear, then to start up a fire so they could have a meal and divide up the money they'd stolen that day. The other six waited outside the gate.

The youngest thief went to the fireplace and got down on his knees to blow up the coals and get the fire started. The cat had his head right down on the hearth, and that man thought its eyes was coals of fire. When he blew in that old cat's eyes, it reached out its claws and, quick as a thought, scratched him down both cheeks. The robber hollered and headed for the door. The dog ran out and bit him in the leg. He shook it off and ran on the porch, and the old donkey raised up and kicked him on out in the yard. The ox caught him up on its horns, ran to the fence, and threw him out in the brush. About that time the old rooster sitting up there on top of the house started in to crowing as loud as he could.

The other robbers, hearing all that racket, ran just as fast they could run. The one they'd sent into the house finally got up and started running like a streak, and caught up with them in no time. They said to him, "What in the world was that in there?"

"Oh, I'm dying. I'm dying!" says the man. "I won't live another fifteen minutes!"

The others said, "Well, before you die, tell us what it was caused all that racket back yonder."

"That house is full of men, and they've even got one on the roof. I went to blow up the fire and a man in the fireplace raked me all over the face with an awl. I started to run and a man behind the door stabbed me in the leg with a butcher knife. By the time I got out the door, another man hit me with a huge club and knocked me right off the porch. In the yard was the biggest and strongest of them all. He picked me up with a pitchfork and threw me over the fence. And then that man up on the roof hollered out, "Bring him to me! Bring him to me!"

"There's no use in us going back there with all those men in the house. Let's leave here for good before they come after us."

So the highway robbers ran for their lives, and kept on running until they were over the mountains and out of the country.

Jack and the ox and the old donkey and the dog and the cat and the rooster, they took possession of that house, and they lived well. They had plenty to eat and plenty of money to buy food whenever they needed it. But the last time I was down that way, Jack had gone on back home to his mother. He was out in the farmyard cutting his mother a big pile of stove-wood. He seemed happy to be back home.

The Ride of Betsy Dowdy (a True Story)

December 1775. The war was not going well for the American colonists. Lord Dunmore was marching an army south from Virginia to resupply his men with the famous ponies of the Albemarle Sound area of North Carolina. These wild ponies were well known not only for their speed, but also for their incredible stamina. The only force that could stop Lord Dunmore was the small army of General Skinner, which was camped in Perquimans County. But Lord Dunmore had been secretive, and swift with his advance into Carolina, and General Skinner knew nothing about the impending dangers approaching Albemarle Sound.

There was one person, though, who was determined to stop the British from stealing her beloved ponies. That was sixteen-year-old Betsy Dowdy. She overheard a neighbor tell her father about the British army coming their way to secure the area for the Crown and to round up all the horses they could find. It was a cold winter night, but young Betsy determined to get the word to General Skinner. Betsy wanted not only to keep the British out of her colony, but also to save her beloved ponies. She had to get word to General Skinner and tell him of Lord Dunmore's plans.

Silently she made her way out to the barn to saddle up her favorite pony, Black Bess. She had named the horse after the highwayman Dick Turpin's famous horse that saved him so many times from the tyranny of the British system in England. She hoped her Black Bess would do the same tonight.

Betsy and Black Bess started off, sliding down the sandy banks and then swimming the icy water of Currituck Sound. The cold water almost took Betsy's breath away, but her sturdy little mare just swam on, as if she knew how important this night was to everyone including ponies like her. After they crossed the sound they sped across the Dismal Swamp. The light-footed Bess ran across the swamp, picking out the firm places and seeming to fly across the bogs. They passed Camden and Hertford. Finally, near dawn, Betsy rode into General Skinner's camp, exhausted but triumphant, on the back of Black Bess. Nearly frozen, Betsy told the general what she had learned.

General Skinner mobilized his men and marched to meet the unsuspecting British army, defeating them at the Battle of Great Bridge. That part of North Carolina was saved from British occupation, and Betsy's wonderful ponies were also saved. After she and Black Bess recovered from their cold night ride, they returned home to Betsy's proud father. Betsy had shown the courage to help the new nation, and her Black Bess proved to be the equal of Dick Turpin's famous Bonnie Black Bess.

Laying Out Mrs. Fox
(a True Story by Donald Davis)

When I was a little boy growing up in the mountains of North Carolina, my favorite place in the world was my Grandmother Walker's house. It was a big log house way back over Rush Fork Gap in the Smoky Mountains, the house in which she was born, my mother was born, and the same house in which even my great grandmother had been born.

You could take me there blindfolded to this very day, carry me inside in my sleep in the middle of the night, and I could wake up telling you exactly where we were from the smell of the place.

It smelled like wood that had never been painted or finished in any way; wood smoke from years of cooking and heating fires; fried pork, which was the main meat of the diet; mildew from the perpetual dampness and humidity of those deep mountains; and . . . snuff spit!

Somewhere in every room, behind a curtain on the windowsill, behind the back leg of a chair, was hidden my Grandmother's spit can. She always had her lower lip filled with snuff, that powdered tobacco favored by women who did not smoke in public, and the spit can was a necessary accessory.

We visited Grandmother (and Granddaddy) Walker almost every weekend, but my favorite times there were the times when I got to stay and visit on my own without my mother to stop and correct either one of us for our behavior.

I was about eight years old when, in the middle of the summer, my mother made the announcement, "Guess what? Your Grandmother Walker wants you to come and stay with her for a whole week! Get your stuff ready . . . we're going out there this afternoon!"

Since I was six years old, there had always been at least one full week of the summer when I got to go alone to my Grandmother's house. This week would make my whole summer!

The log house had three rooms downstairs: the kitchen in the back, where everybody spent all their waking time; my grandparents' bedroom in the front; and a third room called the "front room," which could have been a living room except that there were also two beds in it.

Mama was one of nine children. All seven girls slept in the sleeping loft upstairs, and her two brothers had the beds in the "front room." Now they were grown and gone, and this was my room for the week.

Every day was full. We picked blackberries (and had nothing but multiple servings of blackberry pie for supper). "Don't tell your mama!" was Grandmother's only advice. We worked in the black dirt of her garden and cooked what we picked there. We walked the mile and a half to Ferguson's Store and got not only the sewing thread Grandmother came for, but the news of Rush Fork. I felt very important with her.

Granddaddy was, of course, also there. He slept late, ate long, and pretended to do a little work on the farm.

Early on the morning of the third day, I was awakened by someone loudly knocking on the door of the house. I heard Grandmother come from the kitchen to the door. She opened the door and began to talk with someone who refused her offer to come inside. I could hear only her end of the conversation.

"When did she die? Well, she'd been sick a long time. She turned eighty-nine in June, I know that. Yes . . . you know I will. I'll be down there in about an hour."

I crawled out of bed and met her just as she got back to the kitchen to report to Granddaddy.

"Well," she started, "Old Mrs. Fox finally died. That was her son, Robert. They want me to come down there and lay her out. I told him I'd be there in an hour."

"Do you want me to watch the boy?" Granddaddy thought all his grandchildren were named either "the boy" or "the girl."

"No," Grandmother answered. "He can go with me. I'll leave him outside."

For the life of me, I could not figure out what was happening. What did "laying out" mean? Sounded like what happened in a fight to me. But how could Grandmother fight with Mrs. Fox if she was already dead? My Grandmother wouldn't fight anyway, but if she did, I knew very well that she could "lay them out!" I was glad I was going so I could see what this was all about.

While we had our breakfast, Grandmother and Granddaddy kept talking about the whole Fox family. Old Mrs. Fox had two sons, Robert and Charles. They were both married, and Charles had children. Granddaddy thought that the grandchildren were all boys. "It's a family of boys!" he concluded.

After breakfast, I got dressed while Grandmother got herself ready to go. I could hear her puttering around in their bedroom. When she came out, she was all dressed like she was going to town and she had a little cardboard suitcase in her hand. "Let's go," she spoke to me.

The Fox house was down the old road on the way to Ferguson's Store. The county had built a new road on the other side of the valley, and the only people who ever used the old road, unpaved, were the people who lived nearby. We walked down the old road under the shade of the overgrown trees. Finally Grandmother said, "This is going to take me about an hour. I want you to wait out in the yard." Somehow what she said didn't sound like an invitation to ask questions.

The house where Mrs. Fox lived was a big, old, two-story house with a porch running most of the way around the downstairs. We went up on the porch and knocked on the door. Robert came to the door.

Grandmother spoke right up. "Is the coffin here yet?"

"Yes," Robert nodded. "Silas Smart made it. He just came with his wagon and put it on the back porch. Where do you want it?"

"I'll get it," she said. "Why don't you and Anita go down to the store and hang out there for an hour or so. That ought to be enough time for me. Oh, this is one of my grandsons," she pointed to me. "He's Lucille's older boy."

I nodded, but didn't say anything. Grandmother continued. "Do you happen to have a couple of tow sacks? If it's okay with you, I'm going to let him stay out in the yard. If he had a sack, he could pick up walnuts under that tree while I'm laying her out." The way she said "walnut" made it sound like it could be spelled "warnet."

Soon Grandmother had disappeared inside the house, Robert and his wife were gone, and I was sentenced to pick up walnuts and wonder what was going on.

It didn't take long until curiosity won out over calm, good sense. I had to know what "laying out" meant. The tow sack was left on the ground and I made my way quietly up to the big porch.

The closest windows were the living room ones. I could easily see inside. No one was in there. Around to the right was the kitchen. Most people lived in the kitchen, but, when I looked inside, no one was in there. There was only one choice left: the downstairs bedroom.

Creeping low down so that not much of me would show, I eased to the bedroom window. Grandmother could be heard softly singing to herself, "Come ye disconsolate, where 'ere ye languish," an old song from church.

When I looked into the room, the scene was clear. I was looking at Grandmother's back. She was standing, leaning, over the big double bed. I could see old Mrs. Fox's pale white feet toward the foot of the bed. I could see Mrs. Fox's long white hair streaming down off the side of the pillow at the head of the bed. Grandmother blocked the rest of Mrs. Fox, but I could see that she had a small pan of water with soap and a washcloth. She was bathing old dead Mrs. Fox.

While I watched, she patted her dry, and then began to brush and braid Mrs. Fox's long, white hair. Now I knew what "laying out" was. She was preparing old Mrs. Fox for her burial. I also knew that if I got caught looking, I might be next in line!

I started to leave, but when I did, I saw my own shadow move on the wall of the room straight in front of my Grandmother.

No one on the face of this earth ever picked up walnuts faster than I did in the next few minutes. When Grandmother came out on the porch of the house, I had two sacks almost full.

"I'm finished," she called to me. "I bet you wonder what I've been doing all this time."

"No ma'am," I lied. "I've just been thinking about walnuts."

She chuckled. "Well, leave the walnuts alone and come on up here. Let me show you before Robert and Anita come back." I followed her into the living room of the house.

There, in what most people called "the parlor," was a wooden coffin perched between two diningroom chairs. I wondered how my small Grandmother had gotten the coffin from the back porch into the front of the house. As we walked up, I wondered how she had done all of this. There in the coffin, not scary at all, but calm and beautiful and looking rested and at peace, was old Mrs. Fox, dressed in blue, her hair neatly braided, ready now for her funeral, all with the help of my own Grandmother.

"It was time for her to go," Grandmother softly said. "She has been so sick . . . she has had such a good, hard life. It was time for her to go."

We waited on the porch until Robert and his wife came home. "What do I owe you?" he asked Grandmother.

"I've already been paid," she answered. "My grandson paid me." I didn't understand this either.

But as Grandmother and I walked back up the road to her house, I knew that she was the most important person in the whole world.

People came to get my Granddaddy when they needed help putting up hay. People came to get Mr. Duckett when they needed a horse shod. People came to get my mother when their child needed help in school. But only my Grandmother was called on when someone they loved had died so she could "lay them out" to go "home."

Copyright 2009, Donald Davis, Storyteller, Inc. Used with permission.

Hatteras Jack (Based on True Events)

The passenger approached the captain of the sailing vessel. The ship had suddenly taken in sail and was making lazy, slow circles in the water.

"Excuse me, captain," the man said, "what are we doing?"

"We, sir, are waiting," replied the captain.

"Waiting for what?" the man asked.

"We, sir, are waiting for our pilot, who will guide us through the maze this channel becomes with almost every tide, and take us safe to harbor."

"Couldn't we challenge the way ourselves?" asked the man.

The captain turned an eye of disgust on the passenger only partially hidden by politeness. "Why would I risk my ship, crew, and even my passengers to unsafe waterways when the best, most reliable pilot I have ever worked with will take me through safely and with never a mistake? He should be here soon."

The passenger scanned the water around him. "Here soon? I don't see any boat bringing a pilot out to help steer us."

"He doesn't use a boat to come to us, because he does not get on board the ship." The captain turned to his first officer and said, "That would be a sight to see though, Old Jack at the wheel guiding us from my deck." The captain and first officer laughed.

"I don't understand why it's so funny," said the passenger, a bit embarrassed that he was the source of their joke.

"It's funny because Hatteras Jack isn't a man. We are waiting for a porpoise sir, we are waiting for a porpoise."

The passenger was too shocked to speak, but the captain went on, telling the story to the man's shocked silence.

"Jack showed up a few years ago when shipping started using this lane to get into Hatteras. At first we thought he was just a playful old harbor porpoise, but he would swim out in front of a ship, and if the captain didn't follow, old Jack would come back and do it again. Now some of us were willing to try anything. Before Jack came along, we had to creep along the waterway with a man with a chain calling off depths to make sure we didn't go aground. Once we started following Jack, well, we never needed to have a man with a chain again; and we could go as fast as Jack, and I'll tell you that is pretty fast. We have to stay right behind him. It seems that almost every other tide brings a new channel, and Jack always knows where it is. He never leads any ship aground. All these years, and no one who follows Jack has ever hit the bottom. Jack will even dive when he has a new ship to check their size, and he won't lead them on until the tide can handle them. Once we get to harbor, Hatteras Jack does a show for us. He dances on his tail and does barrel rolls and flips all the way out of the water and back in again in a perfect dive. The shipping lanes here would be lost without Jack. I would never even attempt to go through that channel without him."

Suddenly the captain stopped his story and turned to the first officer and said, "He's here; set some sail and let's follow Jack home." The passenger watched in amazement as a beautiful albino porpoise leapt from the water and turned in midair and started to swim in front of the ship. As the crew cheered, the passenger found himself cheering along. Old Hatteras Jack was on the job, and the sailors all knew, as their captain did, that they were in good hands.

North Carolina Glossary

Jack tales: Stories that feature a young boy named Jack, who appears as either a very clever boy or a wise fool, and sometimes a mix of both; traditional tales brought over by immigrants from Great Britain and now found throughout the southern mountains and as far north as upstate New York.

North Carolina: One of the states called Carolina. Both states were named in honor of King Charles I of England. Its capital is Raleigh.

Porpoise: A marine mammal known to have a brain that, in relation to its overall body size, is one of the largest of any mammal on earth. Numerous stories of how these remarkable creatures have saved drowning people and led ships safely to harbor are told around the globe.

Wild ponies: Small horses, descendants of Spanish horses, that still roam parts of North Carolina's Outer Banks to this day; they are well-known for their stamina.

Story Sources

American Folktales from the Collections of the Library of Congress, Volume 1

American Folktales from the Collections of the Library of Congress, Volume 2

American Myths & Legends, Volumes 1 & 2

Blackbeard's Cup & Stories of the Outer Banks

Buying the Wind

Donald Davis, Storyteller, Inc.

Folk Stories of the South

The Grandfather Tales

The Greenwood Library of American Folktales, Volume 2

Homespun: Tales from America's Favorite Storytellers

How Rabbit Tricked Otter & Other Cherokee Stories

The Jack Tales

Legends of the Outer Banks & Tar Heel Tidewater

Myths & Legends of Our Own Land, Volumes 1 & 2

North Carolina Legends

Outer Banks Mysteries & Seaside Stories

Southern Indian Myths & Legends

Tar Heel Ghosts

A Treasury of Southern Folklore

Why the Possum's Tail Is Bare & Other Classic Southern Stories

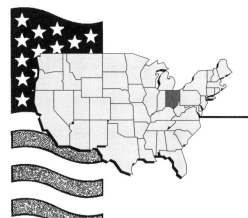

Ohio

Ohio was admitted into the union in 1803 as the seventeenth state. Before the European settlers arrived, this was the home of the Shawnee people, and one of their tales is found in this chapter.

Everyone likes a ghost story, and "The Cursed House" tells an Ohio legend to its scariest end. Real people often become legends, and so it was with Johnny Appleseed, who traveled the Ohio River Valley and planted his orchards throughout the region. The Ohio River is an important part of the state's history, and the clever tale of the flying boat is a fine example of river lore. We end the chapter with a tall tale about a hat out for a walk down one of Ohio's muddy roads.

Johnny Appleseed (Based on True Events)

John Chapman was born in Massachusetts. In 1774 he headed west to the Ohio River Valley. He came to Ohio with bags of apple seeds, and it was in Ohio that he got his famous nickname, Johnny Appleseed. Now most of the old stories talk about Johnny spreading out seeds as he walked along, but that is far from the truth. Johnny actually bought plots of ground and created nurseries that he fenced in to protect them from animals, and he left the nurseries in the care of nearby farmers, who sold the trees for a share of the profits. Every couple of years Johnny would return to work on the orchard and settle accounts with his managers. Unlike trees in most apple orchards, Johnny's trees were grown from seeds rather than by grafting. Johnny thought that the wild varieties produced from seeds were better than those grown through the practice of grafting and creating new types of apples. He got most of his seeds from cider mills that were eager to have more orchards that would eventually bring in more business.

Even in his day, Johnny's generosity was legend. He often left instructions with his managers that if someone was too poor to afford apple trees, that they should give them to that person on account, or for free. No one was to be denied the prospect of food.

In Ohio's Green Township, the Hunter family came under the shadow of hard times. The father and mother each died within two years of each other, leaving their family of nine children to be cared for by their oldest son David, who was only sixteen at the time. One day David met Johnny on the road, and the two sat down to share some lunch. Johnny asked David how they were getting along and if they had planted any apple trees as yet.

David Hunter replied that they didn't have the money to purchase any apple trees. Johnny smiled and told him not to worry about the price of the trees, he would give them fifty or sixty trees if they promised to plant them right away, since, according to Johnny, it was the best time of year for apple tree panting. That gift grew into an orchard of over 600 trees.

Johnny was also aware of the natural world around him, and he often lived off the land as he traveled. He was always mindful that he shared this world with other creatures; and he went out of his way to be respectful of animals, even insects. One story has him putting out a campfire one night because too many mosquitoes and moths were attracted to the flames and died in the fire. Other folks often turned out their old horses into the woods to die, but Johnny searched for these old timers and nursed them back to health. Then he would give them to people who would take care of them and use them in their elder years. He even mourned a rattlesnake that he accidentally killed after it had bitten him when he was mowing grass with a scythe. Johnny told his friends that the snake was only acting in the way nature had intended.

One part of Johnny's life that even the most outlandish folktale could not equal was the way he dressed. He often wore discarded burlap coffee bags with holes cut out for his arms and head. He hardly ever wore shoes, and the soles of his feet were thick with calluses. He went barefoot, even in the dead of winter.

As he grew older he often stayed with pioneer families when he traveled. These people thought him odd, but also saw the goodness in the man. Throughout the Ohio River Valley the Native Americans all thought that he was a holy man and respected him and his ways.

When Johnny died in Fort Wayne, Indiana, he left his sister over 1,200 acres of nurseries and apple orchards worth a fortune even in those days. But his real legacy, both in his own life and in the stories people tell about him, was the kindness he showed to everyone he met and the way he lived his life in his own way.

The Cursed House

The old farmhouse that belonged to a man named Herman stood near the town of Gallipolis, Ohio. Old Herman never paid any attention to his farm or the house. The roof leaked, and the paint on the side of the house had worn away years ago. His fields were always filled with more weeds than crops, and his neglected animals seemed to tend themselves. The old man never seemed to have much money; but he always seemed to have what he needed.

Many people said the old man had once been a thief or a pirate. He called his farm the Isle of Pines, the name of an island that had been used by pirates in the West Indies. The local preacher and his son William were the only visitors to old Herman's house. They knew that it was filled with strange pieces of art from faraway places and unusual weapons from far off lands.

As the preacher's son grew older, he became more and more curious about the old farmhouse. He was convinced that the old man had indeed been a pirate and was hiding a fortune in the old house. The old man often paid for his groceries in old, curious Spanish gold coins. The people of the town often joked about Herman's past, saying that he was a famous pirate, but to William it wasn't a joke. He believed that old Herman was a pirate sitting on a treasure of gold doubloons.

William tried to befriend the old man and learn his secrets, but the old hermit never told him anything about treasure or gold. When the old man died he took whatever secrets he had to his grave.

Now the preacher had been away when the old man died, so he knew nothing of his death. As he was returning home, he got caught in a terrible snowstorm and saw a light in the distance. After walking toward the light, he found himself on the front porch of old Herman's house. He knocked and knocked, but there was no answer. Finally, thinking there was somebody in the old house, he put his shoulder against the door, pushed it open, and walked in, calling out the old man's name. Still, no one answered.

The old man came around the corner and ignored the preacher. The preacher started to talk to the old man, but Herman just wandered around talking to himself and mumbling about this or that. He would walk up to a wall and tap on it and listen, then walk on to a cupboard and open it up and look inside. He seemed to be searching for something. The preacher asked if he could help the old man find what he was looking for, but he was ignored. Old Herman just kept walking around, looking here and there, and never even answered the preacher.

The preacher finally got tired of this bizarre behavior and went into the living room and started a fire. He pulled the old sofa close to the heat and curled up and went to sleep. He woke up to a cry of, "Finally, I found it. I found it."

The preacher ran into the next room, but all he saw was the old candleholder Herman had been carrying during his search and two handprints in the dirt and grime that covered the wall.

The preacher searched and searched, but there was no trace of his old friend. As soon as the storm quieted down, he resumed his journey home.

When he got home, he told his wife and son and his good friend who was a lawyer in town about the strange night. Imagine his shock when his wife told him that the old hermit had died.

William told his father that it was just a dream and pretended not to be interested in the ghostly story, but his eyes glowed at yet another clue to the treasure.

The lawyer said they should go back there and see what they could find of the ghost. The two of them invited William to go along, but he said he had better things to do in town that day.

The two men rode out to old Herman's house. When they got there, they saw the front door open wide. "I know that I shut it tight behind me last night," said the preacher. The men lit candles and moved silently through the old run-down house. Each step they took creaked loudly, echoing from room to room. In the thick dust and dirt on the floor they saw the footprints that the clergyman had made the night before—and a new set of prints right alongside.

"I think there's someone here," said the lawyer. Then the two men heard an unearthly scream, and they rushed to the room where the preacher had seen the two handprints. The door was locked, but they finally broke it down. On the far side of the room they saw that the wall had been torn down. Hundreds of gold coins had spilled out. Lying in front of the wall was William, covered in gold coins. When the father pulled his son into his arms he found him cold and dead, his face a mask of horror.

Most folks say that William saw more than he bargained for that night. Perhaps he saw the blood of all the victims of the pirates who gathered the gold. Maybe he just saw old Herman.

The Flying Boat

Captains often talk about the mates they had during the time they were masters of a ship. Riverboat captains are no exception when they talk about their majestic boats. The *Gordon C. Greene* out of Cincinnati was a packet boat that plied the Ohio River and beyond for many years. Bill Cropper was her first mate and perhaps one of the most famous mates ever to work the rivers. Captain Tom always said he was a lucky man to have Bill as his mate, for Bill had a mind that could work out a solution to any problem.

Once, near Marietta, Ohio, the boat got stuck on a sandbar. Now this was not an unusual situation. The river could change overnight as the water deposited sand here and took it away there, making the river a constantly changing landscape of water, sandbars, hidden logs, and debris. This particular time Bill tried just about every trick there was to getting her off the sandbar and into deeper water. Men tried poles to push her off, but she didn't budge. They tried rocking her free, but stuck she stayed. They used hoses to try to wash the mud and sand loose, but it didn't make any difference. The *Gordon C. Greene* stayed stuck on that bar.

Bill just stood there as the crew tried each and every known method of getting the boat free. One man said that they'd have to wait for high water to float her off. At that, Bill got angry, and when Bill got angry, things started to happen. The lower deck of the boat was loaded with crates filled with turkeys—hundreds of turkeys going to market. Bill had the men go below and bring the turkeys out on deck. He ordered them to tie a rope around the feet of the turkeys, and then the carpenter to fit wooden staples into the deck. The men attached the ropes to the staples. Then Bill had all his deck hands grab towels and sheets and position themselves around the boat. At his signal, all the rousters started to flap their towels and sheets over their heads, yelling as loud as they could. The startled turkeys tried to fly off, but they couldn't go too far for the ropes kept them attached to the boat. The turkeys kept trying though, and with all those turkeys flapping their wings and straining at those ropes, it lifted that boat right off that sandbar and over into deep water.

Yes, Bill Cropper was the best mate on the river. He always could find a solution to every problem.

The Star Sisters (Shawnee)

A long time ago a young Shawnee warrior named Waupee, which meant White Hawk, lived alone in the forest. He was a skilled hunter, and the woods were full of animals and birds, so each day he came back to his home with food.

One day Waupee walked farther than he had ever walked before. He came to a forest that was more open—he could see for miles. Then he came to a prairie where the tall grasses swayed in the breeze. Since there were no paths on the plains, Waupee just wandered through the tall grass, wondering at the size of the prairie. He came to a place where the grass was worn down to the ground and the earth was hard packed in a circle, as if feet had walked around hundreds of times. What Waupee noticed was that there were no trails leading to or from the circle. He could not find a footprint or a bent leaf of grass or a broken stem or the slightest hint that anyone had passed this way.

The young warrior decided to hide himself, watch the circle, and see what all this meant. He had not been hiding long when he heard the faint sounds of music floating all around him. Looking up into the sky, he saw a small speck that seemed to grow by the minute as it approached the earth. As it came closer, the music grew louder and sweeter, and seemed to fill the air around the circle and the prairie that surrounded it. As the speck in the sky grew larger and larger, Waupee could see that it was a huge basket. Inside the basket were twelve young women, whom he took to be sisters. They were beautiful and their laughter seemed to challenge the music in its beauty. He watched as they leapt from the basket and began dancing around the circle, striking a shiny ball as if it were a drum. Waupee was taken by their grace and beauty, especially the youngest. After watching the dancers for a long time, he finally jumped up and tried to grab hold of the youngest dancer. As soon as he appeared, the sisters all jumped into their basket and were drawn up into the sky.

The young warrior watched as they disappeared into the sky. He felt bad that he had startled them into leaving. He thought he would never see them again.

The next day he came back but this time disguised himself as a possum. He heard the music and he saw the basket descend. The sisters jumped out of the basket and started to dance and sing. The music and dancing was even more beautiful than it had been the day before. The young man crept closer. When the sisters saw him, they could see past his disguise, so they jumped into their basket and began to rise into the sky, stopping just out of his reach. "Perhaps he has come to show us how mortals play this game?" said the oldest sister.

"No," cried the youngest. "We should leave as soon as we can." The basket rose into the sky and was soon out of sight.

The next day Waupee came to the circle again. This time he noticed some mice playing near an old stump. He thought that they looked so harmless that maybe he should disguise himself as one of them this time. He moved the stump closer to the circle and changed his shape into that of a mouse. He sat on the stump and looked up toward the heavens for the basket. Soon he heard the music and then the basket came to rest near the circle. The sisters leapt from the basket and began to dance around the circle, even more lovely than the day before. Waupee watched as they danced, sang, and laughed. Suddenly one of the sisters noticed the stump and remarked how it had not been there before when they had visited. They hit the stump with a stick and twelve mice ran out. The sisters killed all but one. The youngest sister ran after the twelfth mouse, which was Waupee, trying to hit it with a stick. Just as she was coming down with the stick, the young warrior changed back to his human form and grabbed her in his arms. Her sisters jumped into the basket and were quickly drawn into the sky and disappeared.

Waupee used all his charms to calm the young girl's fears. He told her stories of his people. He took her for walks in the woods and showed her the beauty of his land. Soon she came to love him and appreciate her new home. Waupee and the sky maiden married and had a son. Though she loved her family, the sky maiden still yearned for the beauty of her own home. She was the daughter of one of the stars, and the earth was beginning to look plain against the memories of her sky home.

Once, while Waupee was gone on a hunting trip, she made a basket that could carry herself and her young son. She began to collect food and things of beauty to take to her father in the sky. She remembered the charm and how she could rise up again into the sky. She took the basket and the things she had collected, and with her son went to the circle in the prairie. She sang her song and began to rise into the sky. Waupee heard the song and ran to the circle, but the basket was already being drawn upward. He begged and cried, but soon it was a speck and then it disappeared. The warrior bent his head and for the first time knew loneliness.

All winter and summer he mourned the loss of his family. During his time of mourning, his wife had returned to the stars and in the beauty and peacefulness there had almost forgotten about Waupee. Her only reminder was her son who, as he grew, asked about his father and wanted to visit the land of his birth.

One day her father said to her, "Daughter, take your son and visit your husband. Ask him to come back with you and live her among the stars. Tell him to bring a bit of each of the animals and birds that he kills when he hunts."

So she and her son made the journey to earth. Waupee, who never strayed far from the circle, heard her voice and came to embrace them as they stepped from the basket. After hearing the message her father had sent, he agreed to come and live in the sky with them. He began to collect parts of the many animals and birds that he hunted. He took a wing from this one and a hoof from that one and a paw from another, and collected them in the basket. When he had collected a bit of each of these creatures, they went to the basket and soon were climbing back to the stars.

When they came to the starry plains, the Star Chief had a great feast for them. At the feast the Star Chief said that each of his people could take one of the pieces of the many animals or birds that Waupee had brought with him to the sky. As they chose, a strange magic took hold. Those that chose a hoof were changed into hoofed animals, and they ran off; those that chose a wing became birds and flew off; those that chose a paw became that animal and padded off; and so it was with each of the star people. Waupee chose a white hawk's feather, and his wife and son chose the same. They spread their wings, and they flew down to earth, where their descendants can still be found today.

Used with the permission of the Ridgetop Shawnee Tribe.

The Sunken Traveler

Roads in the early days of America were often little more than dirt paths that wound their way through the wilderness. When the rains came in the spring, they became almost impassable, and more like swamps than roads. Often travelers actually waded roads like they would a river, coming to places where the mud and water were up to the bellies of their horses.

One day during the rainy season, a man was traveling through Ohio. The roads were very muddy and the journey had been long and hard on both man and horse. As he and his horse picked their way down the muddy road from one safe spot to the next, he saw a beaver top hat lying in the middle of the road. Now beaver hats were expensive and prized in those days, especially by gentlemen. Suddenly the traveler saw that the hat was slowly moving forward on top of the mud. Now the man became frightened, thinking that perhaps a spirit was haunting the hat or that some demon was lurking in the mud to lure him and his horse into the mire and their doom. As he watched the hat make its way slowly down the muddy road, the man decided there had to be a reason. He reached over with his riding cane and knocked the hat over. Immediately a voice reproached him.

"What do you think you're doing, knocking my hat off my head?"

The traveler could see that under the hat there was a head, and it was looking right at him. "Sir," he asked, "do you need some help?"

"Thank you for asking, but I am perfectly fine," said the slow-moving head. "I'm just up to my neck in mud."

"I'll throw you a line and help you out of that horrible slime," replied the traveler.

"Never mind," replied the man in the mud once more. "I'll admit I'm in a rather tight spot, but I've got a good horse underneath me and we are slowly and steadily making our way forward. He's a strong horse and has carried me through worse times than this, and besides he can hold his breath for a long time. Good day to you, sir."

The head, part of a body that was seated on a horse, slowly moved forward.

Ohio Glossary

John Chapman: A man also known as Johnny Appleseed. He traveled all over the Ohio River Valley planting orchards and selling trees. His adventures have literally become legends, and it is difficult to separate the fact from the story.

Ohio: A state whose name comes from the Iroquois word meaning beautiful or great river. The capital is Columbus.

Sandbar: A shifting mound of sand, often underwater, that poses a danger to boats traveling down or up rivers.

Shawnee people: A Native American tribe that spoke the Algonquian dialect. They were one of the few tribes that had a tradition of female chiefs.

Story Sources

American Folktales from the Collections of the Library of Congress, Volume 1

American Folktales from the Collections of the Library of Congress, Volume 2

American Myths & Legends, Volumes 1 & 2

Buckeye Legends: Folktales & Lore from Ohio

The Greenwood Library of American Folktales, Volume 1

Johnny Appleseed: Man & Myth

Myths & Legends of Our Own Land, Volumes 1 & 2

Ridgetop Shawnee Tribe

Sand in the Bag

Songs of the Great Lakes

Tall Tale America

A Treasury of American Folklore: Our Legends, Customs & Beliefs

Yankee Doodle's Cousins

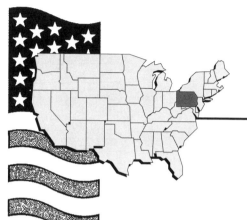

Pennsylvania

Pennsylvania was one of the original thirteen colonies, and Philadelphia was one of the major centers of both colonial America and the new country of the United States. Pennsylvania became a state in 1787, the second state to join the Union. "The Fishing Cow" is an example of the wonderful tall tales from Pennsylvania. "The Avondale Mine Disaster" is a ballad that tells the story of a true event and shows the importance mining had in early Pennsylvania life. "The Last Party at Printz Hall" is a ghost story about a fiddle player and a ghostly dance. Pittsburgh's greatest folk hero, Joe Magarac, represents the steel industry here, while the Pennsylvania Dutch gave us the story "The Rabbit and the Bear." The traditional folktale "Hoop Snakes" is from the telling of Pennsylvania native and storyteller Alan Irvine. Before the settlers came to Pennsylvania it was home to several native tribes, including the Lenape and the Iroquois.

The Fishing Cow

There was an abandoned old mill at Peck's Pond. The pond itself was pretty wild and had an unusual number of pikes. Now a pike is a strong and fierce fish. It'll eat just about anything that moves near the water. Frogs, turtles, bugs, and even young ducks were a big part of its diet.

Now old Hipe Rake started to fish that pond and found that it was a gold mine. He would take his fish to town and sell them for a pretty penny. His business grew fast, and Hipe knew that he could make a load of money, but for that he would need an assistant. He was losing a customer here and there because he couldn't supply them all, and this put old Hipe in a real dilemma. You see the fish had to be sold quickly, so Hipe could never fish two days in a row. But Hipe was also a bit stingy, and the thought of sharing his newfound wealth with another didn't sit well with him at all. But one day all his problems were solved.

Hipe had an old cow that loved to follow him around his small farm. One day she followed him down to the pond and grazed on the green grass that grew all around the water. By noon it was getting hot and the flies were bothering her, so that cow just waded into the water and nibbled at some plants, swiping at the flies with her long tail. Now when she swiped at those flies her tail would skim the water. All of a sudden one of those pike leapt out of the water and grabbed her tail. The cow just swung her tail around, and that pike flew through the air and landed on the shore. One after another of those pike grabbed her tail and found themselves on the shore. That cow used that tail of hers like a combination fishing line and whip. Once those fish caught hold of her tail, she just whipped them around and they flew off and landed in a pile on the grass. Hipe was amazed and pretty happy. He had found his new partner.

Well after Hipe's discovery he hardly had to work at all. He would just lead that cow down to the water every day and then take the fish she caught into town to sell. He made a nice living watching from the shade of a tree as his cow fished in old Peck's Pond.

The Avondale Mine Disaster

This ballad tells the true story of the first great coal mining disaster that happened in Pennsylvania, in 1869. One hundred and ten men and boys were killed.

Good people all, both great and small I pray you lend an ear,
And listen with attention while the truth I do declare.
When you hear this lamentation it will cause you all to weep and wail
About the great disaster in the mines of Avondale.

On the sixteenth day of September, eighteen sixty nine,
Those miners got their call to work down in the mines.
But little did they think that death would soon prevail
Before they would return from the mines of Avondale.

The women and the children, their hearts were filled with joy
To see their men go off to work, likewise their sons and boys.
But a dismal sight in broad daylight soon made them all turn pale
When they saw the breaker burning over the mines of Avondale.

From here and there and everywhere they gathered in a crowd,
Some tearing at their clothes and hair and crying long and loud.
Get them out our men and sons for death is in the mines to steal
Their lives away without delay in the mines of Avondale.

But all in vain there was no hope one single soul to save
For there's no other way to escape from that deep and dangerous cave.
No pen can write the awful fright and the horror that prevailed
Among those dying victims in the mines of Avondale.

A consultation was then held that asked who'd volunteer
To climb down that awful shaft and find their comrades dear.
Two Welshman brave without dismay and courage without fail
Went down the shaft without delay down the mines of Avondale.

When at the bottom they arrived and thought to make their way
One of them died for want of air while the other in great dismay
He gave the sign to bring him up to tell the dreadful tale
That all were lost forever in the mines of Avondale.

The Last Party at Printz Hall

Old Quaker Quidd was sitting at a table at the tavern finishing his meal when young Peter Matthews walked into the room. The young man looked over and a smile slowly spread across his face as he sauntered over to Quidd's table.

"Well now Quaker, what are you doing having your meal here at the inn?" asked young Matthews in a loud voice that everyone in the room could hear. "Oh, that's right, you're just a little bit scared to be staying at your house these days, aren't you? Ghosts got you a bit unsettled, do they? Afraid to sleep in your own bed, that's what I hear."

Quaker Quidd looked up from his plate and stared hard at the young man. "I do believe you may be right, Matthews. But I have a proposition for you. I'll give you five dollars a week to be my caretaker at Printz Hall. You can clean up the grounds, do some maintenance, and you can even live there. What do you say, want the job?" Quaker Quidd was the one smiling now. The young man knew that the older man had just turned the tables on him. If he declined folks would say he was scared of the ghosts. If he took it he'd have to spend the night there, and the young fiddler was quick to tease but he also wasn't keen on facing down a real ghost.

Peter accepted the offer and many a head nodded in the tavern that night. Bets were placed on how long he would be able to live in the old place. Printz Hall stood on a lonely patch of ground outside Chester, Pennsylvania, and was surrounded by a weed-infested garden. The old hall itself was dark and gloomy.

Peter arrived the next day and found a room on the second floor that he could set up for himself. He covered some of the missing panes of glass and lit a couple candles, and the room seemed to brighten up considerably. He started a fire in the fireplace and ate his supper. He thought he'd start working the next day on clearing out some of the weeds that had taken over almost every inch of the garden.

After he'd eaten he took out his fiddle, rosined his bow, and began to play a nice dance tune he had recently learned. Rather than make him happier, the music just seemed to drift through the empty house and sound lost and dull as it swept from room to room, making Peter feel more and more lonely. Sometimes he swore that the tree branch that beat against the shutters was keeping time or that the wind whistling through the cracked and broken panes of glass was trying to sing to the fiddle's tune. After a couple more tunes Peter put away his fiddle, bolted the door, and rolled out his sleeping blanket. He stirred the fire in the grate and then blew out the candle and fell asleep.

Young Matthews didn't know how long he slept, but when he woke he was wide awake. He listened as the house moaned and creaked and seemed to come to life. Then Peter heard a sound outside his room, the sound of heavy footsteps walking down the hall toward his door. Peter knew he had bolted the door, but suddenly it flew open and standing there in the doorway was a tall figure, dark and forbidding, dressed in a dark suit and cloak, a tricornered hat on his head and a long sword on his hip. Peter wanted to run but he found he could not move; he tried to yell but he found he had no voice. He just sat there holding his blankets around his chin, shaking with fear. The grim spirit leaned over Peter and spoke in a deep, rumbling voice, "I am Peter Printz, the governor-general of his Swedish Majesty's American colonies, builder of this house and master of all I see. Tonight my young friend is All Hallow's Eve and my friends will meet here for a party. We will sing and dance the night away until dawn. Pick up your fiddle and follow me, but hear me well, young fiddler: You play for us this night, but you may not speak, not even one word."

The last thing that Peter Matthews wanted to do was follow the long-dead Swedish governor, but it seemed as if his legs were no longer under his control. He followed the dark giant through the hall and down the steps. They walked through a long hall whose walls were covered with portraits of people long dead and gone. The halls echoed with the sound of Printz's heavy boots. They finally came to the old main hall, and when they opened the doors Peter saw that the room was dazzling in the light of hundreds of candles. The floor looked freshly polished, and the paintings and curtains were clean and spotless as if they'd been hung the day before. The room was full of people dressed in clothes that had not been worn in these parts for over a hundred years. They stood laughing and talking, walking from group to group, smiling and enjoying each other's company. When the old governor and Peter walked into the room, all conversation stopped and they all turned and stared at the young man. The governor pointed to a chair in the corner and said, "Sit down, boy, and start playing."

Peter sat in the corner, took out his fiddle and bow, and started to play a jig. All at once the company of guests broke up into couples and started to dance, laughing and twirling around the room. Soon the warmth of the fire began to take its effect on the young man as he played faster and faster. He could not remember a time he had ever played better in his whole life. The dancers whirled and leapt so high into the air that Peter almost lost his place in the song. Faster and faster they danced, laughing all the while. It almost seemed as if a storm had come up in the room and was blowing the ghostly dancers around like an autumn wind blows the fallen leaves.

Suddenly Peter Printz stood in the middle of the dance floor and called for quiet. "You have played well this night, young fiddler, and you shall be paid well for your talent." Two servants brought in a huge chest and placed it next to the governor-general. They opened the lid, and young Matthews saw that the chest was filled with gold coins.

"Give me your fiddle case," he ordered Peter. The young man watched as the ghost filled his case with gold coins. Peter was so overwhelmed at the fortune being placed into his fiddle case that he suddenly forgot what Prinyz had told him and blurted out, "I thank you my lord, I truly do."

As soon as he spoke the room grew dark and the otherworldly laughter that shook the room scared young Peter to his bones. He fell to the ground as if he were dead himself. He awoke the next morning to the same room, but now it was different from the night before. The floor was covered with grime and dirt, and mold grew thick on the walls. The pictures were almost black with age, and the wind blew through the broken panes of glass. Peter looked down at his feet and saw that his fiddle had been smashed into a hundred pieces, and when he opened his fiddle case to look for his night's fee it was filled with dust and old spider webs. Peter ran from the house and kept running until he came to his own home and locked the door tightly behind him. He sat in a chair and thought about his strange adventure. It was not one night later that the old mansion went up in flames, and if anyone asked the young fiddle player how it started he would tell them exactly where old Peter Printz had found the coals to start the fire.

Joe Magarac: The Steel Man

Joe Magarac was a steel man in every sense of the word. They say he was born in the heart of the rich iron ore mountains and had waited for centuries until he was found by a miner, who told him about all the things that were made out of steel in Pittsburgh. When Joe heard about the steel mills he knew that it was the place for him and he headed to Pittsburgh.

Joe took to the work in the mills like a duck takes to water. He worked twenty-four hours a day, only taking a break for meals. At first the other steel men teased Joe about his name. "Magarac?" they laughed. "That means jack ass in the old country tongue."

"Well," said Joe, "I work as hard as any mule, so I guess that suits me just fine."

Joe worked the steel like a true artist. He would gather all the raw ore, the scrap iron, and the limestone blocks and dump them into the furnace. He then would blow on the flames until they were white hot. When everything had melted down he would sit in the doorway of the furnace and with his long, powerful arm he would stir the molten mixture around and around. Most men couldn't get close to a furnace, but Joe just opened the doors to old Number Seven and sat down in front of blasting heat as if it was nothing more than a warm summer's day. He never even worked up a sweat.

As soon as the steel was just right he would pour it into molds. Then as the metal started to cool off a bit, Joe would take it into his enormous hands and squeeze it between his fingers. Through each of the spaces between his fingers out came a perfect steel rail for the train tracks or a steel beam for a new building. The company couldn't sell steel as fast as Joe made it.

Steel workers from all over the country came to watch Joe as he worked. Some companies even sent men to Pittsburgh to challenge Joe in a contest of who could make the best and most steel. Once he had a contest with a man from Gary, Indiana. The two of them worked side-by-side making steel night and day for three days. When they finally stopped, Joe was 3,000 tons ahead of the Gary steel man. That was a close race for Joe!

Now there are two stories about the end of Joe Magarac. The first is that he produced so much steel that they had to close Furnace Number 7 for a week to give the salesmen time to sell all the steel. When they returned they couldn't find Joe. Finally they looked into Furnace 7 and there he was, cooking in a huge ladle filled with molten steel. He had been cooking for a week. He looked at his friends and the bosses and said, "I just couldn't stand not working, so I decided to melt myself down. Now when I'm all gone I want you to make me into steel beams and build a new building right here." Some folks say that's just what they did, and that Joe's spirit is still there in the pure steel beams that surround Furnace Number 7.

Others say that the bosses came to Joe and said that he worked so hard and so many hours that there wasn't enough work for the other men. These men had families to support, and the steel company bosses would have to lay them off unless Joe could cut back a bit. Joe could see that the work needed to be divided up so everyone could have their fair share.

"But I don't know what to do if I'm not working," said the giant steel man.

"What did you do before you came here, Joe?" they asked.

"Well, I was in mine just resting for the day when I came here," replied Joe.

"Well why not take a little rest again?" said his fellow workers.

"Good idea," said Joe. "I haven't had a rest in almost twenty years. I think I'll just find a nice secluded spot and take a nap."

And some folks say that's just what Joe did; someday when we need his tireless strength, he'll come back to us and start to make steel again.

The Rabbit and the Bear (Pennsylvania Dutch)

Once there was a rabbit who lived with her children in a warren in the earth. Her nest was safe from outsiders, but when she left to get food she always told her children to make sure that they saw the paws of whoever came to the door. They were never to let anyone in that didn't have white paws like hers.

When she returned she would always call out, "I'm back with leaves and milk for you."

The children would always cry out, "Show us your paws." She'd laugh and show them her white paws and they would let her in.

Now Bear was hungry, and he knew that there was a warren of plump little rabbits in a hidden nest in the thicket. He hid himself and watched and waited. He saw the mother leave and then saw her return and he heard the exchange. The next day when she left he waited for a little while, then he crept close to the rabbit's home.

"I'm back with leaves and milk for you," he called out.

"Show us your paw," sang the little rabbits.

When Bear showed them his huge black paw the little rabbits refused to let him in. "Our mother's paw is white like the snow," they cried.

Bear ran to the mill and covered his paw with flour and then ran back to the little rabbits' nest.

"I'm back with leaves and milk for you," he called out.

"Show us your paw," they asked.

When Bear showed them his now white paw they opened the door. He rushed in and swallowed them all. Bear settled down after his meal and waited.

Mother Rabbit came to the door of their home and called out, "I'm back with leaves and milk for you."

But instead of the sweet voices of her own children she heard Bear's rough voice growl out, "I'm going to eat you just like I ate your children."

Rabbit turned and ran as fast as she could. Bear knew he could never catch her, so he ambled back into the rabbit's nest and took a nap.

Rabbit ran until she met Dog and told him the story of how Bear had eaten her children. She and Dog ran and told Cat, then they all went and told Goat. Then Rabbit, Dog, Cat, and Goat went to the nest where the Wasps lived and they told them about Bear's evil deed.

More and more mammals, insects, and birds joined Rabbit and her friends. They all walked back to her nest. The Wasps went in first and began biting and stinging Bear. Bear tried to hit them with his paw, but they were so fast they were only a blur, and he turned and screamed at each bite they took out of him. Bear ran out of the nest, and when he came outside all the animals began to bite and claw and hit Bear. Dog bit his leg, while Cat scratched his eyes, and Goat put down his head and ran right into Bear's backside. They pushed and shoved and threw him down the hill.

Bear stopped at the bottom of the hill, and he wasn't moving. Mother Rabbit took a knife and slit his stomach wide open and out popped her little ones. Rabbit and her children and all her friends went back to the warren and celebrated their victory.

Hoop Snakes (as Told by Alan Irvine)

When the first settlers pushed into the mountains of Pennsylvania, they faced all sorts of dangers. They faced fires and floods, blizzards and droughts, Indian raids and frontier bandits, and wild animals like wolves, bears, and mountain lions. But the gravest danger of all was the dreaded Hoop Snake.

Hoop Snakes were not like any snake they had ever seen before. Hoop Snakes were bright blue and gold in color. They grew to be a foot thick and up to ten feet in length. Instead of fangs to bite with, Hoop Snakes had a stinger on the end of their tales that could be a foot long and was filled with a dark, vile, nasty, purple poison so strong that a single drop could burn a hole through a limestone boulder. Just a whiff of that poison was enough to knock out a black bear for a week. And that was not even the dangerous part.

What made Hoop Snakes so dangerous was the way they went about hunting. They liked to slither along the tops of the mountain ridges, looking down into the valley below. When they spotted a nice, tasty snack—a moose, a bear, a pioneer—the Hoop Snakes would line themselves up directly above their prey. Then a Hoop Snake would flip over onto its back and bend in the middle, lifting its head on one side and its tail on the other until it could take its tail in its mouth, making a perfect circle, like the hoop of a wagon wheel. Then the Hoop Snake would give a little twist and start to roll down hill, picking up speed as it did, rolling faster and faster. If you've ever gone down a hill on a bicycle or roller blades, then you know just how fast you can get moving. These Hoop Snakes could roll so fast that nothing could outrun them. If a Hoop Snake came for someone, they were dead, for sure.

In fact, there is only one man who ever survived a Hoop Snake attack. His name was Jimmy Johnson, and he had a cabin near Loyalhanna Creek, just a mile or so from the town of Ligonier. One summer afternoon Jimmy was in his cornfield, which ran up the side of a ridge, hoeing the weeds out from around the corn, when a shower of pebbles came rolling down over his boots. Jimmy looked up to see what was going on and saw the biggest Hoop Snake he had ever laid eyes on coming down the hill toward him! The hoop alone was ten feet across, and moving fast. Jimmy began to panic; there was nowhere to run. He could not go to the right nor the left; the corn was in the way, and it would not do any good to run downhill since that was the same direction the snake was moving. Then the snake hit a rock, bounced up in the air, and snapped out as straight as an Indian spear, with its stinger coming straight for Jimmy's heart! Without thinking, Jimmy grabbed his hoe, steadied the handle on his shoulder a second, then gave a swing!

It's too bad they did not have baseball back in those days, for Jimmy Johnson could have had a great career in the major leagues. He hit that snake dead on, so hard it knocked that handle right out of his hands, and then Jimmy took off running. He was running so hard, it took him a full hour to remember to breathe, and even longer for him to think to look down and discover that he was, to his surprise, still alive!

At that, Jimmy began wondering what had happened to that Hoop Snake. He turned and made his way back to his cornfield. When he arrived, he was greeted with the strangest sight he had ever seen. That snake had struck that handle so hard that its stinger was stuck fast in the wood of the handle, and the snake was trapped. Jimmy was able to take his hunting knife, cut off the stinger, cut off the head, skin that snake, and have snake stew to eat for a week. And that was not even the strange part!

The strangest part was what had happened to that handle. If you've ever been stung by a bee or wasp, you know how your skin swells up. That swelling comes from a tiny drop of poison that is really not all that strong. But that snake had been stuck with its tail in that handle all afternoon long, pumping that dark, nasty, vile, purple poison into the wood until every drop had gone into that handle. And the wood of that handle had swollen up, and swollen up, and swollen up until that hoe handle was ten feet across!

Jimmy could not believe his eyes! He did not know what to make of it. A hoe with a handle that big around was no use as a hoe any more. He sure could not use it in the garden. In the end, the only thing Jimmy could think to do was to roll that handle down the ridge to the place where he was building his cabin. He got out his saw and cut it up into boards. It made a pile of boards ten feet tall, and that was enough boards that Jimmy was finally able to put a roof on his cabin and move in at last.

Jimmy lived in his cabin, nice and safe, warm and dry, until October. Then came one of those wet autumn days when it rains all day and all night. When Jimmy woke up in the morning, the rain was already pouring down, washing down over the boards of his roof, down the walls of the cabin, through the farmyard, and down the hill to Loyalhanna Creek below. It was all Jimmy could do to dash out to the barn to do the most important chores, then dash back to the cabin. It continued to rain like that all day long and into the evening as well. When night came, Jimmy lay in his bed with the blankets over him, listening to the rain washing down over his roof and down the hillside to the creek below. Listening to that, he was glad to be inside: nice and safe, warm and dry. Listening to the rain, Jimmy drifted off to sleep.

About two hours later, however, Jimmy woke up. He was soaking wet and freezing cold. When he opened his eyes, there was no roof above him, just the rain pouring in!

"What happened to my roof?" Jimmy cried.

And then he figured it out. All that rain washing over those boards all day and all night long had eventually succeeded in washing every drop of poison out of those boards. And with the poison gone, those boards had shrunk down, and shrunk down, and shrunk down to their original size, and there was nothing left of Jimmy Johnson's roof but a pile of little toothpicks.

And that's the truth!

© Alan Irvine. Used with permission.

Pennsylvania Glossary

Iroquois: A league of several tribes that met in a great council to decide policy that would affect all its members. Often tribes are referred to as Iroquois when they were part of this league.

Pennsylvania: A state named after Admiral William Penn, father of the founder of Pennsylvania, William Penn. It means Penn's woodland. The capital is Harrisburg.

Pennsylvania Dutch: Descendants of German immigrants who came to Pennsylvania in the eighteenth century. In some communities it refers to Amish or Mennonite people.

Quaker: Members of the Society of Friends, a religious group that promotes peace and peaceful solutions and a simple, less ritualistic approach to worship. Also called "Friends."

Steel mill: A building where raw iron ore is melted down and turned into steel. The ore is melted in the furnaces at extremely high temperatures.

Story Sources

Alan Irvine

American Folktales from the Collections of the Library of Congress, Volume 1

American Folktales from the Collections of the Library of Congress, Volume 2

American Myths & Legends, Volumes 1 & 2

Black Rock: Mining Folklore of the Pennsylvania Dutch

Buying the Wind

Flatlanders & Ridge-Runners: Folktales of the Mountains of Northern

The Greenwood Library of American Folktales, Volume 1

Legends & Lore of Western Pennsylvania

Myths & Legends of Our Own Land, Volumes 1 & 2

Pennsylvania

Pennsylvania Songs & Legends

Snake Bite: Lives & Legends of Central Pennsylvania

Stockings of Buttermilk

Upstate Downstate

Rhode Island

Rhode Island—officially named Rhode Island and Providence Plantations—was one of the thirteen original colonies. It was the last of the colonies to ratify the Constitution, officially becoming a state in 1790. An Atlantic coastal state, it is the smallest state in the union, covering only 1,214 square miles and measuring forty-eight miles north to south and thirty-seven miles east to west at its extreme points. The Narragansett, a Native American tribe, lived on the lands of Rhode Island when the first Europeans arrived.

The rugged and often dangerous life lived by many along the Atlantic coast is reflected in both "The Lighthouse Keeper," the true story of one woman's lonely vigil and remarkable courage, and "The Ghost Ship," the tale of a phantom ship and the mad woman who haunts it. Like stories of the sea, frightening and often eye-opening tales of witch hunts and creatures who consort with dark powers abound in New England. "The Devil in Red Flannel" is one of these and is truly unique to the area. Finally, in the story of Timothy Crumb, "The Grumpy Man," we meet a fellow who, try though he may, just can't keep himself from being a grump.

The Lighthouse Keeper (a True Story)

The two young soldiers had hoped to get across the bay, but a storm came up and swamped their boat. They clung to the half-submerged boat yelling for help, as the storm grew more intense by the minute. Suddenly from shore they saw a boat coming toward them rowed by the keeper of the Lime Rock Lighthouse. The keeper hauled the two aboard the little rowboat and struggled to turn it around in the storm and head back to the lighthouse. When they reached the lighthouse, the two soldiers were astonished to find out that their rescuer was a woman. It was not the first time that Ida Lewis had braved a storm to save a life in her career as the keeper of the Lime Rock Lighthouse.

One winter she defied the cold to crawl over the frozen water with a rope to save two men who had fallen through the ice. On another occasion, two men were transporting a prize sheep, and when the animal got out of control and jumped overboard, they capsized their boat trying to get it back. Ida rowed out and saved the two men, and then went back and saved their sheep.

Ida Lewis was born Idawalley Zorada Lewis in 1842 in Newport, Rhode Island. Her father was the lighthouse keeper ,and after his death her mother took over. After her mother retired, Ida kept up the family tradition. She was the keeper of the lighthouse for thirty-two years, until her death in 1911. She enjoyed the solitude of the lighthouse. When word of her heroism spread and folks came to interview her, or others just came to see the famous lighthouse lady, she was seldom to be found.

Ida saved more than twenty lives during the years she lived at that lighthouse. She was awarded the Gold Life Saving Medal by the United States Coast Guard for her dedication and willingness to put herself in danger to save the lives of others. Years later, the lighthouse was named after her, the only time such an honor was awarded a keeper of a lighthouse.

The Ghost Ship

The ship appears during storms. Sometimes it seems as if it's on fire. Other times, there is a mad woman at the wheel steering the doomed vessel. *The Palatine*, the name of the spectral ship, usually appears between Christmas and New Year's Day, haunting the Rhode Island coast with sails on fire and unearthly wails and screams. That is the legend. What actually happened is almost as strange.

The ship *Princess Augusta* was bringing German Palatine immigrants to America. These immigrants were seeking religious freedom in the New World. On Christmas morning in 1738, the ship was anchored a few miles off the Rhode Island coast. As the ship prepared to continue her voyage, a winter gale rose up and battered her, running her aground on Block Island. At first the acting captain refused to abandon ship, but eventually he allowed the passengers and his crew to be rescued and brought ashore. The *Princess Augusta* broke free and was destroyed on the rocks.

Aboard the ill-fated ship were 150 survivors of the original 340 passengers. During the voyage a fever had raced through the ship, killing passengers and crew alike, including the captain. After the passengers and crew were looked after, they resumed their journey on land for their new homes in Philadelphia.

Now the legend is something completely different. One story found on Block Island is that the people who lived there were kind and took the sick passengers and crew into their homes and nursed them until they were well enough to continue their journey. The story that's told by people off the island is that the islanders lured the ship with false signal lights that caused it to run aground. Once it was helpless, the islanders looted it and stole whatever was valuable. In some versions of the tale they even murdered the crew and passengers. To hide their crime, they burned the ship, but there was one passenger left hiding on the ship, mad with the fever that had taken the lives of so many. When the ship was set on fire, she ran to the wheel screaming, trying to steer the ship.

In 1867 the poet James Greenleaf Whittier used the second version for the basis of his poem "The Wreck of the Palatine." To this day, most people refer to the ship as *The Palatine*.

What is the ship that visits Block Island at night in December with its fiery sails? Is it the *Princess Augusta*, coming to take revenge on the folks on Block Island for the murder of her crew and passengers? Is it the mad woman who is still trying to steer the ship ashore and find some peace? Is it the souls of the passengers and crew who died of the fever still trying to make it to the New World? We'll never know.

The Devil in Red Flannel

There once lived a farmer, Benny, and his wife, Debby, who tended to their work from morning to night, worked hard, minded their own business, and were good neighbors to everyone they met. Because they worked so hard on their farm they thrived and grew richer all the time. They grew so rich and prosperous that the townspeople, at least those who were lazy and spent their time gossiping, said that they had made a pact with the devil, and that Old Nick was helping them to greener crops and fatter sheep.

Now there was one little sheep that Debby loved more than all the others. A white, woolly creeper sheep it was, with short legs and long snowy wool. In the morning she combed it, at noon she fed it, and at night she tucked it away to sleep in a pen she and Benny had built on the back porch. She even put pretty ribbons around it on Sundays and played with it as if it were a dog. That sheep followed her around the garden and the farm, always just a few feet behind her like a faithful old hound. When the townspeople saw this, they were sure that Debby was a witch and that sheep was her familiar.

"Some witches love cats," they sneered, "but this one loves a creeper sheep."

One day, early in March, when the sun was shining bright, the sheep went to graze in the meadow, nuzzling and jostling each other for young grass. Soon a great, wild snowstorm arose. It snowed so thick and blew so hard that you couldn't see in front of your eyes. Benny rushed out, gathered the sheep, and drove them into the shelter.

The next morning, when Debby went to look for her favorite sheep, it was nowhere in the flock. She ran out into the fields, into the meadows, but she saw only snow and ice. She cried and she wept, but all her crying and weeping did not bring her favorite sheep back.

Benny, her husband, promised her three nice new baby creeper sheep, but she only wanted her own sheep back again.

So the days passed, while the wind blew cold, and the earth was covered with snow.

One day, like every day and for the thousandth time, Debby and Benny went out looking for the sheep. They looked and they looked, but there was no sheep in that white world of snow and ice. They were on their way home, walking across a meadow, when they saw a tiny breathing hole, the kind of hole often made by an animal's warm breath when it is buried under snow and ice.

"Oh Benny, we have to dig here. I know that it's my sheep," cried Debby.

They chopped the snow and ice, and there was Debby's little creeper sheep, shivering, quaking, bleating, and blowing sadly, and . . . its long white wool completely gone. The poor sheep had been under the snow and ice six long days, and having no other food, had eaten its own white wool.

Debby carried the half-frozen little sheep back home in her arms, fed it warm milk and bread, and covered it with a warm blanket. Every day the little sheep grew stronger.

The sun shone warmer, the ice and snow melted away, and all the sheep played in God's sunshine looking for young grass. But the little creeper sheep did not go out. Without its woolly coat, it was just too cold outside for the little creature to be outside very long. It bleated and cried all the time. Debby thought and thought about it until she had a good idea.

"I'll make a jacket for you so you can go out with the rest of the sheep. This will keep you warm as toast until your wool grows back again." she said. The little sheep crooked its head to one side as if it knew just what she was saying.

Debby took an old red flannel petticoat and cut and sewed. Soon she had a nice little jacket fitting the creeper sheep, covering it all over except for its four legs and black little snout.

"It'll look funny on you, my little friend," she said, "but it'll be nice and warm, and you can be in the sunshine and play with the other sheep."

Well, the sheep was a sight! If you had traveled up and down the length of America and maybe Europe, you couldn't have seen a funnier sight. But the little animal didn't mind it a bit. It ran and played in the sun, nuzzled the other sheep, ate all the green grass it could find, and was warm as a feather bed in its red flannel jacket.

One day Hester, the town's worst gossip, passed by Debby and Benny's farmhouse. No sooner did she see the strange creature, four hairy legs and a black hairy snout sticking out of the red flannel jacket, than she ran quaking and screaming "The Devil's dressed in red flannel, and it's in Debby and Benny's farmyard."

By the time she came to the village all tuckered out from the running, the story had become even more detailed. She told one and all that the Devil was dressed in red flannel and was dancing with Debby in the meadow, singing a song with fire flashing in his eyes and flame from his mouth.

The townspeople took sticks and stones, scythes and brooms, and even old flintlock guns, and ran to burn the two witches and drive the Devil in red flannel out of their county. They had always known that Debby and Benny were in league with the Devil, and now they had proof. They'd burn them and drive Old Nick out of their village. So they ran through the woods and fields, the Mayor in front, a big hammer in his hands. They came to Debby's home. It was noon by then, and she and her husband were eating bean soup and bread. The sheep was in the kitchen, too, munching on a crust of old bread.

"Come out, you witch, and bring the Devil in red flannel, too!" a hundred voices screamed.

Debby and Benny came to the door to see what was wrong. They saw the crowd, fury in their eyes and clubs in their hands.

"What's eating you now?" Debby asked, for, having done no wrong, she wasn't afraid of anyone.

"You're a witch," they screamed at her. "The Devil is with you on your farm, but we'll put an end to both of you. Hester saw the two of you dancing in the meadow with flames and smoke coming out of Old Nick's eyes and mouth, and him wearing red flannel."

"Oh, so that's it," snapped Debby at them. "She saw me, did she? Evil does as evil thinks. You're a pack of silly fools. I'll show you the Devil in red flannel!"

She pulled out the sheep that stood behind her, by the ear. "Here is the Devil of whom you are frightened, you blind fools!" she cried. "It's my poor sheep that lost its wool. I made a jacket for it from an old red flannel petticoat so it wouldn't freeze." And she and her husband started to laugh and the more they laughed, the louder their laughter got.

Well, the people of the town surely felt silly. They told Debby and Benny how ashamed they were, and they silently went back to their homes. Even old Hester, who had started the whole silly rumor, apologized, and seemed a bit sheepish, which was the right way to feel after all.

From then on no one ever called Debby or any other woman in the village or surrounding farms a witch, for they always remembered the sheep in red flannel that they thought was a Devil.

The Grumpy Man

A long time ago in Rhode Island there was a young man named Timothy Crumb, but everyone called him Grumpy Tim. They called him Grumpy Tim because nothing satisfied him and he always thought that everything he did was wrong. His favorite phrase was, "Just my luck." The more often he said it, the more he believed it and the more things went wrong. That's the way it works; when you think things will go wrong they almost always do go wrong.

He was working for Squire Chample, whose house and farm were near the Chipauxet River. He worked on the Squire's farm every day except Sunday, when he went to church. It was at church that he first saw Sally Brown, the preacher's pretty daughter. It wasn't long before Tim liked Sally and was pretty sure that she liked him, too. The problem was that he was so grumpy all the time. He was always complaining about this or that so loud that most folks were pretty sure that most of Rhode Island knew about Grumpy Tim's complaints.

One day he walked up to Sally and asked her if he could pick her up the next Sunday and walk her to church.

"I'll be waiting on my front porch, Tim," replied Sally. "But could you please try to bring a smile with you and not a frown?"

"I'll try, Sally," said Tim. "I'll try really hard because it's you that's asking me. Really Sally, I'd be smiling all the time, but everything just seems to go wrong all the time."

"Hard luck never follows people who are cheerful. Remember that."

"I'll, try Sally," said Tim. "I really will try."

Sunday came and it was a beautiful day. Tim got up extra early and had a big breakfast, did some grumbling to Squire Chample and the other farm hands, and then went down to the creek to bathe so he'd be clean when he picked up Sally.

First thing he did was to take off his bright red shirt and hang it on the branches of a berry bush. Next he took off his shoes and put them under the bush. He then thought about the creek and how the water might be pretty cold that time of year, so he walked down to the creek in his stocking feet to test the water. He was too busy swatting at flies and gnats to see the flowers or hear the birds singing. He was too bothered by all the stones he was stepping on to see the butterflies or smell the scent of the sweet shrubs that he was passing by. He didn't see Old Wrinkle either, eating his fill of grass in the meadow that the creek flowed through. Old Wrinkle was the preacher's bull, and they called him that because when he was mad he wrinkled his forehead just like a person.

Now Old Wrinkle saw Tim's shirt hanging off that berry bush, and he did what most bulls do when they see something red flapping in the wind: he charged right at it. He tore that shirt down and began to trample and stomp on it.

Tim turned just in time to see Wrinkle begin to trample his shirt. "Just my luck," said Tim.

Now this was Tim's best going to church shirt, and he just started to run toward that bull without thinking. When Old Wrinkle saw Tim running toward him he forgot about the shirt and started running after Tim. Now Grumpy Tim was no coward, but he did think quickly and saw that the bull outweighed him by at least a thousand pounds and the fight would be too short to remember, so he started running back to the creek. He ran as fast as he could through the water in his stocking feet, shouting at the top of his lungs, "Just my luck!"

When he got near the old swamp oak that grew next to the creek he grabbed a low-hanging branch and swung himself up into the tree. Old Wrinkle stomped and shook under that tree, looking up at Tim with an evil eye.

"Just my luck," moaned Tim. "I'm stuck in this tree when I should be picking up Sally."

Then Tim looked up and saw a hornet's nest. It was just about the same time that the hornets noticed Tim. Grumpy Tim's eyes opened wide as those hornets dove down and started to sting him. He lost his grip on the branch and fell out of the tree and right onto the back of Old Wrinkle. Tim took hold of the bull by the horns just as the first swarm of hornets hit the face of Wrinkle. When those hornets stung the soft nose of that bull he went wild and started charging across the pasture. As Tim held on for dear life he screamed, "Just my luck!"

Old Wrinkle snorted and bucked and ran wildly through the pasture as the hornets attacked him and Grumpy Tim. That animal ran until he came to the rail fence that surrounded the pasture and went through that fence like it wasn't even there. Neither Tim nor the bull had time to admire Sally Brown's flower garden as the bull plowed most of it up as he headed for the barn. Sally was sitting on the front porch in her Sunday best, watching in horror and amazement as Old Wrinkle and Grumpy Tim rounded the corner and came into view. Wrinkle was determined to make it into the barn and hide from those hornets, and the bull ran straight for the barn door. Unfortunately for Tim that door was closed. As the bull hit the door, Tim sailed through the air and landed on the preacher's front porch right on top of Sally.

The sight that Preacher Brown saw when he came out of his house was a half-dressed young Tim Crumb and his daughter lying on the ground. The preacher began to bellow as loud as old Wrinkle and started to chase Tim. But before he took more than two steps, Tim was on his feet and running down the road as fast as he could, yelling at the top of his voice, "Just my luck!"

Tim disappeared from the area and wasn't seen in those parts again. Some folks say they saw him in Connecticut; others say he moved west to Indiana or beyond. I'm pretty sure that Grumpy Tim is still running as fast as his legs can carry him in his stocking feet, with no shirt and a lot of hornet stings all over his body, but let's face it, that's just his luck!

Rhode Island Glossary

Creeper sheep: A sheep that eats the wild vines or creepers that are often found in woods or rocky outcroppings.

Flannel: A soft, warm cotton cloth usually used for winter clothing.

James Greenleaf Whittier: A Quaker and early American poet.

Lighthouse: A tower or high building fitted at the top with a light, magnified by mirrors to increase its power. This light was used to warn ships of rocks, shoals, reefs, or any treacherous water along the shore and also was a beacon that guided ships back to land. The lighthouse keeper usually lived at the lighthouse, either in a portion of the tower or in an adjacent house. Most lighthouses are now automated.

Narragansett people: Native Americans living for generations, before the arrival of Europeans, in areas of what is now Rhode Island. The Narragansett were well known as warriors. They usually had two homes: a winter village, where they lived in longhouses, each of which held as many as twenty people, and a smaller summer home, where they lived in birch bark wigwams built usually along the seashore.

Old Nick: A nickname for the devil.

Palatine Germans: People of the West Franconia area of the Rhine Valley in Germany. Palatine Germans have a highly distinctive accent that sets them apart from other Germans.

Rhode Island: A state whose name comes from the Dutch "Roodt Eylandt," meaning Red Island; its capital is Providence.

Story Sources

American Folktales from the Collections of the Library of Congress, Volume 1

American Folktales from the Collections of the Library of Congress, Volume 2

American Myths & Legends, Volumes 1 & 2

The Greenwood Library of American Folktales, Volume 1

Jonathan Draws the Long Bow

Legends of the New England Coast

Myths & Legends of Our Own Land, Volumes 1 & 2

New England Bean-Pot

New England Legends & Folklore

Spirit of the New England Tribes: Indian History & Folklore

A Treasury of New England Folklore

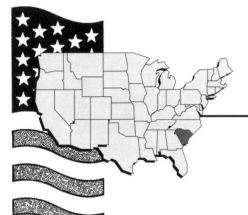

South Carolina

Before it was settled by the British, South Carolina was home to Native American peoples, including the Catawba. It was one of the thirteen original colonies that fought for independence from Great Britain. One of the heroes of that fight was known as "The Swamp Fox," a man whose incredible story is represented here in the story by that title.

"Flying Africans" and "Elija's Remarkable Gift of Prophecy" are part of the African American heritage, both coming from the days of slavery, and each revealing an important aspect of the human will to not only survive but overcome. Another story, "The Mule That Could Talk," is found in both the European and African American traditions, a gentle reminder of the fact that human intelligence is not the only intelligence.

The Swamp Fox (a True Story)

As the British soldiers marched down the road, they looked from side to side nervously, alert at every sound and movement in the trees. They were moving prisoners and delivering supplies to the British army in Charleston. They were worried about the American militia that roamed these parts of Carolina. These men seemed to appear out of nowhere and struck with such speed that stories had already grown around them and their leader, Francis Marion, the Swamp Fox. The nickname had been given to him by Lt. Colonel Banastre Tarleton, who had chased the elusive Marion for over seven hours, covering over twenty-five miles before finally giving up.

Suddenly the British soldiers heard the sound of hoofbeats and the shouts of men. Before they knew what had happened, the Swamp Fox and his small militia had surrounded them. The supplies were captured and the prisoners freed.

This was the kind of fight that Francis Marion waged against the mighty army of England during the Revolutionary War. Francis Marion was born in 1732 in Berkeley County, South Carolina, on his family's plantation. At age twenty-five he volunteered to fight for the army in the French and Indian War. After watching the Cherokee use the natural landscape to hide and ambush, then escape, he began using the same tactics during the Revolutionary War. His band of men were not paid or supplied by the new Continental Congress. They brought their own arms and horses with them, and they lived off the land or the supplies they took from the British.

In the South Carolina of 1780 it looked bad for the American cause. The British had defeated the American army and were in control of the cities as well as much of the countryside. Marion used the swamps and forests to conceal his men and make daring raids on the British. His first success freed 150 American prisoners.

Francis Marion had a network of spies that provided him with all the information he needed to keep the pressure on the English. Since he used speed and concealment, the enemy never knew where he would strike next. The British had to divide their army, which weakened their defensive positions. After every raid, the Swamp Fox and his men would simply melt into the countryside, hiding in the swamps and lowlands.

One famous painting of the Swamp Fox and his men depicts a scene from a favorite story about their exploits. A British officer was meeting with the group to arrange a prisoner exchange. Marion offered him breakfast, sweet potatoes roasted in a fire. The officer remarked that this was a poor meal and probably didn't happen often. Marion replied that in fact this was a good meal, that he and his men often had little to eat unless they took it from the English; and that they were not paid for their loyalty. When the officer returned to Georgetown, he resigned his commission. He could not fight against men who held such high ideals.

After the war Francis Marion retired from public life, but not before advocating amnesty for all the Loyalists, Americans who had served the British during the war. He died on February 27, 1795.

Flying Africans (African American)

There was a time when birds flew through the air and the Africans flew among them. After awhile the people forgot why they had been blessed with this gift and they lost it. There remained, here and there, hidden in the sea islands and in out-of-the-way places in the low country, some who had kept their faith and their wisdom and still had the power to fly. They hid among those who could not fly, and no one could tell them from their neighbors.

Now many Africans were sent to live their lives on plantations in the New World, and among them were those who still had the power to fly. On one of the plantations on the sea islands there was a cruel master who worked his slaves until they died in the fields. When one died, he brought another to take his or her place, and continued killing them with overwork in the burning summer sun.

One day, when all his slaves were dead of overwork, the master bought a company of native Africans who had just been brought into the country. He put them to work in his cotton field at once.

He drove them hard. He sent them to work at sunrise, and they did not stop until dark. They were driven cruelly all day long—men, women, and children. There was no pause for rest during the heat of the midsummer noon, though there was shade nearby. But through the hardest hours, when fair plantations gave their slaves rest, this man's overseer pushed the work along without a moment's stop for breath, until all grew weak with heat and thirst.

Among the slaves was a young woman who had recently had a child. It was her first baby, and she had not fully recovered from the birthing. She should not have been sent to the field until her strength had come back, but there she was with her child straddling her hip, as the other women carried their babies.

The newborn cried, and the young mother spoke in her native tongue to quiet it. Then she went back to chopping the tall grass. Finally, being very weak and sick with the great heat, she stumbled, slipped, and fell.

The driver struck her with his whip until she rose and staggered on, protecting her baby from the blows of the cruel man.

She spoke to an old man near her, the oldest man of them all, tall and strong, with a forked beard. He replied. Because they talked in their own language, the overseer could not understand what they said.

She returned to work, but in a little while she fell again. Once again the driver lashed her until she got to her feet. Again, she spoke to the old man, but he said: "Not yet, daughter, not yet." So she went on working, though she could barely stand.

Soon she stumbled and fell again. But when the driver came running with his lash to drive her on with her work, she turned to the old man and asked, "Is it time yet, father?" He answered, "Yes, daughter, the time has come. Go, and peace be with you!"

The elder stretched out his arms toward her, and with that she leapt straight up into the air and was gone like a bird, flying over field and wood.

The driver and overseer ran after her as far as the edge of the field. But she was gone, high over their heads, over the fence, and over the top of the woods, gone, with her baby on her hip, laughing as they flew through the air.

The driver hurried the rest to make up for her loss. Now the sun was very hot indeed. So hot that soon a man fell down. The overseer himself lashed him to his feet. As he got up from where he had fallen, the old man called to him in an unknown tongue. And when he had spoken, the man turned and laughed at the overseer, and leapt up into the air, and was gone, like a gull, flying over field and wood.

Soon another man fell. The driver lashed him. He turned to the old man. The old man cried out to him, and stretched out his arms as he had done for the other two and he, like them, leapt up, and was gone through the air, flying like a bird over field and wood.

Then the master cried to them both, "Beat the old devil! He is the one who has the magic! Stop him."

The overseer and the driver ran at the old man with their whips ready. The master ran too, with a large branch he had picked up from the ground, to beat the life out of the old man who had caused those slaves to fly away.

But the old man laughed in their faces, and in a loud voice he called to all the slaves in the fields, new and old alike. As he called to them, their memories flooded into their minds, and they remembered their old ways and their old power. One by one the slaves stood up, and shouting as one they jumped into the air and began to fly away like a great flock of birds toward the horizon. The old man flew behind them like a great mother hen moving her flock away as they all laughed and sang. The children and the men and women smiled, and the cares of their slavery seemed to fall away from them as they soared through the sky, free once again.

The master, the overseer, and the driver watched them in wonder and fear as they disappeared into the heavens, never to be seen again.

Where did they go? Who was the old man? Did the cruel slavers mend their ways?

Those questions are left unanswered. The only important thing is that they were free.

The Mule That Could Talk (African and European American)

Once there was a farmer who had a mule. Now this mule had always appeared pretty normal to the farmer and his family. And for almost the mule's whole life he had worked every day of the week except Sunday. It was a day of rest for both the farmer and the mule. One Sunday the man was called over to help a friend who had had an accident on his farm. The farmer sent his young son into the barn to saddle up the mule.

The boy took down the saddle blanket and pushed on the side of the mule and said, "Come on boy, let's move over."

"Do I have to work on Sunday now too?" said the mule.

The boy dropped the blanket and ran out of the barn as fast as he could. He went straight to his father. "Have you finished saddling the mule?" asked the farmer.

"The mule said he doesn't want to work on Sundays," replied the boy.

Now the father thought his son was telling a tall story to get out of working. He went down to the barn with his son, picked up the bridle, and moved toward the mule.

"Did you bring me anything to eat?" asked the mule. The man dropped the bridle and ran out of the barn, his son right behind him. They stopped right outside the barn and the man said, "I can't believe it. I've never heard a mule talk before."

"Neither have I," said one of the barn cats.

The farmer and his son ran as fast as they could for the house and went in, slamming the door behind them.

"What's wrong with you two?" the farmer's wife asked.

"The mule talked," they said together, "and then the cat said 'neither have I'."

"Well, that is the most ridiculous thing I have ever heard," said the farmer's wife.

"Me, too," said the dog. "Everybody knows a cat can't talk."

It was a long time before that family ever stopped running.

Elija's Remarkable Gift of Prophecy
(African American)

Elija was a butler in the big house. He was a clever man, clever enough not to let too many folks know how clever he really was. But sometimes life just gets the better of you.

Elija became very fond of one of the cooks. Now in those days, the cookhouse was separate from the big house. Every morning Elija would pass by that cookhouse and stop in to say hello to the cook ands pass a few minutes in conversation. While they talked, he always took a look at what was cooking in the pots on the big wood-burning stove.

One day as he was passing the master of the house, he decided to impress him and said, "Sir, I know what you are going to have for breakfast. "

"Really, Elija, and what am I having today?"

"Eggs, hominy, ham, biscuits, and coffee," said Elija confidently. "You see I have the gift of prophecy."

The owner of the plantation walked on by, amused at his butler's newfound gift.

Later that week, Elija spoke to the owner and said, "Sir, I know what you're going to have for supper tonight. You are going to have fish and green beans and cornbread."

"Well, Elija, you were right about my breakfast a few days ago. We'll see how you do with this meal."

That evening the master of the house was called to supper; on the table were fish, green beans, and cornbread. A few days later he was talking with another plantation owner and told him about Elija's extraordinary gift of prophecy.

"You don't really believe that he can tell the future, do you?" asked his neighbor.

"I do," said the man, "and I'll put up $500 in a wager to prove it to you."

The wager was accepted, and the two men agreed on the sum of $500 each. The neighbor kept the money, and said, "I'll keep all the money until I test your butler."

Elija's owner went back and told him about the wager and how he had bet $500 on Elija's "gift." "Now Elija, Mr. Williams from the next plantation will call you over sometime this week to test you. Don't disappoint me."

Elija was worried to death. He couldn't tell the boss that he had lied to him or that he couldn't tell the future at all, because then his master would lose his bet and would really be angry. But how could he go over to Mr. Williams's place and be tested? Eliza got so worked up over this predicament that he became ill. The boss sent for a doctor, but he couldn't find a thing wrong with the old butler.

Finally at the end of the week, Mr. Williams sent for Elija. Elija walked very slowly down the road toward the Williams's plantation.

In the meantime, Mr. Williams had taken a possum that he used to train hunting dogs from its cage and placed it underneath a tub. He was going to see if Elija could tell him through his gift of prophecy what animal was under the tub.

When Elija arrived Mr. Williams met him and took him around back to the tub. "Now Elija, let's see if you can predict the future and tell me things that are hidden or not. Under this tub I have put an animal. Tell me what it is."

Elija was scared. His whole body felt like it was going to shake itself apart at the seams. He looked at the tub, then he gazed up into the sky, then he closed his eyes. The tub was too small for a hunting dog. The he heard Mr. Williams's dogs barking. They were penned up. Elija knew that meant that the animal under the tub was one that would attract the dogs. That eliminated chickens and ducks and even cats, because those animals roamed all over the farm. The dogs would see them all the time and wouldn't be that curious or anxious to chase them. Now Elija knew that Mr. Williams, like the other plantation owners, used certain animals to train the dogs. Those animals would drive the dogs crazy. Most of the farmers used raccoons and possums, but which one was it? He figured that raccoons were a bit more aggressive, and they might not like being put under a tub; but a possum was more docile and would just curl up and play dead. Elija made his choice.

"Mr. Williams, I believe you have a possum under that tub."

Williams lifted up the tub and there was a possum curled up "dead" asleep. "You've won the bet, Elija. I do believe you have a gift."

"I do, Mr. Williams, I do," cried Elija. "I can even tell you about Judgment Day. I can tell you about the day you are going to meet your Maker."

Mr. Williams turned pale and said, "That's enough, Elija. Don't say another word. Here, take this money and give it to your boss."

When Elija gave his boss the money, he said, "I told him that a possum was under the tub, and it was. I told him I could even tell him about Judgment Day. I can even tell you the day you're going to die too, sir."

His owner took a step back and said, "Enough, Elija. Don't say another word. I don't want you using your gift anymore, you understand me?"

From that day on Elija was treated with a certain respect he had not had before from the big house. If he wanted something a little special, all he had to do was lift a finger and point up to heaven and wink, and he usually got it.

South Carolina Glossary

Big house: The home of a plantation owner and his family.

Catawba people: Native Americans who settled much of South Carolina. Among the Catawba, both men and women took leadership roles, and there were several prominent female chiefs in their history. When Europeans first arrived, the Catawba lived in wooden framed, bark-sided houses and often had a large round meeting house and a field for sports. Both men and women wore tribal tattoos.

Gift of prophecy: The ability to predict the future correctly.

Plantations: Very large farms in the South that usually were worked by slaves, many of whom picked cotton, the primary money crop of the South.

Slavery: The practice of taking away people's freedom, considering them to be property, and holding them in bondage, usually to work for little or no compensation. The slave period in this country was an evil time, as is illustrated in the story "Flying Africans." Slaves were not only bought and sold, but members of slave families were often separated from each other, husbands and wives from one another and parents from their children, never to be reunited. The work was hard, conditions were harsh, and beatings were not uncommon. The stories that come from this period in America's history often reveal the conditions under which slaves lived, but they also often reflect the humor and resiliency of African Americans who outwit their owners, as Elija did with his "remarkable gift of prophecy."

South Carolina: One of the Carolinas, states named in honor of King Charles I of England; its capital is Columbia.

Story Sources

American Folktales from the Collections of the Library of Congress, Volume 1

American Folktales from the Collections of the Library of Congress, Volume 2

American Myths & Legends, Volumes 1 & 2

The Book of Negro Folklore

The Doctor to the Dead: Grotesque Legends & Folk Tales of Old Charleston

Folk Stories of the South

The Greenwood Library of American Folktales, Volume 2

The Legend of the Lowcountry Liar

Myths & Legends of Our Own Land, Volumes 1 & 2

The People Could Fly: American Black Folktales

Southern Indian Myths & Legends

Tales of the South Carolina Low Country

A Treasury of Southern Folklore

Tennessee

In 1796 Tennessee became the sixteenth state to join the union, but things could have been different if John Sevier and his friends had had anything to say about it. The story of the state of Franklin is a true tale from Tennessee history. We couldn't tell the stories about Tennessee without including one about the state's most famous son, Davy Crockett. Though he was a real person who served as a congressman for Tennessee and died at the Alamo, this story might just be a tall tale—you decide.

Races between horses and steamboats were common in the old days, but the story "The Race" might be about two of the most unlikely contestants. Mike Fink was a keelboat man, but the story "Higgins and the Bear" gives us another keelboat hero from Tennessee by the name of Jim Higgins. "The Bell Witch," included here, might be America's most famous witch story of all time.

Davy Crockett and the Raccoon

One day Davy Crockett was walking home. He had been out hunting all day, but he hadn't seen one animal worth shooting, and he was in a bad mood. He hated to return home without something to show for his day in the woods.

As he passed an old oak tree, he looked up and saw a big fat raccoon curled up on a branch, quiet as a church mouse and trying as hard as it could not to be seen by Davy.

Crockett brought his gun, "Old Betsy," to his shoulder and was just about to fire when that raccoon raised his paw and spoke.

"Sir, are you Davy Crockett, the most feared hunter in all of Tennessee?" asked the raccoon.

"I am Crockett," replied Davy, flattered by the way the raccoon spoke about him.

The raccoon looked sad and said, "Well sir, please wait a minute while I climb on down from this tree. Don't trouble yourself about shooting me off this branch."

The raccoon slowly climbed down and stood right in front of the great hunter. He looked sad and resigned to his fate as just another raccoon shot by the great Davy Crockett. Davy was moved by the way the raccoon just sat there, his eyes closed, waiting for the final moment.

"Well little friend, you are a true and thoughtful gentleman; I'm not going to shoot you after all," said Davy.

"Really?" replied the raccoon.

"Yes sir," said Davy. "Any animal that shows that kind of respect deserves some of it back."

The raccoon started to back away from Crockett toward the edge of the woods. "Thank you, Mr. Crockett. That is very kind of you, sir." The raccoon kept inching his way backward.

"Wait a minute, friend," said Davy, "where are you going in such a hurry?"

"It's not that I don't trust you, sir, but sometimes a man's hunger takes hold of his kind deeds." With those words the raccoon ran as fast as he could into the woods and left Davy Crockett standing there laughing at the clever animal that had just outfoxed him.

John Sevier and the Lost State of Franklin (a True Story)

John Sevier was a brilliant and daring character. The frontiersmen recognized the qualities they admired in this natural born leader, and they nicknamed him "Nollichucky Jack." Back in Sevier's day the whole of Tennessee then belonged to North Carolina, but the settlers on the far side of the mountains were so far removed from the seat of government that, practically, they were without government. Sevier and his friends conceived the idea of organizing a new state. The new state was named Franklin, in honor of Benjamin Franklin, the Philadelphia philosopher, statesman, and patriot.

Of course the state of North Carolina did not recognize this new state. In fact, they decided that the frontier people were leading a rebellion against them. For four years North Carolina tried to end the separatist movement. "Nolichucky Jack," the governor of the new state of Franklin, was arrested for "high treason against the state of North Carolina" and taken to Morganton for trial.

The prisoner's chivalric and gallant military services and the extraordinary nature of the indictment gave the trial a great deal of publicity. As the trial neared, the village streets became crowded with politicians, old soldiers, and settlers from far and near, eager to catch a glimpse of the court and the renegade governor of Franklin. The frontier people, or Franks as they were called, who had risked their lives to find a home in the new state of Franklin, had followed their hero across the mountains. They were determined to "rescue him, or leave their bones."

On the day of the trial, two of the Franks left their companions concealed near the town. Hiding reliable sidearms under their hunting shirts, they rode up before the courthouse. One of the men was riding on "Governor," Sevier's fine race mare. He dismounted, and with the rein carelessly thrown over her neck, stood with the manner of an indifferent spectator. His companion, having tied his horse properly, went into the courtroom. Sevier's attention, by a slight gesture, was directed to the man outside.

During a pause in the trial, Sevier's rescuer stepped up to the bar, and with a firm voice addressed the judge: "Are you done with that man yet?" The scene was so unusual, the manner and tone of the speaker so firm and dramatic, that both officers and audience were thrown into confusion. Sevier sprang like a fox from his cage. One leap took him to the door; two more and he was on his racer's back. The quick clash of hoofs gave notice of his escape. The silence of the bewildered court was broken by the exclamation of a bystander: "Yes, I'm sure you are done with him."

With a wild shout, Sevier's supporters joined him, and they all rode safely back to Franklin. No one followed, and no attempt was made to rearrest him.

The state of Franklin died from various causes, but a few years later the new state of Tennessee honored "Nolichucky Jack" with the first governorship. Later he was elected to the U.S. Senate.

The Race (Based on True Events)

It was bound to happen. And finally, one summer day, it did. The train came into Cairo, Illinois, from the east with a few hundred passengers. Most of the passengers were on their way to Memphis, planning to continue their journey on the train, but when they saw that majestic riverboat sitting at the dock near the train station, they sent word to see if there was a chance that they could book passage. The captain, who only had a few passengers, told them that he had room for as many as wanted to ride down the river on his boat. In fact, he told them all that he would get them to Memphis faster than the train, or their passage would be free.

"That's impossible," said the railroad agent.

"Really?" replied the captain. "I am sure that my boat can beat that train into Memphis."

The railroad agent tried to make a bet with the riverboat captain, but the captain said he had already put a great deal of money on the trip by promising to refund his passengers their fare if he lost. But the race was on. Word spread throughout Cairo and started down river faster than either the train or riverboat could ever hope to travel.

As the passengers started to come aboard the boat, the captain and his mate greeted them. One elderly lady stopped and looked worriedly at the captain. "They say that many men have drowned in this river. Is that true, captain?"

The captain smiled and replied, "My dear lady, you should not believe everything you hear about this great river. I assure you that I have never yet met a man who had been drowned in the Mississippi." The woman looked relieved and walked past the captain and his mate as they winked at each other over her head.

The next day the time for each departure was set, and the boat heaved into the mighty Mississippi just as the train left the station. The riverboat took a bit longer to settle down, but as the train roared out of the tunnel on the Kentucky side, they were side by side. Since the tracks ran parallel to the river, the passengers of both could see each other as the race went on. The train and the boat both poured on the steam. It must have been a sight as that huge boat went flying down the river. People stood on the banks and shouted encouragement to the captain and his crew as they steamed ahead. The ducks and geese were caught off guard as the boat moved fast through the water, catching the fowl as they were eating. Birds went flying in every direction. Looking over the side, passengers swore that even the catfish were scurrying to get out of the way, looking back at the boat angrily with their big round eyes. The old riverboat must have knocked a lot of fish senseless, because there were dozens of small skiffs in the water picking up fish in her wake.

It was neck and neck for an hour or two, but then very slowly the riverboat started to pull away from the train. The conductor made all the passengers stay in their seats and closed every window to stop the drag, but inch by inch the boat still crept past the train. As the two giants roared into Memphis, crowds waited for them. The riverboat beat the train by a quarter of a mile and won the contest. Not one passenger complained, and they gladly let the captain keep their fares. They all knew it was the ride of a lifetime.

Later that day, members of the city council of Memphis came to the dock with a set of horns, the prize that had always been given to winners of races on the river. The captain and his crew proudly mounted the antlers outside the windows of the pilothouse. The great days of the river may have ended long before that race, but there was still some pride in the old riverboats, and they wouldn't give up their crowns as the queens of the mighty Mississippi without a fight.

Higgins and the Bear

Jim Higgins was almost as famous a keelboat man as Mike Fink, and his adventures were just as colorful. Jim had just taken a boat full of flour down to Memphis when he decided to tie his keelboat up along the Mississippi and do some bear hunting in the forests of Tennessee. Higgins treed a huge bear, the biggest ever seen in those parts, and he began to shake that tree to dislodge the bear right out of those branches. He shook it until the teeth in that poor bear's mouth started to rattle and chatter. He shook it some more, until the bones of that poor creature started to tremble. Soon that huge beast just fell from the tree. Higgins and the bear began to wrestle, until the bear finally gave up and Higgins brought him on board his keelboat as meek as a lamb. Jim secured the bear to the anchor chain.

Over the next few days Higgins began to notice that every time he played his fiddle, the bear started to sway with the music. Higgins had an idea. He slowly began to teach the bear to dance. Many an hour after that, the two of them sat on the deck of the keelboat, Higgins playing his fiddle and the enormous beast dancing to the tunes.

The two of them were starting to become good friends. The bear seemed to like the fiddle, and Higgins enjoyed the company, especially company that enjoyed his fiddle playing. One day as Jim fiddled and the bear was learning a new step, they heard a sound that stopped them in the middle of their fun. It was horrible and loud, and it seemed to startle the whole world. In fact, it was the first steamboat on the Mississippi—and it was coming straight at them. The big boat was chasing every creature that lived in the old river before it—fish and alligators, and even a few dead logs. The bear had never heard anything like it, so when he saw the big boat belching steam and coming right at them, well, he spooked and dove off into the Mississippi. By this time the steamboat had passed them by, and the bear was so scared that he pulled the keelboat off the sandbar where it had been resting and right into the water. Then the bear seemed to overcome his terror. He got a little mad at the big boat and took off after it, towing the keelboat behind him. In a half hour, the bear and Jim had caught up with the steamboat. It was neck and neck for a long time. The crew of that steamboat was piling the wood into that boiler, but they just couldn't shake the bear and his keelboat. After a long time, the bear began to pull away, and the huge beast and his fiddling friend passed the steamboat. Jim just kept playing every fiddle tune he knew; and that old bear just kept swimming as fast as he could. Higgins played a little of "Old Joe Clark" and then some of the "Arkansas Traveler," and finally a tune called "Liza Jane." The bear just loved those fiddle tunes, so he kept swimming all the way down toward New Orleans. They plowed through the water day and night, so fast that the breeze kept Jim cool. They went by sunlight and moonlight and never stopped.

The bear and Higgins and his keelboat beat that steamboat to the docks in New Orleans by almost a day and a half. When they got there, they saw a huge catfish chasing the bear, and when they finally stopped, that catfish made a leap with its mouth open, trying to swallow that bear. The bear ducked, and the catfish jumped sixty feet out of the water, landing on the other side of the nearest levee. He was so huge that he kept all the folks who lived along that levee fed for over a month. Jim and his bear went back up the river with another load of cargo, fiddling and dancing all the way home, the best of friends.

The Bell Witch

John Bell and his family moved from Turkey Knob, North Carolina, to the Red River area of Tennessee. He had several land grants in Tennessee, and soon he was buying up more and more of the surrounding farms. People said that Bell had been a large landowner in North Carolina and that he had actually killed his overseer on his North Carolina plantation for beating a slave. Soon Bell and his family had cleared the land and had built a fine house. Because they had nine children, they also built a schoolhouse nearby for their own children and those of some neighbors. Bell was a hard-working man, a leader in his church, and was mostly admired by his neighbors.

Now Bell bought one piece of land from an old widow woman named Kate Batts. Folks always spoke her name a bit quieter than others because some thought she was a witch. She and John Bell bargained and talked and haggled over the price until she finally came down to an amount he was willing to pay for the land. Now Kate started thinking about the price, and she started to feel she had been cheated. She went to Bell to discuss the problem, but he just told her that a deal was a deal—she had agreed to the price and had taken the money. Old Kate was angry. She told Bell and anyone else who would listen that she would get even and make his life a misery.

Not long after her threat, strange things began to happen in the Bell home. They began to hear noises in the walls of the house—knocking, scratching, and whispering a little like beetles would make. Then the children complained that they saw eerie lights around their beds at night. They also said that the covers were pulled off from their beds and thrown on the floor. Sometimes the children were actually dumped out of bed and awakened in the middle of the floor. The noises grew louder day by day, and the tormenting of the children became worse every night.

One evening the family gathered around the fireplace while John read aloud from the Bible. Then they all heard a noise that started like someone just learning to whistle. Then the noise changed to a kitten's meow, then a dog's whimpering, and then to a soft eerie whisper, before changing to a woman's voice low and threatening that said, "John Bell, who was the last poor widow you cheated out of her rightful share? You had better go tomorrow and make it up to her for stealing her land." It was the voice of Old Kate Batts. John Bell was scared, but he was too proud to give in to any intimidation no matter how powerful the source. He told his wife and trembling children that he would deal with this witchcraft himself.

Meanwhile, the harassment of the family grew worse and worse. The children were kicked by unseen feet and pinched by unseen hands, and their hair was pulled as they walked through their house. Dishes, pots, pans, and glasses were thrown at John and his daughter Betsy. Cream was skimmed off the milk so that they couldn't make any butter; sometimes the cows were already milked when they got to the barn, and their milk spilled all over the floor.

Word soon got around the community about the strange noises, voices, and goings on in the Bell home, and neighbors took to visiting in the evenings hoping to experience the haunting of the witch. Usually they weren't disappointed. They heard a voice interrupting the conversation with abuse of John, calling him names that would make a sailor blush. Some of the visitors were so scared that they took off across the fields and down the road, screaming at the top of their lungs, and diving under the covers when they got into their own homes.

One of their neighbors suggested that John consult Sid Moore, who practiced white magic and lived up in the hills. The neighbor warned John that Sid's price would be high, but John Bell had become a desperate man. It cost him twenty-five dollars, a lot of money in those days. For that, he was given complete instructions to stop the witch's harassments and a plan to get her out of the community for good. Sid's instructions were that the breastbone of a black hen should be buried in front of the doorstep to keep the witch from entering the house. But, in case she did, John was to sleep with his Bible under his pillow to prevent the witch from bothering him. Further, each child was to wear a small sack containing the dried toe of a toad around his or her neck, and when the children went to bed at night, they were to turn their stockings wrong side out. If any of them should meet the witch, they were to wrap their fingers around their thumbs in a fist. If they wanted to get rid of Kate Batts once and for all time, then the last Bell child who had been christened would have to leave a branch from the mountain ash tree in a place where Kate would have to touch it. That would mark her as the next soul the Devil was to carry off.

Even after paying Sid Moore the money, Bell just couldn't believe enough in all the spells and charms to use them, until one night when it seemed as if a huge swarm of bees was buzzing just outside their door. The door burst open and Old Kate's voice echoed through the house. "You'll never get rid of me, John Bell. I'll hound you as long as I live, and I'll haunt you once I die." John Bell and his family did everything Sid had told them to do to protect their house and themselves. Betsy, the youngest, took the branch of mountain ash up near Kate's house and placed it where the witch would have to touch it.

It seemed to work for a while. Kate didn't die, but it seemed she did get some religion and she stopped harassing the Bell family. Finally though, she went back to her old ways and started to drink and play her witch tricks on people, especially the Bell family. One night she went by their house and cursed them again and again, especially John, telling him that she would hound him to his grave, that she would make life miserable for young Betsy for leaving the mountain ash branch near her doorstep. A few days later Kate Batts died of a fever.

At first John Bell and his family were relieved; but if Old Kate was evil when she was alive she was twice as bad now that she was dead. She screamed and beat John and Betsy with invisible fists that left very visible bruises, threw food across the room into their faces, and cursed them at every chance. The Bells thought of moving away, but almost as if she could read their minds, she warned them that no matter where they ran to, she would follow.

Betsy, now grown into a beautiful young woman, was seeing a young man named Josh Carter. Josh had not been fond of Old Kate when she was alive and had cursed her openly in front of several people. The witch visited Betsy in a dream and told her that if she married Josh Carter, she would live to regret her decision. When Betsy tried to go out with Josh, she would find her dresses ripped apart and burrs all over her clothes. If she saw any other boy, she had no problems at all. Betsy Bell and Josh Carter went to a picnic where they intended to announce their engagement. When Josh stood up to make the announcement, a loud voice said, "Well, well, here we are. I've come back to make sure that horrible Bell girl don't marry that mean Carter boy. If you do, Betsy, I'll make your lives hell on earth, just like old John Bell's was." Then the voice faded away. In the confusion people ran from the picnic, and the announcement was never made. Betsy gave Josh's ring back to him. Later she and Richard Powell, the schoolmaster at the Bell school, were married. They stayed in the community and raised a large family and were never again bothered by the Bell witch ghost.

News about the Bells' witch spread far and wide. President Andrew Jackson heard about the witch and her ghost that visited the Bells, so he and some friends decided to go and visit the Bell Witch, as she was now known. The moment Jackson's carriage crossed the county line near the Bell home, the wheels locked. The driver coaxed and whipped the horses, but nothing happened. When President Jackson poked his head out to speak to the driver, a voice above his head said, "You can go now. I'll see you tonight, General." At that the carriage began to move.

Sure enough, Old Kate kept her word. That night Busby, one of Jackson's companions, heard her say, "All right, you coward, you threatened to shoot me. Here I am. Now shoot and be damned."

Busby pulled out his gun, loaded it with a silver bullet, aimed it in the direction from which the voice had come, and pulled the trigger. The hammer clicked, but the gun didn't go off. Suddenly Busby began to squirm and twist and went hopping and yelling about the room as if someone were leading him by the nose. The door flew open and he went sprawling down the steps. As soon as he hit the bottom step, he got up and took off for the woods, yelling at the top of his voice. Right then and there, Jackson and the rest of his friends got up and headed for home.

About a year later John Bell was found dead in his room, a bottle of poison beside him. After this the house was no longer haunted. Old Kate Batts seemed to rest easy in her grave.

Tennessee Glossary

Old Betsy: The name of Crockett's musket. Many hunters named their weapons and actually gave them personalities of their own.

Tennessee: A state named after the Tennessee River, which comes from the Cherokee word "tanasie." The capital is Nashville.

Story Sources

American Folktales from the Collections of the Library of Congress, Volume 1

American Folktales from the Collections of the Library of Congress, Volume 2

American Myths & Legends, Volumes 1 & 2

American Witch Stories

Buying the Wind

Davy Crockett: Legendary Frontier Hero

Davy Crockett's Riproarious Shemales & Sentimental Sisters

God Bless the Devil

The Greenwood Library of American Folktales, Volume 2

How Rabbit Tricked Otter & Other Cherokee Stories

Myths & Legends of Our Own Land, Volumes 1 & 2

Myths of the Cherokee

Old Greasybeard: Tales from the Cumberland Gap

Southern Indian Myths & Legends

A Treasury of Mississippi River Folklore

A Treasury of Southern Folklore

Vermont

Before European settlers arrived, Vermont was home to the Abenaki people. At one time part of the colony of New York, it became the fourteenth state to join the union, in 1791. The citizens of Vermont have always had a reputation for independence. Even before the Revolutionary War they fought as a colony led by Ethan Allen for their freedom against the Crown and the colony of New York. An old story about that Green Mountain Boy is included.

Two of Vermont's traditional occupations are showcased here—one in a story, and one in a ballad. Religious leaders are often some of our most colorful characters, as illustrated in the story about Lorenzo Dow.

Finally, just about every state has a monster or creature that haunts some remote part of its wilderness, and Vermont is no exception, as we see in the tale about the Bennington Monster.

The Tale of the Tail of a Bear

In the old days, it was bear time in Vermont. There were more bears up around the Green Mountains than in any other state from north to south, and the pioneers and settlers, men and women, boys and girls, had their hands and homes full of the big hairy beasts.

There are many tales about the bears of those bear days. Some are sad, and some are not sad at all. Here's a tale of the tail of a bear, and you'll soon know whether it'll bring tears to your eyes or laughter to your face.

There once lived in Vermont a man named John, whose wife one day asked him to go to town to get her needles and thread, sugar and salt, and many other things besides. So he and his neighbor James took a boat and went by way of Chimney Point to fetch the things that bring cheer and comfort to the home.

As they rowed along the waters of the great dancing lake, they suddenly saw afar a big swimming thing.

"It's a deer!" cried James.

"It looks as if it might be," said John, "and we can use the meat and hide well enough."

They turned their boat and swiftly paddled toward the beast, but when they got nearer, they saw it was no deer at all—but a giant she-bear paddling slowly in the water, sort of pleasant-like.

"Bear meat is just as good as deer meat, and a bear's pelt is the warmest thing I know on a cold winter night," said John.

"But we have no gun," said James ruefully.

"We have an axe," said John. "Now, James, you row alongside of the animal while I hit her on the head with the axe."

In a few strokes the boat glided alongside the big bear.

John raised the axe high and brought it down as heavily as he could, plunk! on the bear's head. But this was a bear of bears, maybe the strongest, smartest bear in all Vermont. The heavy blow of the axe bothered the beast no more than a dropping apple from a tree. She just turned her face, looked at them, opened her mouth grinning-like, and paddled along a little faster.

That made John mad. Again he raised his axe and brought it down with all his might. But, not judging his distance as he had before, he hit the bear's tail instead, this time with the sharp side, cutting a gash, which began to bleed. It angered the giant bear just a little. She turned around and raised her paws and chug-plunk! hit the boat. It turned over, and both men were deep in the water together with the bear.

Do you think that bear bothered with John and James? Not one bit. She did not even look at them; it was just that kind of a bear. Instead, the animal climbed on the boat and laid its great big body across, watching the two coughing and spluttering men. And if a bear can laugh with might and main, that bear was doing it. She opened her jaws wide, turned her head from side to side, and shook her body up and down.

Once, and only once, John and James tried to get hold of the sides of the boat, but the bear just hit their hands with her great paw, and they didn't try again. So the two swam to shore as best they could and went their way, while the bear with the cut tail got off the boat, paddled to the shore, went into the woods, and jogged along a-thinking.

Now I told you this bear was a bear of bears, a bear who could think near as good as any man. She just kept a-thinking as she jogged along to the cave where her two young 'uns were playing. In the end, she thought out something that would teach John the lesson not to hit a bear that never did him any harm, with an axe. She took her cubs and went off to find John's house.

The sun set, and the stars came out. The bear and her cubs trotted along the leafy ground in the woods. Trot trot, trot trot, they kept on trotting on leaves, moss, and ferns, led by the smell of John, which, as you know, is to a beast in the woods of greater help than eyes are to a man. After a time, the three bears made it to the clearing where John's log house stood.

In the house was Mistress John with her children, never dreaming she'd have visitors that evening. She was sitting on a stool near the fireplace, watching the hanging kettle in which bubbling samp (which is corn meal mush) was cooking for the evening meal. On the rough wooden table stood a pitcher full of milk, and around were plates with wooden spoons.

Mistress John sang a little song to her babe. She was just turning to the black kettle to ladle out the dancing samp, when she heard a funny noise at the furry blanket that served as a door to the house.

She turned around, and there stood a great big bear and two little cubs, one on each side, looking all around.

Mistress John, she did her thinking quick. She picked up her babe and cried to the others:

"Hurry up the ladder into the loft above."

The children scampered up as fast as they could; Mistress John followed with the babe and drew the ladder up after her. Up above they all sat down on the wooden poles and looked through the chinks to see what the bears would do.

The big black bear came in with the two cubs close behind her. They looked and sniffed at this and that and looked and sniffed at everything. So they came to the rough wooden table, where dinner sat. Mother bear thought she'd first drink the milk. She stuck her snout deep in the pewter pitcher, but it wasn't wide enough and fell, the milk spilling all over. The little baby bears licked it up and thought it very good.

Next the great big mother bear came up to the kettle of samp that was still steaming and bubbling a little. It smelled good, and the mother beat wanted to taste it. In went her open snout, and she took a great big mess in her mouth and—jumped back and let out a fierce, spluttering growl! She shook her head, stamped her paws, and danced all around so that it shook the planks and rocked the rafters. The samp was burning hot, and the bear had burned her snout, tongue, and mouth.

Up in the loft the children were shouting with glee and laughter at the dancing, growling bear. Mistress John also laughed till the tears ran down her face.

When the great big bear heard the laughing, she became even angrier and ran up and down the room, knocking down everything that came her way, while the two baby bears sat down at the table, watching their mother's strange behavior, not knowing just what to make of it.

The burning pain in the bear's mouth would not go away with all her running around, so she tried to get up to the loft from which the shouts of laughter came. She raised herself on her paws and tried to jump, but with all her trying, she couldn't do it, so she sat down, spluttering and pawing her mouth without end.

There they were, the three bears, the two little bears looking with their little eyes and the great big bear pawing and growling. A funnier sight there never was. The baby gurgled, and Mistress John and the children rolled on the poles with laughter. And as they rolled they pushed against an old axe lying on the poles, and it fell down through a wide chink . . . right on the mother bear's tail, right on the sore where the axe had cut her before.

The great big bear felt a sharp pain on the wound and stopped pawing and growling. Then the beast began thinking and wondering.

"John's axe is a fierce, magic axe. It followed me from the lake to his house and hit me now for the second time, and I'll not wait for the third time to be hit. Besides, John's home is a magic home where snout and tongue are burned without fire. It's no place for me or my cubs."

So the great big mother bear rose and lumbered out of the cabin, the two cubs following. Mother John and her children laughed and came down. When father John came home and heard the tale, he laughed, too, and was very happy that nothing more had happened.

So ends the tale of the tail of the bear.

Lorenzo Dow and the Thief

Lorenzo Dow was one of the most theatrical, flamboyant preachers of his day. While preaching from the pulpit, he would do just about anything to get his congregation's attention and get his message across to them. His nickname throughout Vermont was "Crazy" Lorenzo Dow. But despite his theatrics, he was a popular preacher and drew great crowds to his Sunday sermons.

One day as he walked along a forest path he came upon two men who were cutting down trees. Dow jumped up on a stump and declared, "Six months from this day at 2:00 p.m. Lorenzo Dow will preach from this stump." Six months to the day a huge crowd was waiting for the famous preacher. Crazy Dow could draw a crowd.

One day as Lorenzo walked to the church to begin Sunday services, he came upon a man who was in obvious distress. The man, dressed poorly, seemed to be looking for something.

"Neighbor," asked Dow, "what is the problem?"

"Well sir," replied the man, "I was chopping wood here next to my house early this morning, and now my axe is gone. I don't have the means to replace it. I'm sure that someone has stolen it, but I can't think who. With winter coming on I need that axe to cut the wood; I'll need to warm my family."

"My dear man, don't think about it again. I'll find out who took your axe when I get to church this morning and have it returned to you."

The man thanked the preacher. Crazy Dow then bent down and picked up a good-sized stone from the side of the path and put it into his pocket and walked to church. Dow delivered a powerful sermon that day. It shook his congregation to the core. He thundered, and sang, and roared from the pulpit. Then he got very quiet and spoke almost gently to his flock.

"There is a man in our community who has had his axe stolen. He is not a rich man, but a poor man trying to keep the winter from the door of his family's home." Dow reached into his pocket and took out the stone. "Now I have here a stone, and I know that the man who stole that axe is here among us. I am going to throw this stone, and I know for certain that God will guide this stone so that it will not hit an innocent person, but it will hit the head of the thief." Lorenzo Dow pulled his arm back as if to throw, and a man in the second row ducked his head behind the back of the man in front of him.

Lorenzo walked over to him and said, "You have your neighbor's axe; now return it." The thief returned the axe to the poor man, who thanked Crazy Dow for the rest of his days.

The Vermont Farmer's Song

This song, which is sung to the English ballad "The Lincolnshire Poacher," dates back to before 1850. The original poem was by John G. Saxe. Merino sheep were first introduced into Vermont around 1810. The song celebrates the beauty of the land and the independent nature of its people.

Did you ever hear tell of the farmers that live among the hills,
Where every man's a king and owns the land he tills,
Where all the girls are beautiful and all the boys are strong?

Chorus
It's my delight on a summer's night to sing the farmer's song.
It's here the tall and manly Green Mountain Boys are seen,
So called because the mountains and not the boys are green.
They'll always fight to win the right or to resist the wrong.

Chorus
It's here the Morgan horses and the Black Hawk steeds abound
For grace and beauty, strength and speed their equals can't be found.
They always race with the wind and always finish strong.

Chorus
It's here the true Merinos of pure imported stock
Are often seen to range the green in many a noble flock.
Their forms are large and beautiful their wool is fine and long.

Chorus
You've often read the wonders of Ancient Rome and Greece
And of Jason's expedition to find the Golden Fleece.
The Spanish got the fleece away and brought the sheep along.

Chorus
And now success to Bingham and all true shepherd men
May heaven keep him and his sheep until shearing comes again.
Then may we be here to see and help the task along
And take delight from morn until night to sing the farmer's song.

The Bennington Monster

The bogs and ponds that fill the landscape of Beaver Meadows on Woodfield Mountain are shrouded in mystery. When the fogs and mists of night and early morning descend on the wetlands, imaginations are stirred and monsters, real or imagined, take form and reach out to the living.

One evening during a sudden and heavy rainstorm, the nighttime stagecoach passed along the ridges that bordered Woodford and Glastenbury mountains. As lightning streaked the sky and thunder rumbled through the valleys, the driver was forced to slow down to avoid having the horses lose their footing in the rising mud. Suddenly the driver was forced to stop, as he saw a large section of the road ahead was washed out. The horses were nervous and they moved uneasily from leg to leg, whinnying their disapproval of the dark night and the surrounding wilderness. The driver got down from the coach and brought his rifle. He went to examine the washout to see if he could get past it. Exploring the area with his lantern, he saw gigantic footprints in the mud that went across the road in a straight line. It must have been recent, just a minute or two before or the tracks would have been washed away with the rain. The space between the circle-shaped prints told of an animal or creature of enormous size, and they were deep, very deep. Whatever made these tracks was not only tall and long but also very heavy.

The driver called to the passengers to come look at the tracks and see if any of them had any idea what sort of animal had made them. As they stood looking down at the huge footprints, the horses screamed and reared up. Suddenly the coach shook as if hit by some enormous hammer, and a roar filled the night. The driver and passengers hurried back to the stagecoach, shaking in fear. As they huddled inside the coach the passengers looked into the rain-soaked forest. Staring down at them were two large, glowing eyes.

They could make out the form of a huge beast, partially hidden by the woods, watching them. Then the creature roared once more and made its way through the woods and into the darkness.

The creature soon became known as the Bennington Monster. Was it just a story that early settlers told to frighten their children, or did the bogs and wilderness of the area breed a creature that was large and forbidding? True, sightings of the Bennington Monster have been few, but other occurrences in that area give rise to possibilities.

Middie Rivers, a well-known guide for hunters and fishermen in the Glastenbury Mountain region, had grown up in the area. The seventy-four-year-old was in perfect health and knew the land like the back of his hand. In November 1945, he led a party of hunters into the mountains. On their return walk to their camp, Rivers got a little bit ahead of the others. They never caught up with him. The old guide disappeared, vanished completely. Police and volunteers combed the area and searched for over a month, but no sign of Rivers was ever found.

This was just the first of five disappearances that took place in the Glastenbury Mountain region between 1945 and 1950. No sign of any of the people was ever found, not a drop of blood, not a piece of cloth, nothing.

Was it the Bennington Monster come back to terrorize the area once more? Was it a phenomenon like so many other places on earth where people just disappear? We may never know.

Every Hero Needs Some Help
(Based on True Events)

Ethan Allen is a legend. He fought injustice as he saw it before the Revolutionary War broke out, when New York tried to take away part of Vermont. He and his Green Mountain Boys fought the king's soldiers for their right to keep their colony whole. Legend has it that the New Yorkers had actually put up a big reward for Allen, so big that even he had to find out about it. He rode alone into the capital at Albany, walked into a tavern frequented by politicians, ordered a drink, and announced. "I'm Ethan Allen. Anyone interested in claiming that reward?" Not a man moved. Allen finished his drink and walked out, not at all impressed by the politicians' bravery.

Now one evening he was on his way to the Richards's house, where he was to meet his fellow Green Mountain Boy Eli and discuss their next move. The Richards were friends and loyal supporters of their cause.

When they walked through the door, their noses and eyes were met by the smells and sight of a feast waiting for them. There were ham and mutton and pies of all sorts with homemade cider to quench their thirst. They were almost finished when they heard voices in the yard; looking out the window, they saw a half dozen British soldiers coming toward the house.

Ethan and Eli grabbed their muskets, but Mrs. Richards just smiled and said, "Boys, I can handle this now, just trust me. Run up to the attic and put your hats on your guns and lean those muskets so the hats show in the light of the attic lantern. I'll take care of everything down here." The two men ran up into the attic and did as they were told.

They were barely in place when the soldiers banged on the door and yelled, "In the name of the Crown open this door."

Mr. Richards walked to the door and asked, "What do you want this time of night?"

"We have reason to believe," replied the officer in charge, "that Allen and Eli are inside. We're here to arrest them in the name of the King and the Governor of New York."

Mr. Richards opened the door and the soldiers crowded in. "We know that they're here. Where are they?" they demanded.

Mrs. Richards walked over to the men and bowed her head a bit and said, "You are right, gentlemen. They are upstairs, eating. But tell me, what's the hurry? There is only one way up and one way down. Let Allen and Eli eat and drink their fill. Once they have some hard cider in them, they'll be easier to capture. I hear that Ethan Allen is a bear of a man. No need for any of you soldiers to get hurt when all you have to do is wait until they have their fill. You might as well join us and have your own meal with us. Allen and Eli are safe enough upstairs. You can look up at the attic window and see them as they eat."

Allen's strength was known across the colonies, and the last thing these soldiers wanted was a hard fight with him and Eli. One of them went outside and looked up and saw the silhouette of two hats bending down as if the folks wearing them were eating. He told the officer in charge that what Mrs. Richards said was true.

"Well ma'am," said the officer in charge, "it would be nice to share a meal with you and your husband before we take Allen and Eli." All six of the soldiers sat down and started to eat. Mrs. Richards brought more meat and fresh bread and pies to the table, and she brought more homemade hard cider. Every once in a while one of the soldiers would go outside to check that the two fugitives were still eating their food, and come back inside to tell his friends that they could go on eating and drinking.

The British soldiers hadn't had a meal this good in a long time. They ate, drank, and started to tell stories and sing their camp songs. The cider started to have its effect, and their voices got louder, and the songs harder to understand. Mrs. Richards snuck upstairs and told Allen and Eli that they could probably sneak out now if they were very quiet, "I'll lower your guns and hats to you after you're safely out of the house." Allen went first, hugging the wall of the attic stairway, slowly making his way out the kitchen door unseen. Eli was next, and soon the two were waiting below the attic window. Mrs. Richards lowered the muskets and hats and whispered for them to take her husband's mare. "She's strong and can carry you both," she added.

Allen and Eli went to the barn and silently led the mare away until the beating of her hooves wouldn't be heard by the troops inside. Soon they were off, and the threat of arrest was just a memory.

Inside the house the soldiers had eaten and drunk so much that they couldn't have followed the two Green Mountain Boys even if they wanted to. One of them walked outside rather unsteadily and looked up at the attic window. He ran into the house, yelling, "They're gone. Allen and Eli are gone."

The officer looked at Mrs. Richards and said, "Madam, you have helped two wanted men escape the King's justice. I should arrest you and your husband."

Mrs. Richards smiled sweetly and said, "They escaped through no fault of mine. I've been here serving you food and drink all night, and my husband has never left his chair. Now if you had tried to take them, my house would have been the scene of murder and mayhem and not fit to live in again. You have all had a wonderful meal and have entertained yourselves with story and song. No one is hurt, and nothing is damaged. What more could you want?" She smiled at them all, and her twinkling eyes silenced their anger.

The soldiers knew she was right, and though they grumbled as they left, they were also just a bit relieved. Allen and Eli went on and did their country proud when the colonies fought for their independence.

Vermont Glossary

Abenaki people: A Native American tribe found in Vermont, New Hampshire, and Maine. They were part of the Wabanaki Confederacy, a group of several tribes that banded together. The Abenaki lived in birch bark houses called wigwams or lodges and were famous for their birch bark canoes.

Crown: A term used to identify the power of the king or queen of England. For example, "The Crown commands" means that the king or queen commands.

Green Mountain Boys: A group of Vermonters led by Ethan Allen who resisted the colony of New York taking over part of their land. Later they were involved in the Revolutionary War as part of the Continental Army.

Merino: A breed of sheep known for its fine wool.

Morgan horse: Often credited as the first true American breed of horses. The line was developed by Justin Morgan of Randolph, Vermont. Black Hawk was a famous Morgan horse.

Samp: Corn meal mush.

Vermont: A state that got its name from the French "vert mont," which meant green mountain. The capital is Montpelier.

Story Sources

American Folktales from the Collections of the Library of Congress, Volume 1

American Folktales from the Collections of the Library of Congress, Volume 2

American Myths & Legends, Volumes 1 & 2

The Faithful Hunter: Abenaki Stories

Green Mountain Ghosts, Ghouls and Unsolved Mysteries

The Greenwood Library of American Folktales, Volume 1

Jonathan Draws the Long Bow

Mischief in the Mountains

Myths & Legends of Our Own Land, Volumes 1 & 2

New England Bean-Pot

New England Legends & Folklore

The New Green Mountain Songster: Traditional Folk Songs of Vermont

The Parade of Heroes

Spirit of the New England Tribes: Indian History & Folklore

A Treasury of New England Folklore

Vermont Folk-Songs & Ballads

Vermonters: Oral Histories from Down Country to the Northeast Kingdom

Virginia

Long before the arrival of Europeans, the Tuscarora and Yuchi made their homes along the shores and among the hills of the lands that became Virginia. One of the thirteen original colonies, Virginia played a prominent role in both the Revolutionary and Civil Wars. In the story "The Angel of Marye's Heights," you will learn how one soldier became a very different kind of hero during one of the Civil War's bloodiest battles.

The wonderful character known as Jack, whose stories are found throughout the east and south of America, appears in "Jack and His Lump of Silver," a fine story of the wise fool from the Anglo-American tradition.

The hills of Virginia—famous not only for their beauty, but also for their dark and misty nights—are the source of "Old Mother Leather Coat," in which we find out how a well-known Virginia mountain was named by one of the state's most famous citizens. Our last story is a ghost story from the Bull Run Mountains about a specter with a special message.

Old Mother Leather Coat

The young surveyor and his small party had been in the Bull Run Mountains for several days. They were tired and hungry when they spotted a small cabin that clung to the south side of a small mountain. Before they could even get off their horses, an old woman appeared in the doorway. She was oddly dressed in a leather apron and jacket, but her smile and warm welcome assured the travelers that they had found refuge for the night.

The old woman cooked them up a wonderful supper of venison and vegetables from her own garden. A dessert of cobbler filled with fresh fruit from the side of her mountain made the perfect ending to their meal. They sat around for hours, listening to her tales and stories about the area where she lived, and then told her stories about their travels. They laughed and talked, and even sang a song or two before they all retired.

The next morning the old woman had breakfast ready for the survey party before they even woke up. She sent them on their way with smiles, full bellies, and enough stories to keep them happy for many a night around the campfire.

When preparing his maps of the area, the young surveyor couldn't resist remembering her kindness by naming the mountain where she lived Mother Leather Coat Mountain. And so it is today, to the west of Thoroughfare Gap in the Bull Run Mountains. Mother Leather Coat Mountain stands in permanent tribute to kindness and hospitality, named by that young surveyor, George Washington.

Jack and His Lump of Silver
(Anglo-American; Collected by Rex Stephenson from Raymond Sloan)

Jack tales are common throughout the British Isles, and when immigrants came to this country from that part of the world, they brought stories like this one with them.

This is the story about Jack and his lump of silver. Jack lived in a village that had a few shops. There was an apothecary shop, a tavern or two, a carriage shop, a bakery, a rooming house, and a marketplace. Both of Jack's parents were dead, so a kindly silversmith, who lived at the edge of the village, took Jack into his home and tried to teach him the trade. Now it was a combination of Jack just not being too bright and also being very lazy that kept him from learning the silversmith's trade. Jack could only learn to fire the furnace and sweep the floor. Even though the silversmith was discouraged that Jack was dull, he was fond of him, and he did need him to keep the place clean and help with the easy tasks around the shop.

After many years, Jack, felt the urge to go to the big city, so he asked the old silversmith if he could pay him for his work during the seven-year period. He wanted to take his money and go to a town where he could find a job and try to find out what he was good at in life.

The old silversmith, since he was getting older and had no family to whom he could leave his business, decided he would do something special for Jack. Around the shop he found bits and odd pieces of silver that had accumulated over the years. These bits of silver had been thrown into drawers and placed in small boxes and had accumulated into quite a lot of silver. These pieces he put into the furnace and melted it into a huge silver lump. When it was cool, he called Jack in and said, "Jack, here is your money. You can go to the big city now and trade it in for whatever you want. But be careful, this is a lot of silver, and you should get a lot of money for it."

So Jack said good-bye to the man who had taken him in and been so good to him for all those years. Both of them had tears in their eyes, but Jack promised to come back to visit him soon.

Well, Jack put the lump of silver in his pack, which he slung over his shoulder. Under his arm he put a loaf of bread, and then he started out on his journey. He hadn't gone very far when he met up with a man leading a donkey. The man said, "Good morning, my young friend. Where are you going?"

Jack said, "I'm going to the big city."

The man said, "Well, you should be riding, not walking. I have a donkey here that I'd be willing to trade if you had anything of value."

Now Jack thought that sounded pretty good, and he did have that lump of silver. When the man looked at the lump of silver, he realized it was his lucky day. He quickly agreed to let Jack have the donkey for the lump of silver. Now the donkey looked around and saw what was going on, but didn't speak until the man had gone on his way with Jack's fortune.

As Jack climbed up on the donkey's back the donkey turned around to Jack and said, "Hee haw, you sure made a terrible trade there. I'm worth a lot, but I'm not worth that lump of silver."

Jack said, "Well, I wanted to ride."

The donkey said, "Well, I'm hungry. Do you have any money left to buy me some oats?"

Jack said, "No. The only money I had was the lump of silver."

So the donkey said, "Well, I can't get by on just nibbling grass at the side of the road. I'm not sure I want you to ride me. I don't think you'll be a very good master—you're definitely not a very good trader."

Jack and the donkey argued and argued until the donkey finally said, "Jack, I think maybe you're a little too heavy. You ought to get off my back and walk along side of me and see how it feels to be back on the road again; after all, I'm getting hungry and you don't have any oats and nothing to buy any with."

Jack was pretty dissatisfied with the trade, and so was the donkey. Pretty soon in the distance, they saw a man walking along, coming toward them leading a cow. As they approached each other, the donkey turned around to Jack and said, "Now here's a man you can trade with. I'm sure he'll treat me better than you. He'll probably take me to his farm and give me plenty of oats and corn and things for me to eat. You're going to the big town; you won't be able to feed me once you get there."

Jack said, "Well, all right. We'll see what sort of a trade we can strike up."

When Jack got close enough he said, "Hello neighbor, would you like to trade your cow for my donkey?"

And the man studied the donkey and said, "Yes, but I don't have anything to pay extra. Could we swap even? I could use a donkey on my farm to pull a plow and ride around the farm a little bit."

The donkey seemed to be pleased with the arrangement because he wanted to get off the highway, and he certainly didn't want to go to the big city. So they made an even swap, and the man with the cow said, "Now you have a back to ride on, but when you get hungry, you can milk her. So you'll have milk and a ride, too."

Jack thought that sounded really good.

Well, Jack led the cow on down the road. Before long he tried to climb up on the old cow's back, but the cow started to buck and Jack fell off.

The cow said, "Moo, I don't like for people to ride on me. I'll tell you what. You just might as well take me on down here and trade me to somebody else, because I don't think you're going be a very good master. I heard the donkey say that you don't have any corn or oats to feed me on."

Jack said, "Well, I don't, but I thought maybe you could give me some milk."

The cow said, "Well, you can try, but I don't know whether you'll find much milk or not."

So Jack took off his hat and sat underneath the cow and tried to milk her. Finally the cow turned around and said, "Look, Jack, it's not my time of the year to give milk."

Jack couldn't get any milk in the hat at all. "It looks like I've made another bad trade here."

The cow said, "Well, you sure did. You'd better trade me off to somebody else you meet along the road."

Pretty soon a man came up the road leading a hog. The man had tied a rope around the hog's neck and was pulling him along. It wasn't an old hog; it was a young shoat. So when he got up close, Jack said, "What've you got there?"

And the man said, "This is a young shoat that I'm taking on over to the farm. Want to do some trading? I could use a cow."

Jack said, "Yeah, I guess so. Would you want to swap even?"

The man said, "That sounds good to me. You take the young shoat and when you get to town you can sell it for a good price."

So they swapped even and Jack started on down the road. But it wasn't long before the shoat said, "Jack, I don't want to go to town. When we get there, I'm afraid someone will take me over to the butcher's shop, and I certainly don't want to go there. What I'd like to do is to live on a farm somewhere, someplace with a bunch of little pigs and have a family and a happy life. You're taking me to the big city where I don't know what might happen to me."

"Well, that is true. What would you suggest that I do?"

The shoat replied, "First farmer you meet up with, trade me for something and then maybe he'll take me on to his farm, and I'll be happy there for a long time.

Now Jack was sympathetic to the young hog's future, so he said, "All right, we'll see who we run into."

A little further down the road came a man carrying a grindstone on his back. And as they got closer together, they both looked at each other hard. The man put his grindstone down and asked, "Jack, what have you got there?"

And Jack said, "Well, I got a young shoat that would like to live on a farm if he could. I'm going to the city, and I don't know what I'd do with a young shoat after I got into town." And the farmer said, "I'll tell you what. I'll swap you this grindstone for the pig, and I'll give that pig a good home."

Well, the pig was pleased with the deal, and Jack was as pleased as he'd been with any other deal that day.

So Jack picked up the grindstone and the man went on down the road with the pig. The further Jack went, the heavier the grindstone got. He hadn't realized how heavy a grindstone could be. In the distance Jack could see the steeples, and all the buildings in town. He knew he was getting close to the big city, but he had walked so far with only a loaf of bread to eat. He had shared most of that with the donkey, and now he was really hungry and thirsty. In the distance he spied a well, all walled up in rock and brimming full of water. As he got closer and closer to the well, he said, "Somebody has already put a nice fresh bucket of water on the edge." Sure enough, there was a bucket of cool water, just within reach. Jack walked over and set his grindstone down. But when he reached over to get a drink of water, that grindstone slipped and SPLASH!! it fell right down into the bottom of that well. Jack looked down at the bottom of the well and said, "Good riddance. That grindstone was too heavy to carry around all day. Now I don't have a thing in the world to worry about. I never was good at tending property in the first place. I'll just walk on into town and see if I can find something to do there."

I'm not sure what ever happened to Jack. He probably got a job working for some other silversmith, firing furnaces and sweeping floors and making a living that way.

Used with permission of Rex Stephenson.

Raymond Sloan had been part of the WPA Federal Writer's Project in Franklin County, Virginia. He collected folk songs, tall tales, play party songs, and tales of ghosts and witches. Mr. Stephenson collected this Jack tale from Mr. Sloan in the late 1970s.

The Angel of Marye's Heights
(Based on True Events)

The Battle of Fredericksburg was one of the bloodiest and most lopsided victories in the American Civil War. General Burnside sent his Union men charging toward the Confederate forces who were entrenched in the hills. The Union casualties were staggering. As he looked out over the slaughter, General Robert E. Lee said, "It is well that war is so terrible or we should grow too fond of it."

There was one soldier who had surely not grown fond of the horrors of war. Sergeant Richard Rowland Kirkland of the 2nd South Carolina Volunteer Infantry of the Confederate Army sat with his fellow soldiers and listened to the cries of the hundreds of Union soldiers. He and his unit were stationed behind the cover of a stonewall at the base of Marye's Heights. They had been in some of the thickest fighting in which the Union army had suffered the most. He could hear the wounded crying out and pleading for water through the cold winter night on December 13, 1862.

Kirkland went to his commanding officer and asked for permission to take water to the Union wounded out on the open field in front of the Confederate lines. His commander, General Kershaw, gave him permission, but would not allow him to take a flag of truce or call a ceasefire. If Kirkland wanted to tend to the enemy, he would have to risk being shot.

Richard Kirkland gathered as many canteens as he could and filled them with water. He climbed over the stonewall that protected the Confederate soldiers from the Union snipers and started to provide water to the wounded Union soldiers who were left lying on the battlefield. In broad daylight he went out with water and blankets, taking care of the wounded for over an hour and a half as soldiers from both sides watched and kept the peace. No one fired a shot as Kirkland moved from soldier to soldier, giving them water, covering them with blankets and coats and speaking a few words to ease the loneliness and pain. Because the Union soldiers who were watching could tell that this Confederate sergeant was taking care of their wounded, they held their fire. Richard Kirkland did not stop his mission of mercy until he had cared for every wounded Union soldier at that end of the battlefield.

Richard Kirkland was called "The Angel of Marye's Heights" and became a legend of the Civil War. Today at the Fredericksburg and Spotsylvania National Military Park there stand a statue and memorial honoring this brave man who tried in a small way to bring humanity to the battlefield.

The Quaker's Gold

A long time ago there was a Quaker community up in the Bull Run Mountains. Now an old man and his wife lived in that community on a small farm. The man was learned and helped his neighbors with their letter writing and any legal issues that needed a fine pen. He never charged for this service but did it because he thought it was part of being a good neighbor. He rented out most of his land and took his fee in food. Though he and his wife never made much money, they always seemed to have plenty. They never wanted for food or a good horse to pull their wagon. Most folks thought they probably had some money put aside that no one knew about. When the family had first moved there they had several children, but they all died in a small pox epidemic that came through the area. They were buried behind the house near an old cedar tree. Not long after the last child was buried his wife also died, most folks said of grief over her lost babies. The old Quaker continued to live alone in the house for many years. He was still friendly and always there for any neighbor in need, but he stayed to himself more and more as the years went by. One winter there was a terrible storm and the roads were blocked for several days. Some neighbors noticed as they passed the old man's house that there was no smoke rising from the chimney, so they stopped to investigate. Sure enough, they found the old man dead in his cabin.

Now because of the rumors that had run through the community, everyone felt he had been robbed of his gold. They even arrested a young man until the doctor's testimony proved that the old man had died of natural causes. The cabin was sturdy and well-built, so it was eventually rented out, but that's when the trouble started. One tenant after another left after only a day or two. They talked about hooded ghosts and wandering souls and cries in the night. They said that the old Quaker would come and stand at the foot of their beds and just stare at them until they ran screaming from the cabin.

At last the new schoolmaster of the nearby Quaker school rented the cabin and brought his wife and children. The very first night he and his wife woke to find a hooded man standing at the foot of their bed. Before they could even sit up, he disappeared. The young teacher was also a Quaker and decided that the ghost was trying to communicate. The very next night when the hooded figure appeared in their bedroom, the young husband said, "What dost thou want?"

The ghost did not respond, so the young man took a step toward it and repeated his question. "What dost thou want?"

Suddenly the ghost turned and faced him and a faint whisper came from the hooded figure. "Go to the small graveyard where my family is buried. Dig one rod east from the cedar tree. Thou will find a pot of gold. Give one half to the poor and keep the rest for thyself and thy family. God bless thee." With those words the ghost disappeared.

The next day the young schoolmaster went to the small graveyard and dug just where the ghost had told him to dig. Soon his shovel hit an iron pot that was filled with gold coins. True to the ghost's wishes, the young man distributed half of the money to the poor. The rest he kept for his family but was always generous with those who needed a helping hand.

The old Quaker never bothered the cabin again. Finally, his ghost was at rest.

Virginia Glossary

Apothecary shop: An old-fashioned name for a drugstore or pharmacy.

Civil War: The war between between the Union, the states of the north, and the Confederacy, the states of the south, which divided the nation. The Civil War lasted from 1861 until 1865, the year when General Robert E. Lee surrendered the Confederate army to General Ulysses S. Grant. In military history, the American Civil War is considered to be one of the first modern wars. The Battle of Fredericksburg, with extremely heavy Union losses, was one of the bloodiest battles of the war and a resounding victory for the South. also known as the War Between the States.

Quaker: A member of the Society of Friends, a religious group. The Quakers are believers in nonviolence and have historically been concerned with human rights issues. Quakers often used the more formal "thee" and "thou" when addressing each other.

Surveyor: A person who uses instruments and angles to determine the boundaries of a piece of land.

Tuscarora people: Native Americans who were members of the Iroquois League and lived in the lands of Virginia and North Carolina before the time of colonization. The traditional dwellings of the Tuscarora were longhouses.

Virginia: A state named in honor of Elizabeth I, the first queen of England, often referred to as the virgin queen because she never married; its capital is Richmond.

Yuchi people: Native Americans living in the lands of Virginia and parts of Tennessee and Kentucky when Europeans first arrived. The Yuchi traditionally arranged their homes around a square, where ceremonies and dances were held.

Story Sources

American Folktales From the Collections of the Library of Congress, Volume 1

American Folktales From the Collections of the Library of Congress, Volume 2

American Myths & Legends, Volumes 1 & 2

A Civil War Treasury of Tales, Legends and Folklore

Folk Stories of the South

The Greenwood Library of American Folktales, Volume 1

Myths & Legends of Our Own Land, Volumes 1 & 2

Outwitting the Devil: Jack Tales from Wise County, Virginia

Southern Indian Myths & Legends

Tall Tales of the Devil's Apron

Traditional Ballads of Virginia

A Treasury of Southern Folklore

Virginia Folk Legends

Virginia Ghosts

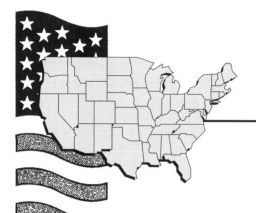

Washington, D.C.

Washington, D.C., the capital of the United States, became so when Maryland and Virginia donated land for a federally supervised seat of government. Originally known as the District of Columbia, it is now officially Washington, D.C. It has been home to many colorful characters, but none as colorful as Anne Tyler and her persistent pursuit of lawmakers. The events in the story included here, "Anne Royal and the President," probably didn't happen, but you might notice that the president isn't named, so maybe it did happen after all. During the War of 1812 the British Army captured Washington and burned down the Capitol, the Treasury, and the White House.

The White House still produces ghosts, some from before that burning. You'll meet a few in the story "Who Haunts These Halls?" Abraham Lincoln was one of our most famous presidents, and the story "The Whetstone" gives us an idea why he was so beloved. President Calvin Coolidge was an odd man in a town where talking was almost as important as breathing. His nickname was "Silent Cal," and in the short tales about him, you'll see why he so frustrated the rest of Washington.

Anne Royal and the President

In beautiful Washington, in the capital of America that is full of statues, presidents, and senators, folks are no different than in other parts of the land. They are merry and they are sad, they are frightened and they are glad.

Stories told there are made of the same stuff as those told anywhere else in the country, from up in Maine clear to California, and now I'll tell you some of them.

Listen.

In the days that are gone, gone not very far, there lived a battling lady in Washington whose name was Anne Royal. She was tall and thin, with an angry face and strong beliefs. And she always carried a green umbrella under her arm.

Folks from the President down were scared of Anne Royal. She printed a newspaper by hand, called it the *Huntress*, and in it scolded and nagged and badgered anyone who did not agree with her. None was safe. Presidents, generals, and senators talked of rigging up an old-fashioned ducking stool in the Navy Yard to duck Anne to keep her quiet.

But that never stopped Anne Royal. She just kept on pestering people to make them talk and buy her paper.

One day she could not think of a thing to complain of nor a person to attack, so she decided to write about the President and his politics. She tried to get into the White House to talk to the President, but the guards wouldn't let her in. She stomped along the grand Potomac, right before the capital in those days, and she tried to pass the guards, but it did her little good. The President wouldn't see her.

One hot morning very early, when the sun had just begun to peep over the housetops, the President decided to take a swim in the cool waters of the river that ran right near the White House.

He went down to the water, took off his clothes, and jumped in the moving stream. It was so pleasant and refreshing that he never noticed the tall, thin lady with a green umbrella coming toward him.

It was Anne Royal!

Anne Royal saw the President in the water, and saw his clothes on the bank. Surely the President would speak to her now!

She sat down on the clothes and cried out sharply, "Good morning, Mr. President."

The President took one look and felt hot in the cooling water.

"I want you to tell me about the troubles between the U.S.A. and England, and I'll print it in my paper," she said, cool as the running stream.

"Get off my pantaloons," the President cried, "and leave at once so I can come out and have my breakfast."

"I won't get off your clothes, and you won't get out of the water for breakfast until you tell me all the troubles between America and England for my paper."

The sun was rising, and people would be passing soon. A President should not be bathing in the river while ambassadors are waiting to decide who should rule the world. Besides, the President was hungry, just like any other man at this hour in the morning.

The President grumbled and growled and spluttered, but he told Anne Royal all about the troubles in the world.

The lady with the green umbrella went off satisfied, and the President had his clothes back, and even more important, his breakfast.

Who Haunts These Halls?
(Based on True Events)

The servant was sent into the study to prepare it for a meeting. As he opened the door, he looked across the room. There he saw a figure standing with his back to the door, hands clasped behind his back, staring out the window. His face was half turned away, but even so the man knew that the expression was one of deep sorrow and that the face was one of the best-known faces in American history. He also knew that the man had been dead for over seventy-five years. The man at the window was Lincoln, and the room was the Oval Office at the White House.

Carl Sandberg, the poet and Lincoln biographer, once stood at that very window while President Franklin D. Roosevelt sat nearby. Sandberg didn't actually see Lincoln, but he felt his presence in the room, a room in which Lincoln often came to stand at the window and look toward Virginia and the battlefields of the War Between the States. However, Lincoln has reportedly been seen throughout the White House—in his bedroom sitting on the bed taking off his shoes, in the Oval Office, in the hallways walking to a meeting that happened so long ago. Many a presidential dog has stood outside Lincoln's old bedroom, barking furiously but refusing to step inside it. But he is not the only ghost in America's most famous house.

During President Taft's tenure in office, the gardeners were asked to move some old rose bushes from one spot to another in the garden. A few hours later servants throughout the household saw Abigail Adams through the windows looking sadly around the garden for the roses she had planted so many years before.

White House staff members have said they saw Abigail Adams, the wife of the second president, walking right through the closed doors of the East Room in the early morning hours. It was there that she hung up the family laundry to dry. Years later people claimed they saw her there, still doing that simple task as if she and her family still lived there and she still needed to wash their clothes.

Others say they have heard laughter coming from the bedroom where Andrew Jackson slept, seen Ulysses Grant walking down the halls, and even seen the ghost of William Harrison, who died in the White House. Are they all there, these great men and women who helped shape the country? Are they still watching over every new president, hoping their spirit will guide each new leader? Or maybe it's just hard to leave the White House when your term is up, and these ghosts have all decided to hang around a bit longer?

The Whetstone (Based on True Events)

The old couple had stood in line for what seemed like hours to get a chance to shake the hand of the new president of the United States. He was from Illinois, just like they were, and from the same part of the state as well, and they had traveled all the way to Washington to see him. They had met him many years before when he was running for Congress; they wondered if he would remember them.

The couple finally came to stand in front of Abraham Lincoln. The president smiled as he shook their hands and called them by their names.

"You remember us?" the old farmer said, amazed at Lincoln's legendary memory.

"Of course I do," said Lincoln. "I came to your home asking for your support when I first ran for Congress. I was talking to you in your field when the dinner bell rang. You invited me to eat with you and your family, but I declined."

"That's not all," said the farmer. "You took the scythe and cut several rows for me while I ate. When I returned to the field you had stacked what you cut and placed the scythe up against the fence post. You did a fine job with that scythe, Mr. President."

"Thank you, sir."

"One thing though," said the old man. "I found you had sharpened the scythe, but I couldn't find the whetstone. What did you do with it?"

Lincoln laughed as he looked down at the short old man and replied, "I put it on top of the high gate post."

When the old man and his wife got back to Illinois, they got a ladder and looked at the top of the high gate post, a spot where only a very tall man like Lincoln could ever reach. There they found the whetstone, still sitting there after all those years.

Silent Cal (Based on True Events)

President Calvin Coolidge was a man of few words, and even that might be an exaggeration.

Once he was attending a dinner in Washington and was seated next to a well-known society woman. She leaned over to the president and said, "Mr. President, I am so thrilled to be your partner at dinner. I know of your reputation for being silent, but I did make a bet today that I could get you to say three words in a row."

The President looked at her for a moment and as he turned away he remarked, "You lose."

At one of his press conferences reporters were asking questions of President Coolidge and getting their usual responses.

"Sir, have you anything to say about Prohibition?"

"No," replied Silent Cal.

"Sir, have you anything to say about the World Court?"

"No."

"Sir, have you anything to say about the farm situation?"

"No."

"Do you have anything to say about the upcoming election?"

"No."

As the defeated reporters filed out of the White House meeting, the President called out to them and said, "And don't quote me."

He might have been quiet, but he had a sense of humor.

Washington, D.C., Glossary

Abigail Adams: The wife of John Adams, the second president, and the mother of John Quincy Adams, the sixth president. Abigail Adams was one of the most influential American women of her day.

Abraham Lincoln: President, 1861–1865 (died in office).

Andrew Jackson: President, 1829–1837.

Calvin Coolidge: President, 1923–1929.

Oval Office: The office of the president of the United States.

Ulysses S. Grant: President, 1869–1877

Whetstone: A sharpening stone used on knives and farm tools.

White House: The official residence of the president of the United States.

William Harrison: President, March 4, 1841 to April 4, 1841 (died in office).

William Howard Taft: President, 1909–1913.

Story Sources

American Folktales From the Collections of the Library of Congress, Volume 1

American Folktales From the Collections of the Library of Congress, Volume 2

American Myths & Legends, Volumes 1 & 2

Myths & Legends of Our Own Land, Volumes 1 & 2

A Treasury of Southern Folklore

Upstate Downstate

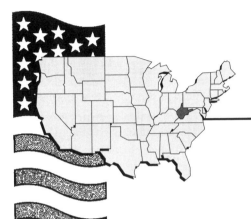

West Virginia

West Virginia was the only state to secede from a Confederate state during the Civil War. It left Virginia and was admitted as the thirty-fifth state of the union in 1863. West Virginia has produced some legends that match its rough geography. John Henry appears here both in story and ballad. He is a hero to people who feel that they are being shoved aside because of progress.

Many people went there to settle and brought their stories with them. We have a story here that came from Ireland with the immigrants who came to work in the mines and on the farms of West Virginia. Often mine owners would make sure that there were always people from different countries on every shift ,and since most didn't know English, it prevented them from talking to each other and organizing unions to protest their working conditions. Tony Beaver is the West Virginia version of Paul Bunyan, and the tall tale that appears here has all the great ingredients of an American legend. The last story is a ghost story that comes from the mining tradition and is about a faithful friend.

The Cherokee people occupied parts of West Virginia before the European settlers came.

John Henry

John Henry lived on a farm deep in the valleys of the eastern mountains. He was a big baby who loved to sit on his mother's knee and listen to her sing him songs while she knitted. He would stare up at her and laugh and laugh at her songs. His father worked on the railroad and sometimes would be gone several weeks laying down new track as the railroads pushed west. One day, when he was old enough to talk, John Henry told his mother that someday he would work on the railroad just like his father.

John Henry grew to be a giant of a man. He worked hard around the farm, tending the animals, clearing the fields, and planting the crops. When he was old enough to leave home he went to the C & O Railroad and got a job as a steel driver on the new Big Bend Tunnel outside of Talcott, West Virginia, that was just under construction. Steel drivers were the men who used heavy sledgehammers to bore the holes in the rock for the dynamite. It was hard work, and it was dangerous. Steel drivers always worked with a partner called a shaker, who held the long steel spike that made the hole in the rock. The shakers used to sing while the steel drivers swung their hammers. The songs kept the drivers on a steady rhythm and also made the work go faster. John Henry was the strongest and fastest of all the steel drivers working on the Big Bend Tunnel, swinging two twenty-pound sledgehammers in perfect timing against the mountain.

One day the boss of the work gang made an announcement.

"Well boys, we might not need some of you after tomorrow. The company sent down a new steam drill to bore the holes in the rock."

Now this meant that some folks might lose their jobs, and they weren't happy about that at all.

John Henry stepped forward. "A man can work harder than a machine. We have hearts, and we feel pride about our work. No piece of clanking metal can outwork me. Before I let that steam drill beat me down, I'll die with this hammer in my hand."

They decided to have a race the next day. John Henry against the steam drill.

John Henry and his shaker stood on one side, and the steam drill and its inventor on the other side. The race was on.

John Henry had a sledgehammer in each hand, and they whistled through the air like a strange music. He turned to his shaker and said, "Shaker, why don't you sing? I've got twenty pounds of hammer swinging through the air. Let's listen to that cold steel ring."

The race went on all morning; the only sound was the ringing of John's hammers and the pounding of the steam drill. All the workers stood and watched as their hero worked on without ever stopping. Suddenly it was quiet. The steam drill had broken down and stopped. The machine had drilled nine feet. John Henry had bored fourteen feet. There was a cheer from the crowd of men. John Henry had beaten the machine. Their jobs were safe.

John Henry stood there with his head bowed, his hammers at his side. Slowly he slumped to the ground. Now some say his poor heart had broken from the strain. Others say he just dropped down to rest awhile, and that years later, when he retired, he went back to that farm in the valleys of the eastern mountains to tend the animals, plant the crops, and listen to his mother sing. Either way, John Henry was the greatest steel-driving man.

John Henry

Most scholars consider this ballad to be one of the best examples of the American folk song. John Henry stands with Paul Bunyan and Davy Crockett as the best-known American folk heroes, and the song has been recorded by such artists as Pete Seeger, Woody Guthrie, Leadbelly, and Bruce Springsteen, as well as being arranged for chamber orchestra by Aaron Copland.

When John Henry was a little baby,
Sitting on his mama's knee,
He picked up a hammer and a little bit of steel,
Said this hammer's gonna be the death of me.
This hammer's gonna be the death of me.

Well the captain he said to John Henry,
"I'm gonna bring that steam drill around.
I'm gonna bring that steam drill out on the job.
I'm gonna pound that steel on down.
I'm gonna pound that steel on down."

John Henry said to his captain,
"A man ain't nothing but a man.
Before I let that steam drill beat me down,
I'll die with this hammer in my hand,
I'll die with this hammer in my hand."

John Henry said to his shaker,
"Now shaker why don't you sing?
I've got twenty pounds of hammer swinging from my hips on down.
Just listen to that cold steel ring,
Just listen to that cold steel ring."

The man that invented that steam drill
Thought he was mighty fine.
John Henry drove fourteen feet,
But the steam drill only made nine.
Yes, the steam drill only made nine.

John Henry hammered in the mountains.
He hammered till the mountains cried.
He worked so hard his poor heart broke.
He laid down his hammer and he died.
He laid down his hammer and he died.

They carried John Henry to the graveyard.
They buried him in the sand.
And every train that comes rolling by sings
There lies a steel-driving man.
There lies a steel-driving man.

Leprechaun Dust (Irish American)

Once there was an Irish girl named Peggy O'Leary. She lived with her father and two brothers. Peggy's mother was dead, and Peggy took care of the house and did the cooking and sewing.

Now Peggy knew she couldn't stay at home forever, even though her father and brothers would have liked her to. She was in love with young Brian O'Neil, a merchant in their village. He was a hard-working young man, but her father would not have his name mentioned in their house. You see, the O'Neil and the O'Leary families had not spoken in many years. Some long-forgotten argument still bothered the families and kept Peggy from being happy.

One day after her chores were done Peggy went for a walk. She came to a beautiful stream and stopped to watch the water as it bubbled over the rocks and as the sunlight bounced on its surface and seemed to bring a thousand diamonds to life. As she watched she became very tired and sat down on the banks of the stream and soon fell asleep. As she slept two leprechauns saw her there and stopped to look at the pretty girl.

While she slept she dreamed of young Brian, and her heart grew sad and she began to weep in her sleep. The leprechauns were startled to see someone cry in her sleep, and they wondered what was bothering the young woman.

Finally they woke her up and asked why she was so sad. Peggy told them about how silly the men were acting about something that nobody could really remember.

"I want to marry Brian, but my father and brothers won't have it. The O'Neil and O'Leary families don't speak, but they can't remember why, and my heart is breaking because of it."

The little men assured her that they would have a solution for her. They told her to be back at that spot by the stream at the same time the next day. The leprechauns disappeared, and by the time Peggy got home she wasn't sure that she hadn't dreamed it all.

The next day she was back at the stream at the right time. Soon after she arrived the two little men popped into sight. They were carrying a large pouch filled with dust.

"Now Peggy lass," one of them told her, "you must take this magic dust and put it into the dough of a loaf of bread and divide the loaf among your father, brothers, and Brian. After they eat that bread they will forget that their families had ever disagreed and will be fast friends for life."

Peggy did just as she was told, and sure enough, it worked. The O'Leary and O'Neil families were united with Peggy's marriage to Brian. It was a great wedding, and most folks say that the music and the bread were especially good, both furnished by the leprechauns as a wedding gift.

Peggy never forgot the kindness of the little men, and for all her days she would put out a bowl of milk at night or a plate of cookies for her friends, who brought her and her true love together.

Tony Beaver: The West Virginia Lumberjack

Tony Beaver lives in his lumber camp up on the Eel River. Now you won't find that river on a map of West Virginia. If you need to find Tony, you just send him a message by the next songbird you meet, and soon enough he'll send you his path to bring you to the Eel River.

How Tony Beaver acquired his own path is an interesting story. Well, he was walking through the woods one day when he felt that he was being followed. He looked down and saw a little baby path not even big enough to be called a trail just creeping slowly behind him. He took that little path home and cleaned it and let it warm itself near the fire. It became the mascot of the camp, and when it grew up it was the only way to get to the Eel River. The only complaint was that the young path moved fast, really fast, and it almost took your breath away. It would fly out across the hills and forests and mountains just like a roller coaster. That path was Tony's personal messenger.

Now the lumber camp at Eel River is a bit unique. The men are all like Tony, really big. They live in huge watermelons that grow around the main camp. The beds and tables and chairs are all carved from the watermelon seeds. These are leftovers from Tony's days as a farmer,. when he grew the biggest watermelons in the world. He also grows peanuts and has a few maple trees just to keep the boys in syrup for their pancakes.

One year it began to rain. The rain kept coming down day after day until the little town of Eel Landing was threatened with being swept away in a flood. The folks were afraid that the levees would break and sweep the entire town downriver.

Word was sent to Tony. He came down to Eel's Landing, took one look at the flood waters, and knew just what to do. He sent all the lumberjacks to the storehouses where the barrels of maple syrup were kept. Then he sent the townspeople to the warehouses where the peanuts were stored. Tony went back to his camp and found the biggest spoon he could and brought it back to Eel's Landing. When everyone was assembled he had the townspeople start to shell those peanuts as fast as they could, and the lumberjacks poured all those barrels of maple syrup into the river.

The peanuts and the syrup clogged up the reeds and the riverbed. Soon the sweetest smell rose from the river as the sun started to bake those ingredients. Tony started to swing that spoon through the river from bank to bank. Bubbles came up along the shore, first little ones and then huge ones, as the river started to boil with its sweet concoction. Tony's huge spoon churned the waters faster and faster, and the water turned a brown color as the river thickened.

Suddenly Tony threw his spoon onto one bank of the river, reached up, and drew a cloud across the face of the sun. The river started to cool. The thick golden brown mass of syrup and peanuts stopped in its tracks and began to harden. Right across the river stretched a dam as hard as a rock. Except for the peanuts that stuck up here and there, the lake behind the brown dam was smooth as glass.

The people of the town cheered. Folks ran home and some of them got their skates and started to glide around on the river. People from all around came down to see the golden brown river and the lake the dam had caused. They cheered for Tony and the way he had saved the town. It was a great celebration, maybe the best that was ever held in West Virginia.

Eventually, folks started to get a bit hungry. Tony reached down and broke a piece of that dam off and started to gobble it down. He turned to the people and said, "Just help yourselves to some of the dam or a piece of the lake. It tastes pretty good to me." The people tried it, and Tony was right, it was delicious.

In one day Tony Beaver had saved the town of Eel's Landing from a flood and invented peanut brittle. Now that's a hero.

An Old Friend

In the old days before heavy machines had been invented, mules did the work of pulling the coal to the shaft and hauling the needed equipment around the tunnels. The animals spent most of their lives in the dark, working longer hours than the miners, who worked long hours themselves. Now Dan had worked in the mines a long time, and his partner had always been a mule, a patient animal with a white star on his forehead. The mule had worked alongside Dan and had even kept him safe from the dangers that lurk in the mines. Dan always brought him a fresh carrot or other vegetables from his garden and talked to the animal just like he would talk to another miner. Dan saw that the mule was getting too old to work much longer and would soon be replaced by a younger animal. He decided that it would be fitting if his old friend came to live on the small farm that he and his family rented on the edge of town. When the mule's time came, that's exactly what happened. Dan took his old friend home to his farm and gave him a comfortable place in the barn where he could live out his remaining days.

Hard times came to the mountains that year. The union went on strike and families were desperate for money. Dan's family fell behind in their rent and soon the landlord was knocking on their door, threatening them with eviction if they didn't come up with the money they owed.

That evening Dan went out to the barn and wrapped his arms around the mule that he had worked with down in the mines for so long and told him all about the strike and the landlord and about losing the place where they lived. The old mule just listened patiently as he had always done before when Dan had come and talked to him about his problems.

The next morning when the old landlord woke up he saw a mule looking in his window. He recognized the animal as Dan's old mine mule by the white star. The mule looked angry, but when the man came back with his gun it was gone. That afternoon when he was walking into town he saw the mule again, running faster than any mule he had ever seen. It was running right at him. The man ran for his life, but the animal kept on chasing him through the streets, between the buildings and down the alleys, all the way to the door of the sheriff's office. The landlord was so shaken that he told the sheriff that Dan and his family could live on the farm rent free until the strike was over, if Dan would only get his mule to stop harassing him. The sheriff, who knew the landlord as a greedy man, agreed to tell Dan the news. When he got to the small farm he was amazed to find that the old mule had died in his sleep the night before. His old friend had saved Dan one last time.

West Virginia Glossary

Cherokee people: A Native American tribe who were removed to Oklahoma during the Trail of Tears. They are the largest tribe in the U.S. today.

John Henry: The character in what is considered to be America's greatest ballad. Most folklorists (people who study the songs, stories, and customs of a people) agree that this ballad is partially true. There was an African American steel driver who worked on the Big Bend Tunnel of the C & O Railroad around 1873. He drove steel spikes into the rock to hold the explosive charges. Those charges tore the heart out of the mountain and allowed the railroad companies to dig the great tunnel. The race is probably fiction, but what a great story. It shows us how one man's pride in his work and his sense of worth can be an example to all.

Shaker: The man who held the iron bar that was hit by the heavy sledgehammer. The blow from the hammer drilled the hole into the rock. The shaker often sang to keep the steel driver in rhythm

West Virginia: A state that kept the name "Virginia" after it separated from Virginia during the Civil War. It also was named in honor of Elizabeth I of England, often called the virgin queen because she never married. The capital is Charleston.

Story Sources

American Folk & Fairy Tales

American Folktales from the Collections of the Library of Congress, Volume 1

American Folktales from the Collections of the Library of Congress, Volume 2

American Myths & Legends, Volumes 1 & 2

Folk Songs from the West Virginia Hills

Folk-Songs of the South

Green Hills of Magic: West Virginia Folktales from Europe

The Greenwood Library of American Folktales, Volume 2

How Rabbit Tricked Otter & Other Cherokee Stories

Myths & Legends of Our Own Land, Volumes 1 & 2

Myths of the Cherokee

Southern Indian Myths & Legends

The Telltale Lilac Bush & Other West Virginia Ghost Tales

A Treasury of Southern Folklore

Yankee Doodle's Cousins

Wisconsin

Wisconsin entered the union as the thirtieth state in 1848. Wisconsin was and still is home to several Native American tribes—the Ojibwa, Menominee, and Sac and Fox people.

One of the worst disasters in our nation's history, when Peshtigo and the surrounding communities and forests and farms were literally burned to the ground, is told in story form here. Two stories from Kevin Strauss, a resident of Minnesota and a son of Wisconsin, provide us with a tall tale about a mythical beast from Rhinelander and a family story about his Aunt Gretchen from Waterloo.

The ballad "The Little Brown Bulls," about a pulling contest in a lumber camp, recalls Wisconsin's lumber camp past. The immigrants' experience can be felt through the traditional story "Brier Rose," which brings to mind the German migration to Wisconsin.

The Great Peshtigo Fire (a True Story)

It hadn't rained for a long time, longer than anyone could remember. The land was dry, and the creeks and ponds disappeared. Work continued on the railroad that was going to run through eastern Wisconsin, and the lumberjacks still cut down trees, piling them up in clearings near roads to be hauled to the mills. So when the fire came, it swept through the forests, across pastures and farmland, and rolled over the towns as if they were just more sticks to be burned. It ate its way across the land, driving the people before its flames and heat.

The people of northeastern Wisconsin were desperate. The telegraph lines, their only fast connection to the outside world, had all burned down, and no help came in the first days after the firestorm. Most of the world's attention was on the south, for the Chicago fire happened at the same time as the great fire in Wisconsin. Even Governor Lucius Fairchild of Wisconsin, unaware of his own disaster, had left Madison with a trainload of supplies for the victims of the Illinois tragedy.

When news finally came to Madison of the Peshtigo fire, there was only one person who acted quickly and decisively, the governor's young wife, Frances Fairchild. Only twenty-four years old at the time, Frances Fairchild organized the first relief effort for the people of the devastated area. She commandeered a train bound for Chicago, put out a call to the people of Madison, and filled it with supplies and blankets and quilts. She sent the train to Peshtigo, guaranteeing its priority over all other train traffic. Then she organized more supply trains and telegraphed her husband in Chicago, who returned to work with his wife to secure more supplies. Her insistence on sending blankets and quilts probably saved many people from dying of exposure.

The Peshtigo fire was the greatest fire disaster in America's history. Over 2,400 square miles were burned to the ground. It was the first firestorm to be documented. The winds reached over 100 miles per hour, and temperatures were a scorching 1,500 degrees Fahrenheit. Seventeen towns were destroyed by the fire, and as many as 2,500 people died in the fire, altering both the landscape and the industry of that part of Wisconsin forever.

The Hodag's Lament (as Told by Kevin Strauss)

The smell is what hits you first. That's what everyone says. It's a combination of rotten eggs, lavender, and skunk spray, and you can smell it half a mile away. The smell alone is usually enough to send people running. That might explain why most people have never seen a Hodag. That is, most people except Gene Shepard.

Shepard was a logger near Rhinelander in 1896. A logging accident had smashed his nose when he was young, and he'd lost his sense of smell. That might explain why one spring day, he was one of the rare people who stumbled upon a Hodag in a swamp. The sight itself made his knees shake. Shepard only saw it from the back, but he said it had the body of an immense bull with a spiked lizard tail and a half dozen dinosaur spikes rising out of its back. When Shepard saw a flash, he realized that the creature could snort fire. Well, that was all Shepard needed to see. He took off running to his cabin and hid under the bed.

But as time went on and the monster never came to eat him, Shepard began losing his fear of the beast. And as his fear ebbed away, he started getting curious. He began watching the creature whenever he got the chance. After watching it from a distance, day after day and week after week, Shepard learned some things about the Hodag. The first thing he noticed was that the Hodag seemed to be crying. Its eyes were always watering, and it would blubber and bellow like a crack of thunder on a sunny day. Looking at the creature's teeth (as it bellowed), Shepard saw that it must eat meat. This made him a little nervous. But after a while, he noticed that the only things the Hodag seemed to eat were white bulldogs, and then he only ate them on Sundays.

Now some folks say that after that, Shepard caught the Hodag in a pit trap (baited with two white bulldogs) and took it on a tour of county fairs. But that can't be true. If it were, then lots of people would have seen the Hodag. Yet these days, it's hard to find anyone who claims to have seen one.

Now, I have it on good authority that the story is a bit more complicated. You see, after watching the Hodag bawling all day, every day, and seeing it snort fire from its nose, they say Shepard began to take pity on the poor beast. What's more, he noticed that since the Hodag could shoot fire from its nose, a crying Hodag was a serious fire hazard. So it was in everyone's best interest to try to cheer the creature up.

Shepard figured out that the only thing that could make a creature so sad was loneliness. So he set off into the woods and swamps around Rhinelander, looking for another Hodag. It took months, but he found a female Hodag in a swamp up near Hurley.

Shepard knew that Hodags must have a good sense of smell, since he had seen a Hodag track a white bulldog by smell before. So he gathered up some Hodag scat (droppings) from that female and made a smell trail from Hurley to Rhinelander. It was a good thing that Shepard had no sense of smell at that point. It wasn't long before that male Hodag followed the trail to the female.

Did they have any young? Who knows? But since those Hodags met up, no one has heard a Hodag crying in the woods, and forest fires are a lot more rare. Coincidence? I think not.

"The Giant Mosquitoes," "Aunt Gretchen's First Drink," and "The Hodag's Lament" have been reprinted from The Reading Ranger's™ Guide to 50 Fabulous Folktales That Everyone Should Read and Hear, *by Kevin Strauss. ©2008 by Kevin Strauss. Reproduced with the permission of Trumpeter Press, Eden Prairie, MN.*

The Little Brown Bulls

Written in the lumber camps of Wisconsin in the 1870s, this ballad tells the story of a contest to see which team, the little brown bulls or the spotted steers, could haul the most lumber in one day. Most lumber was hauled out in the winter on skids that moved through the snow like a huge sled.

Not a thing in the woods had McClusky to fear,
As he swung his gored stick over the big spotted steers.
They were young, sound and quick, girding eight foot and three.
Said McClusky the Scotsman, "They're the ladies for me."

Oh next came Bull Gordon, the skidding was full
When he hollered, "Wah-hush!" to his little brown bulls.
They were short legged and shaggy, girding six foot and nine.
"Too light," said McClusky to handle our pine.

"For it's three to the thousand our contract does call.
Our skidding is good and our timber is tall."
Said McClusky to Gordon, "To make the day full
I will skid two to one of your little brown bulls."

"Oh no," said Bull Gordon, "that you never can do,
But mind you, my laddie, you'll have your hands full,
Though your big spotted steers are the pets of the crew,
If you skid one more log than my little brown bulls."

Oh the day was appointed and soon did draw nigh,
For twenty-five dollars their fortunes to try.
Both eager and anxious that morning was found,
The boss and the scaler appeared on the ground.

With a whoop and a holler came McClusky in view
With the big spotted steers, the pets of the crew,
Saying, "Chew your cud well boys, and keep your mouth full
For today we will conquer those little brown bulls."

Then up came Bull Gordon with a pipe in his jaw
And the little brown bulls just starting to paw.
Said Gordon to Sandy, "We've nothing to fear
For we'll never be beat by those big spotted steers."

Well at sundown that evening the foreman did say,
"Turn in boys, turn in, you've enough for today.
All numbered and scaled, each man and his team."
And we thought that we knew which had knocked down the beam.

When supper was over McClusky appeared
With a new belt made ready for his big spotted steers.
To make it he'd torn up his best mackinaw.
He was bound to conduct it according to law.
Then up jumped the scaler and says, "Hold on boys, you're wild.
The big spotted steers are behind just a mile.
You've skidded one hundred and ten and no more
While Gordon has beat you by ten and a score."

How the crew they did holler and McClusky did swear
As he pulled out in handfuls his long yellow hair.
He said, "I'll just kill them and take off their skins
And I'll dig them a grave and I'll tumble them in."

So here's to Bull Gordon and Big Sandy John
For the biggest day's work on the Wolf River was done.
So fill up your glasses, yes fill them plumb full,
And we'll drink to the health of the little brown bulls.

Aunt Gretchen's First Drink
(Family Story by Kevin Strauss)

Aunt Gretchen was never a tall woman. She barely reached a rail-thin five feet tall as she moved around her tiny apartment's kitchen.

"You know, I owe my life to an oven," she said as she opened the oven door to take out the freshly baked angel food cake.

"What do you mean?" I asked, sitting down at the kitchen table.

"I was a tiny baby when I was born at home, and back then, there weren't incubators for babies. So my father had to make one. He warmed up the wood stove and then snuffed out the fire. He cleaned out all the wood and closed the flue to keep the heat in. He wrapped me in a warm towel and some cotton batting and set me in a shoebox. He opened the oven door and put my box inside. And all through that cold winter night, the warm oven worked just fine.

"But even though I was warm, I was still sickly. Today you'd say I had 'colic.' Days went by and I would fuss and cry and never got any sleep. My parents didn't get any sleep either. After five sleepless nights, my father called for the doctor.

" 'Give her some whiskey. That will put her right out,' suggested the doctor.

"The problem was that we were a good Methodist family. And no good Methodist family had whiskey in the house. So my father had to run across the field to our nearest neighbor. You see, the Moores were Irish Catholics, and they always had a bottle of the stuff. He brought the whiskey home and gave me a drink. It knocked me right out, and I was fine after that.

"It was the first drink I had, and the last," she said as she cut me a piece of cake.

Gretchen Strauss was born in 1918 at her family's home on a dairy farm outside Sun Prairie, Wisconsin.

"The Giant Mosquitoes," "Aunt Gretchen's First Drink," and "The Hodag's Lament" have been reprinted from The Reading Ranger's™ Guide to 50 Fabulous Folktales That Everyone Should Read and Hear, *by Kevin Strauss. ©2008 by Kevin Strauss. Reproduced with the permission of Trumpeter Press, Eden Prairie, MN.*

Brier Rose (German)

In the late nineteenth and early twentieth centuries, many German immigrants flooded to Wisconsin to work in the factories and breweries. They brought this story with them.

In the days of old, there once lived a king and queen. Every day they looked at each other and said the same thing, "If only we had a child." But they never had one.

One day as the queen was bathing in a pond on the castle grounds, a frog spoke to her and said, "Your wish will come true. Before the year is over a child will be born to you, a little girl." The frog's prediction came true, and the queen had a baby girl by the end of the year. The king was so happy that he had a great feast to celebrate the birth. Relatives and friends were invited, as well as the wise women of his kingdom, in hopes they would give wisdom and luck to his newborn daughter. However, there were thirteen wise women in his kingdom, but only twelve golden plates left for the guests, so one of them was not invited.

The twelve wise women gave wonderful gifts to the baby. One gave her virtue, another beauty, and the third wealth, and so on until eleven of the twelve had given her a gift. Before the twelfth woman could present her gift, the thirteenth wise woman, the one who had not been invited, came to the door of the feasting hall. She wanted revenge for being slighted. She cried out, "In her fifteenth year the princess shall prick her finger with a spindle and fall down dead." That was all she said. Then she left the hall.

The king and queen were horrified. They didn't know what to do to stop this tragedy.

The twelfth wise woman had yet to make her wish, and though she couldn't undo the evil curse, she could make it less harsh. "The princess shall not die," she said softly, "but shall fall into a deep sleep for one hundred years."

The king was determined to save his daughter, so he ordered that all the spindles in the kingdom be burned. Meanwhile, all the gifts the twelve wise women who had been invited to the feast gave came true for the young princess. She was wise and kind, sensible and beautiful. Everyone who met her loved her at once.

Now on the morning that she turned fifteen, the king and queen were not in the castle. The princess was alone. She wandered the palace and finally came to a room at the top of a turret that was locked. An old rusty key was in the lock. When she turned it, the door opened. In the room she saw an old woman bent with age sitting with a spindle, spinning flax.

"Good morning, granny," said the princess. "What are you doing here?"

"I'm spinning flax, my dear," replied the old woman.

"What's that thing that keeps bobbing up and down?" asked the girl. She reached out and took hold of the spindle. In that instant, the curse began to work. She pricked her finger on the spindle.

The moment she felt her finger hurt, she lay down on the bed that was nearby and fell into a deep sleep. This sleep spread throughout the entire palace. The king and queen, just returning, had barely stepped into the great hall when they fell down asleep. All the people of the court and all the servants also fell asleep. The horses and dogs, the chickens and cows, even the frogs and the flies all went into a deep sleep. Even the fire in the kitchen went out, and the wind stopped blowing around the walls. The cook who was reaching to scold the kitchen boy stopped and fell asleep, her arm still outstretched. Not a single leaf stirred on the palace grounds.

Soon a brier hedge rose up and surrounded the castle. Every year it grew higher, until the castle was completely out of view. Not even the highest turret was visible.

Throughout the kingdom, the story was told that a beautiful princess was behind the wall of thorny briers, and that she was asleep waiting for a prince to free her. They called her Brier Rose. Princes came from far and near and tried to cut their way through the brier wall, but they all failed. The briers took hold of them and kept them fast. All the princes died there trapped in the thorny wall, their skeletons a warning to all others who tried.

One hundred years passed. A prince, journeying through the land, heard an old man at an inn tell a story about the brier wall, the castle behind it, and the beautiful princess called Brier Rose. He also told of all the princes who had tried to save her, but had failed and paid with their lives.

"I'm not afraid," said the prince. "I will go and see this Brier Rose and break this awful enchantment."

The old man tried to stop him, but the prince would not listen. In the end, the old man guided him to the brier wall. The thorns had entangled and held on to each other. The wall was so tall you could barely see its top. Deep inside the brier wall, skeletons could be seen entangled and held in grotesque poses.

Now one hundred years had just ended. Today was the day that Brier Rose would wake up from her deep sleep. As the prince approached the brier wall, it was horrible to see, but as he got closer, it bloomed with beautiful flowers. When he was within one step of it, the wall opened up and let him through, then quickly closed behind him.

The prince found himself in the castle courtyard, where he saw dogs, horses, and servants, all asleep, lying where they had fallen so many years ago. The pigeons on the roof still sat with their heads tucked under their wings, fast asleep. In the kitchen, he saw the sleeping cook, still reaching for the kitchen boy. In the great hall the king and queen lay, hand in hand, where they had gone into a deep slumber.

One girl was sitting with a chicken in her lap, ready to pluck its feathers, both of them asleep. Even the flies on the wall slept. The castle was so quiet that the prince could hear himself breathe. Every step echoed along the silent corridors.

Finally the prince came to the tower. He walked up its steps and into the room where Brier Rose lay. He saw her lying on the bed; she was so beautiful that it took his breath away. He leaned over her and kissed her, and when their lips touched, her eyes opened and she smiled. With that kiss, the spell was broken and everyone in the palace woke up. The king and queen and the court and all the servants woke from their deep sleep. The horses pranced in the courtyard; the dogs ran and wagged their tails. The pigeons spread their wings and flew off into the fields. The fire came to life, and the roast on the spit began once more to cook. The wall of thorns completely disappeared. All was as it once had been so many years before.

Of course, the prince and Brier Rose fell in love. Their wedding was celebrated with great happiness, and they lived together in joy until the end of their days.

Wisconsin Glossary

Flax: A blue-flowered plant that is used for its raw fiber to make thread and cloth. Its seeds are also used in cooking and making oil.

Menominee people: A Native American people original to Wisconsin. They lived both in round wigwams and rectangular lodges. They were found in Wisconsin and the Upper Peninsula of Michigan.

Ojibwa people: A Native American people also called Chippewa. They are one of the largest tribes in North America. They settled in the Michigan, Wisconsin, and Minnesota area.

Sac and Fox people: Two closely related but separate tribes. They were allies but each had their own chiefs and customs, though many of their traditions were shared.

Spindle: A pin in a spinning wheel used for twisting and winding the thread.

Spinning: Drawing out raw fiber and twisting it and spinning it on a wheel to make thread.

Steers and oxen: Male bovines that were used to haul heavy loads. Lumber camps and wagon trains often used them because of their almost tireless strength and endurance.

Wisconsin: A state named after the Wisconsin river. The Algonquian name for it was Meskousing, but it was later corrupted by the French to Ouisconsin. The capital is Madison.

Story Sources

American Folktales from the Collections of the Library of Congress, Volume 1

American Folktales from the Collections of the Library of Congress, Volume 2

American Myths & Legends, Volumes 1 & 2

Daylight in the Swamp

Firestorm at Peshtigo

Folk Songs out of Wisconsin

Giants in the Land: Folk Tales & Legends of Wisconsin

The Greenwood Library of American Folktales, Volume 1

Kevin Strauss

Lumberjack Lingo

Midwestern Folk Humor

Mythical Creatures of the North Country

Myths & Legends of Our Own Land, Volumes 1 & 2

Paul Bunyan

Paul Bunyan Swings His Axe

Songs of the Great Lakes

Stagecoach & Tavern Tales of the Old Northwest

Tall Timber Tales: More Paul Bunyan Stories

A Treasury of Mississippi River Folklore

Wisconsin Chippewa Myths & Tales

Wisconsin Folklore

Wisconsin Lore

Wisconsin Sampler

Yarns of Wisconsin

Bibliography

Story Sources

People and Organizations

Cultural Preservation Office of the Muscogee/Creek Nation, Okmulgee, Oklahoma.

Donald Davis Storyteller, Inc.

Alan Irvine

Natchez Tribal Nation

Ridgetop Shawnee Tribe

Greg Rodgers, Choctaw/Chickasaw storyteller

Bob Sander

R. Rex Stephenson

Jenifer Strauss

Kevin Strauss

Publications

Adirondack Voices, by Robert D. Bethke. University of Illinois Press, 1981. ISBN 0-252-00829-4.

Alabama, One Big Front Porch, by Kathryn Tucker Windham. New South Books, 2007. ISBN 1-58838-219-2.

Alabama Tales, by Drue Duke. Vision Press, 1994. ISBN 0-9630700-5-3.

The Algonquin Legends of New England: Myth & Folk Lore of the Micmac, Passamaquoddy & Penobscot Tribes, by Charles G. Leland. Houghton Mifflin, 1884. LC 68-31217

Amazing American Women, by Kendall Haven. Libraries Unlimited, 1995. ISBN 1-56308-291-8.

American Fairy Tales, by Vladimir Stuchl. Octopus Books, 1979. ISBN 0-7064-0860-8.

American Folk & Fairy Tales, by Rachel Field. Charles Scribner, 1929.

American Folktales from the Collections of the Library of Congress, Volume 1, edited by Carl Lindahl. M.E. Sharpe, 2004. ISBN 0-7656-8062-9.

American Folktales from the Collections of the Library of Congress, Volume 2, edited by Carl Lindahl. M.E. Sharpe, 2004. ISBN 0-7656-8062-9.

American Myths & Legends, Volumes 1 & 2, by Charles M. Skinner. J. B. Lippincott Company, 1903.

American Traveler, by James Zug. Basic Books, 2005. ISBN 0-465-09405-8.

American Witch Stories, by Hubert J. Davis. Jonathan David Publishers, 1975. ISBN 0-8246-0199-8.

Arab Folktales, by Inea Bushnaq. Pantheon Books, 1986. ISBN 0-394-50104-7.

Ballad Makin' in the Mountains of Kentucky, byJean Thomas. Oak Publications, 1939. LC 39-31805.

Ballads and Songs of Southern Michigan, by Emelyn Elizabeth Gardner and Geraldine Jencks Chickering. Folklore Associates, 1967.

Black Rock: Mining Folklore of the Pennsylvania Dutch, by George Korson. Johns Hopkins University Press, 1960. LC 60-16892.

Blackbeard's Cup & Stories of the Outer Banks, by Charles Harry Whedbee. John F. Blair Publisher, 1989. ISBN 0-89587-070-3.

Bloodstoppers & Bearwalkers: Folk Traditions of the Upper Peninsula, by Richard M. Dorson. Harvard University Press, 1952. LC 52-5394.

Body, Boots & Britches, by Harold W. Thompson. Lippincott Company, 1939.

The Book of Negro Folklore, by Langston Hughes and Arna Bontemps. Dodd, Mead & Co., 1958, ISBN 0-396-08197-5.

The Borzoi Book of French Folktales, by Paul Delarue. Alfred A. Knopf & Company, 1956. LC 55-9281.

British Ballads from Maine, by Phillips Barry, Fannie Hardy Eckstorm, and Mary Winslow Smyth. Da Capo Press, 1982. ISBN0-306-76135-1.

Buckeye Legends: Folktales & Lore from Ohio, by Michael Jay Katz. University of Michigan Press, 1994. ISBN 0-472-06558-0.

Buying the Wind, by Richard M. Dorson. University of Chicago Press, 1964. LC 63-20903.

Cajun & Creole Folktales, by Barry Jean Ancelet. University Press of Mississippi, 1994. ISBN 0-87805-709-9.

The Canaller's Songbook, by William Hullfish. American Canal & Transportation Center, 1984. ISBN 0-933788-44-4.

A Civil War Treasury of Tales, Legends and Folklore, by B. A. Botkin. Random House, 1960. LC 60-5530.

Davy Crockett: Legendary Frontier Hero, by Walter Blair. Lincoln-Herndon Press, 1955. ISBN 0-942936-08-6.

Davy Crockett's Riproarious Shemales & Sentimental Sisters, by Michael A. Lofaro. Stackpole Books, 2001. ISBN 0-8117-0499-8.

Daylight in the Swamp, by Robert W. Wells. Northword, 1978. ISBN 0-942802-07-1.

The Doctor to the Dead: Grotesque Legends & Folk Tales of Old Charleston, by John Bennett. University of South Carolina Press, 1943. ISBN 1-57003-040-5.

Encyclopedia of Urban Legends, by Jan Harold Brunvand. W.W. Norton, 2001. ISBN 0-393-32358-7.

Every Tongue Got to Confess: Negro Folktales from the Gulf States, by Zora Neale Hurston. HarperCollins, 1991. ISBN 0-06-018893-6.

The Faithful Hunter: Abenaki Stories, by Joseph Bruchac. Greenfield Review Press, 1988. ISBN 0-912678-75-5.

Firestorm at Peshtigo, by Denise Gess and William Lutz. Henry Holt, 2002. ISBN 0-8050-6780-9.

Flatlanders & Ridge-Runners: Folktales of the Mountains of Northern Florida, edited by J. Russell Reaver. University of Florida Press, 1987. ISBN 0-8130-0870-0.

"Folk Legends from Indiana." *Indiana Folklore* 1, no. 1 (1968). Journal of the Hoosier Folklore Society.

Folk Songs & Singing Games of the Illinois Ozarks, by David McIntosh. Edited by Dale Whiteside. Southern Illinois University Press, 1984. ISBN 0-8093-0585-2.

Folk Songs from the West Virginia Hills, by Patrick W. Gainer. Seneca Books, 1975. ISBN 0-89092-011-1.

Folk Songs of the Catskills, by Norman Cazden, Herbert Haufrecht, and Norman Studer. State University of New York Press, 1982. ISBN 0-87395-581-1.

Folk Songs Out of Wisconsin, by Harry B. Peters. State Historical Society of Wisconsin, 1977. ISBN 0-87020-165-4.

Folk Stories of the South, by M.A. Jagendorf. Vanguard Press, 1972. LC 70-134672.

Folk Tales of Connecticut, edited by Glenn E. White. The Journal Press, 1977.

Folklore from the Adirondack Foothills, by Howard Thomas. Prospect Books, 1980. ISBN 0-913710-02-4.

Folksongs of Florida, by Alton C. Morris. University of Florida Press, 1950. ISBN 0-8130-0983-9.

Folksongs of Mississippi and their Background, by Arthur Palmer Hudson. Folklorica Press, 1981. ISBN 0-939544-02-4.

Folk-Songs of the South, by John Harrington Cox. Dover Publications, 1967. LC 67-18093.

From the Winds of Manguito: *Cuban Folktales in English & Spanish,* retold by Elivia Perez. Libraries Unlimited, 2004. ISBN 1-59158-091-9.

The Ghost of Peg-Leg Peter & Other Folk Tales of Old New York, by M.A. Jagendorf. Vanguard Press, 1965. LC 65-17371.

Ghost Stories of Illinois, by Jo-Anne Christensen. Lone Pine, 2000. ISBN 1-55105-239-3.

Ghost Stories of the Delaware Coast, by David J. Seibold and Charles J. Adams III. Exeter House Books, 1990. ISBN 0-9610008-9-9.

Giants in the Land: *Folk Tales & Legends of Wisconsin,* by Dennis Boyer. Prairie Oak Press, 1997. ISBN 1-879483-45-9.

God Bless the Devil, by Tennessee Writers Project. University of Tennessee Press, 1940. ISBN 0-87049-475-9.

The Grandfather Tales, by Richard Chase. Houghton Mifflin, 1973. ISBN 0-395-06692-1.

Green Hills of Magic: *West Virginia Folktales from Europe,* by Ruth Ann Musick, University Press of Kentucky, 1989. ISBN 0-8131-1191-9.

Green Mountain Ghosts, Ghouls and Unsolved Mysteries, by Joseph A. Citro. Vermont Life/Chapters Publishing, 1994. ISBN 1-881527-51-4.

The Greenwood Library of American Folktales, Volume 1, edited by Thomas Green. Greenwood Press, 2006. ISBN 0-313-33773-X.

The Greenwood Library of American Folktales, Volume 2, edited by Thomas Green. Greenwood Press, 2006. ISBN 0-313-33774-8.

Gullah Folktales from the Georgia Coast, by Charles Colcock Jones Jr. University of Georgia Press, 2000. ISBN 0-8203-2216-4. (Originally published in 1888 as *Negro Myths from the Georgia Coast.*)

Gumbo Ya-Ya: *A Collection of Louisiana Folktales,* by Lyle Saxon, Robert Tallant, and Edward Dreyer. Bonanza Books, 1945. ISBN 0-517-01922-1.

Half Horse Half Alligator, by Walter Blair and Franklin J. Meine. University of Chicago Press, 1956. LC 56-10082.

Haunted Hoosier Trails, by Wanda Lou Willis. Guild Press, 2002. ISBN 1-57860-115-0.

Homespun: *Tales from America's Favorite Storytellers,* by Jimmy Neal Smith, Crown Books, 1988, ISBN 0-517-56936-1

Hoosier Folk Legends, by Ronald Baker, Indiana University Press, 1982. ISBN 0-253-32844-6

How Rabbit Tricked Otter & Other Cherokee Stories, by Gayle Ross. HarperCollins, 1994. ISBN 0-06-021285-3.

Illinois: *A History of the Prairie State,* by Robert Howard. Wm. B. Eerdmans Publishing, 1972. ISBN 0-8028-7025-2.

In the Pine: *Selected Kentucky Folk Songs,* by Leonard W. Roberts. Pikeville College Press, 1978. LC 78-56599.

Indiana Folklore: *A Reader,* by Linda Degh. Indiana University Press, 1980. ISBN 0-253-10986-8.

Iroquois Stories, by Joseph Bruchac, The Crossing Press, 1985. ISBN 0-89594-167-8.

The Jack Tales, by Richard Chase. Houghton Mifflin, 1943. ISBN 0-395-06694-8.

The Jersey Devil, by James F. McCloy and Ray Miller Jr. Middle Atlantic Press, 1976. ISBN 0-912608-11-0.

Johnny Appleseed: *Man & Myth,* by Robert Price. Indiana University Press, 1954. LC 54-7972.

Jokelore: *Humorous Folktales from Indiana,* by Ronald Baker. Indiana University Press, 1986. ISBN 0-253-20406-2.

Jonathan Draws the Long Bow, by Richard M. Dorson. Harvard University, Press, 1946.

Land of the Millrats, by Richard M. Dorson. Harvard University Press, 1981. ISBN 0-674-50855-6.

The Legend of the Lowcountry Liar, by Brian McCreight. Pineapple Press, 2005. ISBN 978-1-56164337-0.

Legendary Connecticut: *Traditional Tales from the Nutmeg State,* by David E. Philips. Curbstone Press, 1992. ISBN 1-880684-05-5.

Legends & Lore of Southern Illinois, by John W. Allen. Southern Illinois University Press, 1963.

Legends & Lore of Western Pennsylvania, by Thomas White. The History Press, 2009. ISBN 1-59629-731-9.

Legends of the Delaware Indians and Picture Writing, by Richard C. Adams. Syracuse University Press, 1997. ISBN 0-8156-0487-4 (originally published in 1905).

Legends of the New England Coast, by Edward Rowe Snow. Dodd, Mead, 1957. LC 57-12134.

Legends of the Outer Banks & Tar Heel Tidewater, by Charles Harry Whedbee. John F. Blair Publisher, 1966. ISBN 0-910244-41-3.

Legends of the Seminoles, by Betty Mae Jumper. Pineapple Press, 1994. ISBN 1-56164-040-9.

Lore of Wolverine Country, by Stan Perkins. Broadblade Press, 1984. ISBN 0-940404-08-7.

Lumberjack Lingo, by L. G. Sorden. Wisconsin House, 1969. LC 73-10090.

Maryland Folk Legends & Folk Songs, by George G. Carey. Tidewater Publishers, 1971. ISBN 0-87033-158-2.

Midwestern Folk Humor, by James P. Leary. August House, 1991. ISBN 0-87483-108-3.

Mike Fink, by James Cloyd Bowman. Little, Brown, 1957. LC 57-5510.

Mischief in the Mountains, by Walter R. Hard Jr. and Jane Clark Brown. Vermont Life Magazine, 1971. ISBN 0-8289-0117-1.

More New Hampshire Folk Tales, by Mrs. Moody P. Gore and Mrs. Guy E. Speare. Published by Mrs. Guy E. Speare, 1936.

Mules and Men, by Zora Neale Hurston. Harper Row, 1990 (first published in 1935). ISBN0-06-091648-6.

Mythical Creatures of the North Country, by Walker D. Wyman. River Falls State University Press, 1969.

Mythical Creatures of the U.S.A. and Canada, by Walker D. Wyman. University of Wisconsin-River Falls Press, 1978.

Myths & Legends of Our Own Land, Volumes 1 & 2, by Charles M. Skinner. J. B. Lippincott Company, 1896.

Myths of the Cherokee, by James Mooney. Dover, 1995. ISBN 0-486-28907-9.

Negro Folktales in Michigan, by Richard Dorson. Harvard University Press, 1956. LC 56-6516.

New England Bean-Pot, by M. A. Jagendorf. Vanguard Press, 1948.

New England Legends & Folklore, by Samuel Adams Drake. Castle Books, 1993 (originally published in 1883). ISBN 1-55521-925-X.

The New Green Mountain Songster: Traditional Folk Songs of Vermont, by Helen Hartness Flanders, Elizabeth Flanders Ballard, George Brown, and Phillips Barry. Folklore Associates, 1939.

New Hampshire Folk Tales, by Mrs. Moody P. Gore and Mrs. Guy E. Speare. New Hampshire Federation of Women's Clubs, 1932.

New York City Folklore, by B. A. Botkin. Random House, 1956. LC 56-8815.

North Carolina Legends, by Richard Walser. North Carolina Division of Archives & History, 1980. ISBN 0-86526-139-3.

Of Kings and Fools: Stories of French Tradition in North America, by Michael Parent and Julien Oliver. August House, 1996. ISBN 0-87483-481-3.

Old Greasybeard: Tales from the Cumberland Gap, by Leonard Roberts. Folklore Associates, 1969. LC 69-20398.

Outer Banks Mysteries & Seaside Stories, by Charles Harry Whedbee. John F. Blair Publisher, 1978. ISBN 0-89587-006-1.

Outwitting the Devil: Jack Tales from Wise County, Virginia, by Charles L. Perdue Jr. Ancient City Press, 1987. ISBN 0-8941270-42-4.

The Parade of Heroes, by Tristram Coffin and Hennig Cohen. Anchor Press, 1978. ISBN 0-385-09711-5

Paul Bunyan, by James Stevens. Garden City Publishing, 1940.

Paul Bunyan Swings His Axe, by Dell J. McCormick. Caxton Printers, 1936. ISBN 0-87004-093-6.

The People Could Fly: American Black Folktales, by Virginia Hamilton. Alfred Knopf, 1985. ISBN 0-394-96925-1.

Pennsylvania, by James York Glimm. University of Pittsburgh Press, 1983. ISBN 0-8229-5345-5.

Pennsylvania Songs & Legends, by George Korson. Johns Hopkins University Press, 1949.

Pine Barrens Legends, Lore & Lies, by William McMahon. Middle Atlantic Press, 1980. ISBN 0-912608-19-6.

Pioneering Michigan, by Eric Freedman. Altwerger & Mandel Publishing, 1992. ISBN 1-878005-24-3.

Sand in the Bag, by M. A. Jagendorf. Vanguard Press, 1952. LC52-11125.

Seneca Myths & Folk Tales, by Arthur C. Parker. University of Nebraska, 1989. ISBN 0-8032-8723-2.

Singing About It: Folk Songs in Southern Indiana, by George List. Indiana Historical Society, 1991. ISBN 0-87195-086-3.

Snake Bite: Lives & legends of Central Pennsylvania, by James York Glimm. University of Pittsburgh Press, 1991. ISBN 0-8229-5444-3.

Songs & Ballads of the Maine Lumberjacks, by Roland Palmer Gray. Harvard University Press, 1925.

Songs of the Great Lakes, by Ivan H. Walton and Joe Grimm. Wayne State University Press, 2002. ISBN 0-8143-2997-7.

South from Hell-fer-Sartin: Kentucky Mountain Folk Tales, by Leonard W. Roberts. University Press of Kentucky, 1955. ISBN 0-8131-0175-1.

Southern Indian Myths & Legends, by Virginia Pounds Brown and Laurella Owens. Beechwood Books, 1985. ISBN 0-912221-05-4.

Spirit of the New England Tribes: Indian History & Folklore, by William S. Simmons. University Press of New England, 1986. ISBN 0-87451-372-3.

Stagecoach & Tavern Tales of the Old Northwest, by Harry Ellsworth Cole. Southern Illinois University Press, 1987. ISBN 0-8093-2125-4.

Stockings of Buttermilk, edited by Neil Philip, Clarion Books, 1999. ISBN 0-395-84980-2.

Stories of Georgia, by Joel Chandler Harris. American Book Company, 1976. ISBN 0-8103-4082-8 (originally published in 1896).

Storytellers: Folktales & Legends from the South, by John A. Burrison. University of Georgia Press, 1989. ISBN 0-8203-1267-3.

Swapping Stories: Folktales from Louisiana, by Carl Lindahl, Maida Owens, and C. Renee Harvison. University Press of Mississippi, 1997. ISBN 0-87805-931-8.

Sweet Bunch of Daisies: Folk Songs from Alabama, by Jack Solomon and Olivia Solomon. Colonial Press, 1991. ISBN 0-938991-51-5.

Tales & Songs of Southern Illinois, by Charles Neely. George Banta Publishing Company, 1938.

Tales from the Cloud Walking Country, by Marie Campbell. Indiana University Press, 1959. LC 58-12212.

Tales of the South Carolina Low Country, by Nancy Rhyne. John E. Blair Publisher, 1982. ISBN 0-89587-027-4.

The Tales of Uncle Remus: The Adventures of Brer Rabbit, by Julius Lester. Dial Books, 1987. ISBN 0-780803-70271-X.

Tall Betsy & Dunce Baby: South Georgia Folktales, by Mariella Glenn Hartsfield. University of Georgia Press, 1987. ISBN 0-8203-0900-1.

Tall Tale America, by Walter Blair. University of Chicago Press, 1944. ISBN 0-226-05596-5.

Tall Tales of Cape Cod, by Marillis Bittinger. Memorial Press, 1948.

Tall Tales of the Devil's Apron, by Herbert Maynor Sutherland. Overmountain Press, 1970. ISBN 0-932807-27-5.

Tall Timber Tales: More Paul Bunyan Stories, by Dell J. McCormick. Caxton Printers, 1939.

Tar Heel Ghosts, by John Harden. University of North Carolina Press, 1954. ISBN 0-8078-4069-6.

Tellable Cracker Tales, by Annette J. Bruce. Pineapple Press, 1996. ISBN 1-56164-100-6.

The Telltale Lilac Bush & Other West Virginia Ghost Tales, by Ruth Ann Musick. University Press of Kentucky, 1965. ISBN 0-8131-0136-0.

13 Alabama Ghosts & Jeffrey, by Kathryn Tucker Windham and Margaret Gillis Figh. University of Alabama Press, 1969. ISBN 0-8173-0376-6.

13 Georgia Ghosts & Jeffrey, by Kathryn Tucker Windham. University Press of Alabama, 1973. ISBN 08173-0377-4.

13 Mississippi Ghosts & Jeffrey, by Kathryn Tucker Windham. University of Alabama Press, 1974. ISBN 0-8173-0379-0.

Through a Ruby Window: A Martha's Vineyard Childhood, by Susan Klein. August House, 1995. ISBN 0-87483-416-3.

Traditional Ballads of Virginia, by Arthur Kyle Davis Jr. University Press of Virginia, 1957. LC 78-79458.

A Treasury of American Folklore: Our Legends, Customs & Beliefs, by Terri Hardin. Barnes & Noble, 1994. ISBN 1-56619-370-2.

A Treasury of Mississippi River Folklore, by B. A. Botkin. Crown Publishers, 1955. LC 55-10172.

A Treasury of New England Folklore, by B. A. Botkin. Bonanza Books, 1965. LC 64-178948.

A Treasury of Southern Folklore, by B. A. Botkin. Crown Publishers, 1949.

Uncle Monday & Other Florida Tales, by Kristin G. Congdon. University Press of Mississippi, 2001 ISBN 1-57806-384-1.

Up Cutshin & Down Greasy, by Leonard W. Roberts. University Press of Kentucky, 1959, ISBN 0-8131-0176-x.

Upstate Downstate, by M. A. Jagendorf. Vanguard Press, 1949.

The Vanishing Hitchhiker: American Urban Legends & Their Meanings, by Jan Harold Brunvand. W.W. Norton & Company, 1981. ISBN 0-393-95169-3.

Vermont Folk-Songs & Ballads, by Helen Hartness Flanders and George Brown. Folklore Associates, 1968. LC 68-20768.

Vermonters: Oral Histories from Down Country to the Northeast Kingdom, by Ron Strickland. Chronicle Books, 1986. ISBN 0-87701-394-2.

Virginia Folk Legends, edited by Thomas E. Barden. University Press of Virginia, 1991. ISBN 0-8139-1331-4.

Virginia Ghosts, by Marguerite DuPont Lee. Virginia Book Company, 1966. LC 66-14984.

Walking the Choctaw Road, by Tim Tingle. Cinco Puntos Press, 2003. ISBN 0-938317-74-1.

The White Deer & Other Stories Told by the Lenape, by John Bierhorst. Wm. Morrow & Company, 1985. ISBN 0-688-12900-5.

Why the Possum's Tail Is Bare & Other Classic Southern Stories, by Jimmy Neal Smith. Avon Books, 1993. ISBN 0-380-76857-7.

Wisconsin Chippewa Myths & Tales, by Victor Barnouw. University of Wisconsin Press, 1971. ISBN 0-299-07314-9.

Wisconsin Folklore, by Walker D. Wyman. University of Wisconsin Extension, 1979. LC 79-65323.

Wisconsin Lore, by Robert E. Gard and L. G. Sorden. Wisconsin House Ltd., 1962. ISBN 0-88361-008-6.

Wisconsin Sampler, by Sue E. McCoy. Northword, 1983. ISBN 0-942802-03-9.

Yankee Doodle's Cousins, by Anne Malcolmson. Houghton Mifflin, 1941. LC 41-24262.

Yarns of Wisconsin, by Sue McCoy, Jill Dean, and Maggie Dewey. Wisconsin Trails/Tamarack Press, 1978. ISBN 0-915024-08-X.

You Live and Learn Then You Die and Forget It All: Ray Lum's Tales, by William Ferris. Anchor Books, 1992. ISBN 0-385-41926-0.

General Reading about American Folktales, Folklore, and Folk Music

Afro-American Folktales, by Roger D. Abrahams. Pantheon Books, 1985. ISBN 0-394-72885-8.

American Folk Classic Tales Retold, by Charles Sullivan. Harry N. Abrams Publisher, 1998. ISBN 0-8109-0655-4.

American Folklore & Legend, by Jane Polley. Reader's Digest Association, 1978. ISBN 0-89577-045-8.

The American People, by B. A. Botkin. Transaction Publishers, 1998 (first published in 1946). ISBN 1-56000-984-5.

The Ballad of America: the History of the United States in Song and Story, by John Anthony Scott. Southern Illinois University Press, 1966. ISBN 0-8093-1061-9.

Flying with the Eagle, Racing the Great Bear, by Joseph Bruchac. Troll Medallion, 1993. ISBN 0-8167-3027-X.

The Folk Songs of North America, by Alan Lomax. Doubleday & Company, 1960. LC 60-15185.

Folklore in America, selected and edited by Tristram Coffin and Hennig Cohen. Doubleday & Company, 1966. LC 66-17450.

From My People: 400 Years of African American Folklore, by Daryl Cumber Dance. W.W. Norton & Company, 2002. ISBN 0-393-04798-9.

Further Tales of Uncle Remus, by Julius Lester. Dial Books, 1990. ISBN0-8037-0610-3.

The Girl Who Married the Moon: Tales from Native North America, by Gayle Ross and Joseph Bruchac. BridgeWater Books, 1994. ISBN 0-8167-3480-1.

Great American Folklore, by Kemp Battle. Barnes & Noble Books, 1986. ISBN 0-88029-902-9.

The Great American Liar, by James E. Myers. Lincoln-Herndon Press, 1988. ISBN 0-942936-13-2.

The Greenwood Encyclopedia of African American Folklore, Volumes 1–3, edited by Anand Prahlad. Greenwood Press, 2006. ISBN 0-313-33035-2 (set).

Hearts of Fire: Great Women of American Lore & Legend, by Kemp Battle. Harmony Books, 1997. ISBN 0-517-70397-1.

Heroes & Heroines, Monsters & Magic: Native American Legends & Folktales, by Joseph Bruchac. The Crossing Press, 2004. ISBN 0-89594-995-4.

Heroes, Outlaws & Funny Fellows of American Popular Tales, by Olive Beaupre Miller. Doubleday & Company, 1940.

The Hurricane's Children, by Carl Carmer. David McKay Company, 1965. LC 67-17525.

The Last Tales of Uncle Remus, by Julius Lester. Dial Books, 1994. ISBN 0-8037-1303-7.

Latin American Folktales, by John Bierhorst. Pantheon Books, 2002. ISBN 0-375-42066-5.

Legends and Lore of the American Indians, edited by Terri Hardin. Barnes & Noble Books, 1993. ISBN 1-56619-039-8.

More Tales of Uncle Remus, by Julius Lester. Dial Books, 1988. ISBN0-8037-0420-8.

Myths, Legends, & Folktales of America, by David Leeming and Jake Page. Oxford University Press, 1999. ISBN 0-19-511783-2.

Myths of Native Americans, edited by Tim McNeese. Four Walls Eight Windows Publishing, 2003. ISBN1-56858-271-4.

Native American Legends, edited by George E. Lankford. August House, 1987. ISBN 0-87483-041-9.

Sidewalks of America, by B. A. Botkin. Bobbs-Merrill, 1954. LC 54-9485.

Spirits Dark & Light: Supernatural Tales from the Five Civilized Tribes, by Tim Tingle. August House, 2006. ISBN 0-87483-778-0.

A Treasury of Afro-American Folklore, by Harold Courlander. Smithmark Publishers, 1996. ISBN 0-7651-9733-2.

A Treasury of American Folklore, by B. A. Botkin. Bonanza Books, 1983. ISBN 0-517-420570.

A Treasury of North American Folktales, edited by Catherine Peck. W. W. Norton & Company, 1999. ISBN 0-393-04741-5.

A Treasury of Railroad Folklore, by B. A. Botkin and Alvin F. Harlow. Bonanza Books, 1968. ISBN 0-517-168685

Voices of the Wind, by Margot Edmonds and Ella E. Clark. Facts on File, 1989. ISBN 0-8160-2067-1

Featured Storytellers

Phillip Allen, writer
(580) 916-6392
pallen@choctawnation.com

Ceil Anne Clement
PO Box 1
Hettinger, ND, 58639-0001
(701) 567-4218

    Ceil Anne is a performer and educator and is available for programs in schools, libraries, and festivals. She is also on the roster of the North Dakota Artists in Residence Program.

Donald Davis
PO Box 397
Ocracoke Island, NC 27960
(252) 928-2587
donald@ddavisstoryteller.com
www.ddavisstoryteller.com

    Donald has published several books and CDs and is available for concerts, workshops, and festivals.

Dr. Tina L. Hanlon

    AppLit: Resources for Readers and Teachers of Appalachian Literature for Children and Young Adults: www/ferrum.edu/AppLit

Alan Irvine
2704 Tilbury Avenue
Pittsburgh, PA. 15217
(412) 521-6406
alanirvine@aol.com
http://members.aol.com/alanirvine

    Alan has published recordings and is available for concerts, workshops, festivals, and residencies.

Greg Rodgers
6104 NW 54th Street
Warr Acres, OK 73122
(405) 361-2619
grodgers3@cox.net
www.gregdrodgers.com

    Greg has published recordings and books and is available for concerts, festivals, school appearances, and workshops.

Bob Sander
(317) 255-7628
mail@bobsander.com
www.bobsander.com
    Bob is available for concerts, workshops, festivals, school appearances, and residencies.

R. Rex Stephenson
Artistic Director of the Blue Ridge Dinner Theatre
Ferrum College
Ferrum, VA 24088

Jenifer Strauss
1061 West Sager Road
Hastings, MI 49058
(269) 945-4943 or (269) 838-8361 (Cell)
E-mail: jenifer@storybetold.com
www.storybetold.com
    Jenifer has published CDs and is available for work in schools, libraries, concerts, and festivals.

Kevin Strauss
PO Box 6511
Rochester, MN 55903
(507) 993-3411
kevin@naturestory.com
www.naturestory.com
    Kevin has published CDs, DVDs, and books and is available for concerts, school appearances, library appearances, and festivals.

Art Thieme
705 Calhoun, Apt. 7-B
Peru, IL 61354
folkart@ivnet.com
Art has published several CDs.

Dovie Thomason
PO Box 6351
Harrisburg, PA 17112
dovestory@earthlink.net
www.doviethomason.com
    Dovie has published several CDs and is available for concerts, festivals, residencies, and workshops.

Tim Tingle
4417 Morningside Way
Canyon Lake, TX 78133
(830) 899-5678
timtingle@hotmail.com
www.choctawstoryteller.com
    Tim has published books and CDs and is available for concerts, festivals, workshops, and school appearances.

Index

About the Author

DAN KEDING has been a professional folksinger and storyteller for almost forty years. He has written several books, made over a dozen recordings, and has been a regular columnist for *Sing Out: The Folk Music Magazine* for over twenty years. His recordings and books have won numerous awards, including The American Library Association Notable Recording for Children, The Anne Izard Storytellers' Choice Award, and nine Storytelling World awards. In 2000 he was inducted into The Circle of Excellence of the National Storytelling Network. He is also an Adjunct Lecturer at the Graduate School of Library and Information Science at the University of Illinois. One of his hobbies is collecting books on folktales, fairy tales, folklore, and ballads. He has over 2,200 volumes in his library. He lives in Urbana, Illinois, with his wife Tandy and his two Australian shepherds, Jack and Maeve. You can visit him at www.dankeding.com.